"'*Reality emerges and exists everywhere, all the time and all at once, like an endless web of changing content through which we constantly create our unique corridor of action and meaning*'. In a similar manner, this original and fascinating narrative unfolds. Adina Tarry posits that, in the fourth – digital – revolution, 'co-existence and co-evolution', rather than competition with AI, is the key for creating complementary knowledge. But this highly inspirational text also urges that human skills are becoming commodities which need 'restructuring, renewal, re-evaluation and redeployment'. Building stronger human capabilities is necessary in a world shared with AI, characterised by change and complexity. And yet, as the author suggests with a strong conviction, simple acts of dialogue (i.e. crucial aspects of coaching) remain constant. They help 'internal drivers' of individuals to be understood within their emerging realities of work and life. This book is a pure gem, with insights on every page!"

Zorica Patel, *Chartered Occupational and Registered Coaching Psychologist, Senior Lecturer, HRM Department, Westminster Business School, University of Westminster, UK*

"Adina offers us a personal journey though careers coaching to provide a unique insight into both the coach and client experience through a reflective lens. She asks big questions about who we are and what we are becoming, drawing on her own experience as a coach in a growing VUCA-AI world."

Jonathan Passmore, *University of Evora, Portugal & Henley Business School, UK*

"Using a practitioner-researcher perspective and a polymath's thinking, Adina Tarry shares a lifetime of experience combining practice, reflection, research and development. Domains like dialectic thinking, complexity theory and individual development apply a cross-disciplinary lens to the exploration of the development and essence of the human mind and its constructs of reality. In turn this leads to what the author calls 'the third way' – a positive and credible vision for the forthcoming digital revolution and its impact on careers, as opposed to a binary utopian or dystopian view. This book will serve all those who contemplate their own readiness for the future, with a desire to be better prepared for uncertainty and change."

Alexandru Popa-Antohi, *Computer Science, Leadership Development, Executive Coach and Millennial*

Coaching with Careers and AI in Mind

This book presents an integrated overview of work and career options for individuals caught in the wider context of an unravelling world and a new world of work – impacted by the fourth digital revolution – and the tension this context creates. This is followed by a positive message for a way forward that can be found by building a strong personal core, as a point of reference that enables change and flexible adaptation, to meet the future with hope and a better chance for survival and success.

The book brings together an integrated view of extensive career coaching experiential findings, related and relevant scientific thinking, research-based information about the future of the world and of work in the age of the fourth digital revolution, and a call to action for ways to adaptively and positively respond to the seismic changes that await us in the foreseeable future.

Adina Tarry (born Adina Mironovici) is a business psychologist, professional coach, organisation development consultant and visiting lecturer. Her thinking and practice are informed by extensive international business experience, applied business psychology, cross cultural savvy, advancements in science and technology, academic activity and extensive continued personal and professional development. Adina's approach to life and work is integrative, combining strategy and tactics, and drawing from multiple sources. All coming together under the principles of dialectic philosophy and complex systems theory, which in her view provide a most helpful and flexible framework that closely reflects the multifold nature of the human condition and the dynamics of our changing world.

The Professional Coaching Series
Series Editor: David A. Lane

Coaching with Careers and AI in Mind

Grounding a Hopeful and Resourceful Self Fit for a Digital World

Adina Tarry

Routledge
Taylor & Francis Group

LONDON AND NEW YORK

First published 2019
by Routledge
2 Park Square, Milton Park, Abingdon, Oxon OX14 4RN

and by Routledge
711 Third Avenue, New York, NY 10017

Routledge is an imprint of the Taylor & Francis Group, an informa business

British Library Cataloguing-in-Publication Data
A catalogue record for this book is available from the British Library

Library of Congress Cataloging-in-Publication Data
A catalog record for this book has been requested

ISBN: 978-1-78220-583-8 (pbk)
ISBN: 978-0-429-45155-3 (ebk)

Typeset in Times New Roman
by Apex CoVantage, LLC

This book is dedicated to the hundreds of people who – during our coaching work – trusted me with their life stories and their dreams, and collectively offered a mirror, which in turn made me a better person. Their resourcefulness and resilience has never ceased to amaze me.

To my late father, who always believed that I am good with people, and my late school friend Maria, who introduced me to psychology in our teen conversations, resulting in me embracing it as a career and way of life.

Contents

Acknowledgements

My dedication to, and enjoyment of, extensive personal and professional development has been an endless source of joy, inspiration and growth. But knowledge means little without those who help us make sense of it, and we become better in the presence of "significant others" (used in the talking professions to indicate all or any person – friend, colleague, relative, teacher, man, woman, younger, older, etc.) who shape our identity and respectfully value our authentic self, enabling it to flourish without envy or hindrance, in our quest to become a succession of best versions of ourselves and share this transformation with the rest of our human connections, in life and work.

This book is one expression of my evolution to date, and I share it – with gratitude – with all those influencers who helped me get here. Prof. Ion Vladutescu, the wonderfully "mad professor" of philosophy, whose intense presence and total absorption in his subject magically got all his students equally entranced by the beauty of his lectures, and whose A+ grade for my exam is a singularly proud moment of my student years.

The late Prof. George Ionescu, my clinical psychology/psychiatry professor, who told us to watch for psychiatry "extra muros" and pressed the point of developing alertness and keen observation when having to start from barely visible signs in people's everyday behaviour, because of the value in understanding them and in meaning-making.

Annie Hareng, my International Trade Manager at Bristol-Myers Squibb, who fought hard to convince me to take on what was my first real job, because she believed I was her ideal candidate, whilst I was reluctant! She prevailed and then became a stylish, patient and competent mentor in my transition from my former life as a student to my future life of work in business. From her I learned everything that was significant and necessary to create a strong and positive foundation for my future career in the corporate world. Her ability to be gently demanding, embody high standards and praise achievement was exceptional. She seamlessly combined professionalism with humanity, an invaluable mix for the young inexperienced person that I was at the beginning of my working life.

Ross McKay, CEO of Ranier Pty., who hired me as a production manager in his family-owned business, although I had never done that job before, simply because, as an excellent judge of character, he trusted my motivation, work ethic and ability to learn, which under his mentorship indeed swiftly transformed me into a formidable performer.

David Benson, Logistics Director at Alcatel, a man of outstanding vision, who reinvented himself many times over; a committed inspirational force whose mission was to enable, motivate and reward his team, and whose sheer optimism and pragmatism influenced hundreds of people around him to be at their best.

Steve O'Brien, Quality Manager at Alcatel, who believed in and valued my enthusiasm for the job and gave me the opportunity to add my "psychologist mind" to his team of "quality engineers". He opened for me the door to quality management, a function possibly undervalued in many organisations. But I hold my view that quality management offers a unique and magical philosophy to balance aspiration and implementation, and has continued to inspire me to this day.

Murali Raman, my Program Manager at IBM, who uniquely contributed to a positive impression of the corporate world in my last corporate job, due to his exceptional natural ability as a coach and mentor, with outstanding emotional intelligence, backed by deep business savvy, pragmatism and a tactful capability to drive ambitious business objectives.

Dr. John Evans and Prof. Michael Carroll, who have been supervisors and mentors at the time of my career transition to coaching and people development.

Prof. Nigel Marlow, with his uniquely wired and amazingly creative mind, who as Director of Study at London Metropolitan University invited me to become a Visiting Lecturer, and later acted as supervisor for my MSc dissertation on coaching from a complex evolving systems perspective.

Prof. Eve Mitleton-Kelly, a guest speaker at one of my lectures in business psychology, who presented the complex evolving systems theory in a way that triggered a "this is home . . .!" reaction of such magnitude that I promptly decided to make it the subject of my MSc dissertation and embrace it as my most satisfying thinking framework to date.

Dr. Meredith Belbin, who generously appreciated my MSc-based book on complexity *The New Order at the Edge of Chaos: A Unified Coaching Perspective on the Complexities of Evolving Systems* (2006), and noted the similarities in our thinking about complex interplays. This led to us working together on a project where I learned in practice the beauty of applied research methodology – structured scientific scrutiny and how it translates into a useful output.

Collectively, to all my friends around the world, who may have also known me as Adina Mironovici, and caringly followed my geographic and personal journey around the outer and inner spaces, and who have always retained an unwavering confidence in me, my choices and my powers of transformation, even when my individual dynamic was somewhat different to theirs.

Last but not least, my late father, Stefan Mironovici, a first inspiration and bearer of invaluable gifts such as his love of books, boundless curiosity and absolute belief in creativity, knowledge and sheer human kindness. A natural mentor and educator, he believed in the power of nurture and the impact of early influence through education and role modelling. A solid point of reference, with extraordinary insight and situational flexibility, he supremely succeeded in the impossible task of morphing from a protective and patient parent to an inspiring and motivational mentor, who told me "you can . . .", to a supportive and equal friend, as I reached adulthood and maturity, to finally an apprentice, ready to listen and learn from me about my world; respectfully adapting to our changes in age and experience, which naturally took us from me learning from him to him learning from me. An avid learner, he remained compassionate and restlessly curious to his last breath. He taught me the delights of knowledge and creativity, the value of empathy and the gratification of learning from, sharing with and inspiring others.

About the author

Adina Tarry (born Adina Mironovici) embraced science and technology in childhood and was raised with short science fiction stories – instead of fairy tales – as part of her early reading. In her first career Adina worked internationally with blue chip corporations in manufacturing, supply chain and quality management, enjoying the dynamic, innovative and science- and research-driven environments of information technology, communications, pharmaceutical and fashion industries. Adina refocused her second career on the development of "people in business", working as an organisation consultant, business psychologist and professional coach. In her work she combines business savvy, science and technology, cross cultural competence and psychology. An avid learner, she also enjoys her role of Visiting Lecturer, which keeps her up to date with latest thinking and offers opportunities for knowledge exchange. Adina is a published author and speaker who also dedicates some of her time to pro bono work, including with professional organisations, actively supporting high professional standards in communities of practice.

Series editor's foreword

We are increasingly faced with greater complexity in our working and personal life. Sometimes with bewildering speed what we thought we knew that would serve us well for the future has become redundant. Jobs built on hard earned expertise are particularly vulnerable to the rising tide of artificial intelligence. This impacts us all as workers, business owners, professionals or coaches. Past ways of thinking about careers and the models for career planning and development do not fit current and emerging trends.

For some time, we have been considering a book on careers coaching as part of the professional coaching series. To do justice to this area in the climate of an increasingly complex world we needed a coach with a background in thinking about and writing on complexity. The author also had to bring extended experience of working with careers development for multiple clients, alongside a business, global and technological perspective. In keeping with the traditions of this series we needed an informed, reflective, experienced practitioner who was, in addition, able to grasp and place the changed realities, under a cross-disciplinary lens, yet make them more accessible.

Adina Tarry seemed the right author for that task. Why – because she does possess the unusual characteristics we were seeking. Her previous publications on complexity combined with many thousands of hours of practice as a coach, her first career in international business and her enthusiasm for technological advancements, all combined, enabled her to attempt to make sense of what careers coaching will look like as we contemplate our futures. Fortunately, she had also been thinking about writing a book on the subject, so through a number of conversations we were able to agree that she was the person to be trusted with this theme.

The book is an unusual but perhaps not unexpected contribution to our professional coaching series. Consistently, our authors have endorsed the value of being a reflective practitioner as a way to enhance our practice. In most cases this has been reflected in the accounts given in previous books. This time it forms a central theme of the work, as Adina sets out the purpose of her journey and her reflections and learning. Out of these she draws conclusions that lead to advice to our readers for planning future careers. Our authors have also consistently endorsed a practitioner researcher, scholar practitioner or scientist practitioner model of practice. That is, they have drawn upon research findings to inform practice but have also used practice to inform research. This stance is heavily endorsed and illustrated in the book. The ways in which current research and practice are struggling to deal with the rapidly changing work context are thoughtfully explored.

This current thinking is enlivened through adopting an historical frame. Western and eastern philosophical traditions are examined, and these are placed within the emerging complexity sciences to try to address the world as it is in the process of becoming. At each stage this thinking is translated into exercises and questions for the reader to use to reflect upon their own journey and how they might prepare for the increasingly uncertain future.

This new future is explored in terms of the changing industrial landscape and the demands that Artificial Intelligence and other technologies will place upon us both ethically and in the type of work created. We cannot prepare for the future as we did in the past. Career development cannot sit in a frame that assumed it was possible to gradually build your expertise and keep up-to-date with continued professional development (CPD) and thereby ensure your future. The expertise you so painfully built yesterday can become irrelevant tomorrow. Adina embraces this but instead of a picture of gloom, she presents a picture of possibility. She addressees the way in which we can prepare for an uncertain future. We can become adaptable and recognise that how we learn and earn in the future, may look very different to the present but these changes present opportunities.

However, this option is not presented as a matter just for individuals to be better prepared. She also challenges the type of capitalism that the future demands. Industrial models that generated wealth for the few with increasing gaps between those who have it all and those who have barely enough cannot be tolerated. She argues for a cooperative capitalism recognising that the problems we face require collaborative practice. Rather than thinking based in the concept that what is good for business is good for society she urges us to embrace the idea that what is good for society is good for business. She points to a new evolutionary stage in capitalism that refocuses business to the new opportunities in ways that are for the greater good.

Hence the author sets out a picture of the complex and challenging world we face and urges us to embrace a paradigm of shared values. This is a challenge to us as individuals and citizens and to business and the state.

Who might benefit from engaging with the dialogue in the book. Clearly it sits with our coaching series and therefore strongly supports coaches engaged in developmental and career coaching initiatives. It brings new ideas that will benefit clients. However, as with other books in our series it also calls on readers to look at their own development. If you are just starting your career journey or the next step in multiple careers the new world of work will impact. The helpful examples and exercises in the book will prepare you for the experience that awaits you. By adopting the multiple perspectives the author offers, you will not only be better prepared but also be able to actively shape the future. Beyond the individual, the challenge in the book is to the world of business and government to grasp the opportunities for a different approach to wealth creation – for the common good.

Adina has set out her journey and generously shares her learning and in doing so creates inspiring stories which address the challenges of the new world of work.

Professor David A Lane
Professional Development Foundation

Introduction

The book and I: a reflective journey

Looking back at the times when I was reflecting on the contents of this book and how to best present them, I realised that this book had morphed, taking on a life of its own, as a tangible expression of the way my own thoughts were evolving, influenced by external events and by my own thinking, preferences and values and how I was moderating this interplay, by keeping the readers in mind.

I initially considered writing a book, after almost two decades of practice as a career coach, because the work with hundreds of individuals over thousands of hours of coaching had generated a significant amount of information that seemed to structure itself around themes and patterns. I thought that the work done between me and so many clients had co-created a valuable nugget of wisdom, which deserved recognition and needed to be reshaped into an open gift to many others, likely to encounter similar situations and contemplate similar challenges and questions.

But as I went back in time, to collect my material, I could not help paying attention to the signals of the present, about the things to come in the world of work, in the future. With readers in mind, I asked myself again who will this book serve and for what purpose, to conclude that it was imperative for the book to serve not only the present but more importantly the future and those who need to prepare today for the world of work of tomorrow.

The urgency of this new objective was amplified by the increasingly unsettling realisation that the future has become, at this point in our evolution, somewhat impossible to fathom, because it involves changes and transformations never seen before and so making it difficult to extrapolate and predict something for which we have no historic data to work with.

In addition, having worked in the last few years with a younger generation – people aged between twenty and forty – it is a fact that they contemplate up to forty years of an active working life ahead of them with decreasing certainty about what the world will look like, even in the next few years. In this light, and with a need to still be somewhat prepared, it became clear that the only certain resource they could count on was themselves. Meaning that awareness of self, others and volatile contexts, readiness of resources, flexibility, resilience, self-belief and hope were imperative more than ever before; the very domain of personal development and coaching.

And so the book that started as a reflection on the past experience, set to inform the readers of today, acquired the reassigned purpose of also serving the future. I then set about to design the best way I could gather and present the contents to fit this more ambitious purpose of being useful to a wider audience.

Considering the equal importance of various strands of interest, the number of perspectives that I decided to represent increased to six, to cover: my client group, an individual case study, my thoughts on my reflective practice, people who take an interest in actively managing their careers, academics and researchers and, last but not least, my peer coaches. As a result, the relevant content was structured as follows:

- Themes and trends emerging from my clients as a group: positioning this material from the perspective of a practitioner–researcher, which is briefly described further in this section
- Myself as a case study, because specific examples are useful to complement group findings, but restrictions around confidentiality are sensitive and I wanted to have total freedom of expressing such information
- Professional reflective thoughts and knowledge; as a practicing professional psychologist and coach
- Scientific models, theories and research that are used in development work and can be useful to all who wish to go deeper in making sense of themselves and the world
- Useful suggestions and practical tips that everyone can apply in their own career and personal development
- An overview of the capabilities that are likely to be useful in the future, as a way to prepare for the seismic changes that the world of work will experience in the next five to twenty years.

This task has been trying at times – plagued by indecisions between the option of covering a lot of ground and that of focusing on a few specifics – but also useful and joyous; one unintended consequence led me to an unexpected window into my own evolution as a person, thinker, professional and writer. I had the chance to review the way my thoughts have been guided by inheritance, nurture and education; how the seeds of knowledge and ways of thinking planted in my teens and early twenties in school and university have built a scaffolding upon which the rest of my experience and knowledge has found a place to rest and merge with all the other fragments of accumulated experience. Also, I experienced a new confirmation of the importance of understanding the history of our cognitive and moral development as the legacy that founded our adult personal and professional development.

Our actions are an outward expression of our inner worlds and the many sub-personalities and identities that we contain, and so this book is also an artefact of my history and my resulting thoughts, after a meandering journey of months during which it transformed many times under the pressures and conflicting demands of my own considerations and changing perspectives. I am hoping that reading this book will also enable others to do the same, as they move along the chapters; take a moment to reflect, become aware of and own their identity on a deeper level, and embrace the strengths and the foundations that the reading journey will reveal about present and future professional and personal options.

Setting the scene

The scope of this book may be ambitious, and it is by design. It represents an attempt to map our increasingly challenging, divided, volatile and contradictory world, as a result of a rapid succession of major disruptive events that have marked the first two decades of this millennium, followed by suggestions on how to respond to this in an adaptive way.

The social, ideological, political, economic and geographic tensions and conflicts have now spread – all rolled up into one big wave – across the planet, uncontrolled and unresolved, sending clear and alarming signs of a leadership adrift, that lacks answers. Yet we remain unavoidably positioned for a continued, accelerated and massive shift in an unclear direction, with the rapid unravelling and transformation of the world as we have known it. This new world is set to be complex and unpredictable and can no longer be explained, understood or controlled by the usual thinking paradigms. What has worked before may no longer work in the future and there is no clarity on how to get out of this predicament in a swift and easy way. The days of ready answers are gone.

At an individual level, all this calls for an adaptive change. The next level of a developmental stretch involves stepping up to a view of the world and a way of thinking that demands some capability and fluency in complex thinking containing paradoxes and the acceptance of uncertainty as part of a normal life, and proactively builds flexibility and adaptive resilience as a new model to face this unprecedented challenge. Hopefully this book provides content for such a stretch and facilitates a paradigm shift beyond current comfort zones, to mirror reality and mobilise individual and collective strengths.

The lenses here are set to look at the interplay between individual facets, the social context, and the wider global community, shining an integrative and hopefully useful light on complexities within complexities. And we should clearly differentiate between complex and complicated; two completely different concepts. Complexity is about intricacy and subtleties, about a non-linear causality where cause and effect are not directly visibly linked, and where the link between events is so distanced in time that we cannot see it; complexity is also about intended and unintended consequences and about probability instead of certainty. Complexity is unsettling not because it is too complicated, but because often the answers are probabilistic and this requires us to deal with anxiety and uncertainty whilst remaining strong and hopeful. Complexity has its own elegance and dynamic principles that can be understood and explain its inner activity.

Making sense of the world around us is one of the defining characteristics of humankind. We need to find meaning, assign value and find certainty, feed our hopes, and act in the best way we can at a given point in time. Our humanity – personal or collective – has been and may continue to be our greatest strength and weakness. Finding that deep core, that evolving yet still point, from where to flexibly and adaptively adjust to an emerging context, whatever this may be, could provide an answer to successfully riding this storm, from a strong individual inner centre of self-belief, to meaningful connections with others, to the co-creation of an adaptive capability for the future of humankind.

Intended audiences and outcomes

Various categories of readers may benefit from this book in different ways, depending on circumstances. For people in their twenties, who contemplate half a century of working life before retirement at seventy – if today's parameters still hold – it is imperative to become alert to the signs on the horizon and create an integrated picture of the fast approaching new world, in order to develop resilience, flexibility and an understanding of their skills and how they can meet the challenges and opportunities ahead. This, alongside a clear understanding that their working life will be quite different; fragmented across a few changes in profession or activity, with different ways of delivering work, which may include a mix of corporate employment, self-employment, working for a small company, or delivering against successive short contracts, specific sets of skills for a pre-agreed "gig" and amount of money, arrived at by a bidding process. Faced with this future, being prepared and establishing a point of certainty within themselves becomes critical.

For those readers in mid working life, the question is how to adapt, upskill and overcome the technology gap to remain professionally relevant for another fifteen to twenty years and respond adaptively to situations where they may have to step out of their comfort zone, work in contexts they may not prefer, and embrace resilience and change as a way of life. For readers close to retirement, the challenge is how to continue staying active and pledge their wisdom and experience for the greater good, perhaps secure part-time work, in spite of a massive technology gap and generational differences.

For people who contemplate becoming self-employed (start a business) after some time in employment, or those who have never been employed but have always worked for themselves, there is scope to reflect on how this type of work is delivering on what they set out to achieve. Perhaps they will ask some questions about the alignment between who they are and what they have to offer or gain in this exchange with the outer world, or have the need to rethink or change their working path and careers by evaluating their employed or self-employed status, starting from the "self".

Coaches may use this book as an opportunity to have a career review in terms of self-evaluating how fit for practice they are, going forward. The integrated vision of the future of work, presented here, offers a fast and ready digest of what is to come and assists with ways of proactively adapting personal and professional capabilities, thinking and practice, so as to remain relevant and helpful to clients, who face an emerging new world of business and work.

The human resources practitioners, who are the custodians of the recruitment process, may wish to see how "the other half feels" about the recruitment process. And as candidates in their own quest for work, they may also evaluate their own professional position in the future world of work and prepare for the forthcoming changes. Finally, academics may find themes, topics or informed opinions that could capture their imagination and create an appetite for some novel and specific lines of research.

Therefore, whilst attempting to write a book for "everyone" may be too ambitious, the fact is that everyone able, and of age, is actually in work right now and will continue to work for whatever duration applies to their circumstances. As a result, everyone is quite likely to be challenged at several points in their life, by the need to adapt and change, and will have to pause, reflect and decide on the path of their future working life. And do so a number of times, over a number of decades. This is how things are. And the critical difference is in whether we accept to allow such a path to "happen to us" or we help along events, opportunities and change, by exercising a sense of purpose and agency, coming from awareness and active involvement in the dynamic context of our times. And this is indeed a decision that everyone, sooner or later, will have to make!

Contents, style and structure

I have used accessible language and structured the contents in a way intended to make sense and follow an internal organic flow. There are sections where I felt I had to introduce a more rigorous tone, to support opinions, examples and lessons learned, because of a personal belief in the value of formal and scientific backing to our experiential views. This is why the book combines, on the one hand, the information that I have gathered from practice and, on the other hand, in the second chapter, a number of models and scientific thinking that are likely to help in structuring the experiential knowledge, by providing multiple frameworks to explain it.

The book has a structure that looks at the relevance of the legacy of the past experience (Chapter 1) and then consolidates this legacy in the present aided by a scientific underpinning (Chapter 2). It then moves forward with a vision of the future and the world of work in the age of artificial intelligence (Chapter 3) and finally concludes with what are the learnings of past and present that individuals and groups of people could take with them into the future (Chapter 4) to prepare their successful transition and landing into an age of great change, at the cusp of a new unprecedented chapter in the history of humanity. The four chapters are interconnected, but are also structured as stand-alone pieces.

Notwithstanding my own interest, I have introduced scientific theories and models to provide credibility and formal underpinnings and language to real life examples that enable everyone to access the theory. As a result, the formality of some sections has purposely been complemented by accessible case studies and comments in plain language to hopefully remain interesting for all. Guided by primary sources that I have tapped into – for almost two decades – in my own Continued Professional Development (CPD) specifically related to coaching and psychology, I have also used for this book current information that is freely available to all, on the internet. This is why I have given few references, hoping instead, that this will stimulate individual research in readers who wish to further explore some of the themes, and extend to them the invitation to engage their own curiosity and follow their own cognitive style, rather than mine.

The relationship between theory of science and reality is strong. By endeavouring to expand our appreciation of a conceptualised representation of our outer and inner worlds, in the way science talks about them, we can also develop another level of thinking and comfortably work with the intricate and interconnected rules, principles and dynamic factors that have been instrumental in describing, changing and moving our own minds, as well as the world around us.

This aspect is mainly evidenced in sections where I have brought in philosophical and scientific examples, research and other pieces of information that relate to what the future may look like – or what type of higher conceptual structure we need to consider in the way we develop and use our higher level of thinking, in evaluating our opportunities and choices. This we will have to do in the complex and uncertain world – the world of work as it will manifest itself to us – after the fourth industrial revolution; a world dominated by Big Data and the artificial intelligence (AI) of the learning machines of the future.

The themes and subjects covered are not treated exhaustively and there is a lot of information and literature in the public domain that provides great detail to those who wish to pursue a more in-depth exploration. Instead, what is attempted here is the opposite: to create an integrated "big picture", which is not commonly done, because it is challenging. To this end, I have used a "sampling" approach. I selected a number of subjects that could be significant and useful, which I have covered just enough to have an impact and hopefully leave a mark of their own; but also be instrumental when trying to reconstruct the wider view, which in fact reflects reality much better. Because our wider context is dynamic, complex and unbounded; and this is a challenge.

We introduce the linearity of time and the simpler cause and effect or inputs-outputs principles to make sense of reality around outcomes, in some succession and in an easier-to-understand way. But even so, there are many other planes of concurrent activity that continue to happen, even if we have narrowed our field of vision and do not look that way. It would therefore be useful for us to become more capable of holding this wider vision by first using such familiar knowledge islands as markers – like nodes in a flexible mesh or a net – to later re-create the vision of the entire archipelago, which as a result becomes more familiar and easier to understand and navigate. So the subjects and themes covered in the book are meant to become such markers or stepping islands; individually covered enough to leave a useful trace in our minds, as a first step to building a much richer and complex context to our thinking. This can hopefully increase our capacity to work with a dynamic foreground-background flexible interplay, in a concurrent and fluid manner.

In reality, in our shifting, rapidly changing, volatile and uncharted future, where predictability will be low and probabilistic, high background activity will continue even when we may be absorbed with what is immediately in front of our eye. Across this dynamic landscape I felt it necessary to find a thread of certainty, to connect past, present and future, to guide our way, back and forth, across events and history, to also connect us with our human nature and our amazing resources of transformation, adaptability and resilience. Based on my work with clients and my own reflections, I believe that thread to be deeply set in our system of ethics, values and beliefs and our individual identity, to support that unique psychological marker and identifier of who we are.

This personal psychological profile is unique for each one of us, even if we know that it has been forged by many shared and common dimensions across all individuals of our species and under the collective influence of our societies. And it is this synthesised core that makes us who we are both as individuals and as members of our collective humankind, which has been, is and will continue to be our raft – our surfing board – that will hold firm against the waves and the unpredictable winds of the future changes.

If well designed, constantly maintained, upgraded and skilfully used, it will keep us afloat and enable us to navigate and choose the direction of travel that will lead us to a shore where we can start building a new existence, on a new ground and for a better new world. Without a doubt there are going to be casualties on this perilous journey in stormy, choppy waters, but the hope for success and triumph resides still within ourselves and the way we build a strong core as our own strong reliable foundation, whilst otherwise we will need to flex, reshape and transform in whichever way the – sometimes hostile, sometimes auspicious – demands of the future impose on us.

Self-developing or coaching from the centre, from the core, from the inside out, offers a profound and impactful way to adapt to the world of work of the future and to the world as such, because it is within our direct reach. Putting together an experience-based argument in favour of such a personal approach to our responsibility for our adaptation to the future and aspiration for a successful transition also enabled me to reflect on my own transitions and development as a professional. This resonated with the practitioner–researcher framework proposed for coaching in 2011.

Healing the divide between theory and practice: the practitioner–researcher model in coaching

In many ways, the journey of this book is similar to my own journey from childhood to the professional adult that I am today. I was raised with an appreciation for science, technology and the arts. My first years as a professional were spent learning and acquiring knowledge and filtering it through my understanding at the time, which grew with experience, to the point when I eventually had something to offer and share with others. This development reflected the worlds of our existence: an individual one and a collective one.

And there are people who follow a vocation and choose the way in between those worlds, to act as facilitators, "skilled others", as a result of their own quest for development but also because they wish to illuminate the developmental path of their fellow human beings. They belong to the category of occupations known as talking therapies and dialogical professions. Practicing coaches, psychologists, mentors, therapists, counsellors, psychiatrists and advisors have all contributed over time to gathering a significant body of knowledge, which has given rise to models, techniques and scientific scrutiny as a formalised and standardised synthesis, offering a solid platform to that which has been collected in the first instance, intuitively and experientially. And eventually I also joined them.

But in my first business career, in the corporate world, my focus was on the market and the products. Therefore my acquisition of knowledge and the way I processed my thoughts were directed at and related to the scope and objectives set for me by someone else – that is to say, by the job description and by the organisation. And I pursued my other interests on the periphery of this core activity, which I genuinely enjoyed very much.

The world of business fascinates me because it combines people, process, technology, culture and leadership – all so different in nature, yet connected in one dynamic entity that is almost miraculously effective and produces a designated outcome. I have met a lot of interesting and inspiring people in business – who contributed an exceptional human (coaching and mentoring) touch to the excellent training programs and the availability of state of the art technology and methodologies for business and people management. But eventually, I experienced the feeling that a part of me was lost. That side of my Self, interested in the arts, poetry, writing, reflection, people and culture. Adaptively, I navigated towards "softer" business roles. Quality management – with its total quality management (TQM) philosophy and the self-managed teams with shared leadership – was one. Operational HR was another. Yet after a while, I became restless again with a sense that what I could learn in this environment had run its course. Organisations were pushing me hard to be an achiever, an expert, and a "doer"; and with my mother's legacy strong in me, I was happy to be one for a good while. But there was also my father's legacy, sidetracked yet strong and asking for a place in my life. My Self was out of balance and I had for too long neglected to listen, to dream and to be. I had become someone who was not the real me, distorted by my context. It was time to reconsider my purpose and review my values. I needed to move on and rebalance myself by recovering what was missing; my other creative, sensitive, empathetic self. With so much experience acquired, I felt I needed to turn a new page, start working and developing under my own agenda, instead of that of an organisation.

This is how, after decades in international business, I became self-employed and regained full control to self-determine the direction of my development, the acquisition of knowledge, the alignment to my own values and beliefs, the content of my work, the way I delivered it, the people I chose to work with, my creative interests and, most importantly, who I was becoming. This led to my second career, which I began in 2001, as a practicing business psychologist and professional accredited coach, in London.

An important part of my coaching practice has been dedicated to career coaching, which always held a special place in my work due to the holistic aspect that career conversations take. Whilst at first glance career coaching is about updating a *curriculum vitae* (CV) – including CV writing services that are available to purchase – in order to find a new job, in fact it is not. Career coaching is really about a review of a person's entire life; and in my experience, writing the CV is the last thing one does, and when that time comes, it writes itself; with no need to hire other people to write about one's working life. This is because it is done with ease and pride by the client – the person who has now taken full ownership of their working life – with a newly gained, profound and meaningful understanding of their identity, empowered to decide, for themselves, from their core, the direction of travel into their working future.

This highly rewarding work was now enabling me, too, to acquire experience in a new and quite self-determined way; by my choice and in collaboration with people who also chose to work with me. And I also felt that the outcome of that extensive interaction with hundreds of people during thousands of hours was worth documenting, so that its value could be shared with and benefit many more.

Just like other dialogical professions or talking therapies, coaching has flourished in practice, well before being academically researched or peer group self-regulated. Meaning that just like therapy, psychiatry and psychoanalysis, coaching practitioners have initially gathered findings from case studies, which eventually reached a critical mass, significant enough to allow for process, structure, definitions and models to be created, and enable subsequent scientific research to formalise general explanatory principles. This has repositioned coaching as an increasingly credible and professionalised activity, rather than just another occupation.

Codes of ethics, training standards, accreditation criteria, professional associations, scientific papers and publications that have flourished since the early 2000s, have all contributed to formalising and controlling the practice of coaching, for the benefit and protection of the coaching clients and to create and maintain a positive reputation of professionalism for the coaching practice.

The practitioner–researcher model is one such framework that aims to end the academic vs. practitioner divide and put forward criteria that help differentiate the quality of coaching practice and the attainment of a certain level of quality, against competencies comparable to those of the academic researchers. In general perception and in the professional world, the academics are considered outsiders to the reality of practice, preoccupied with questions of a fundamental nature and focused on generalising knowledge and developing theory. To this end they also have access to funds and resources that may be needed for large-scale undertakings. The practitioner, on the other hand, is at the front end of the process, exercising a reflective practice effectively delivering, witnessing and analysing the reality or their client interactions, conducted in the context of a complex working, organisational and personal life. So the questions that they formulate reflect the context of their activity, the other players and their own role in the wider setting of their work.

The increasing reputation of coaching as an effective method, the accumulation of evidence, the involvement of science and rigour in the processing of evidence have all made the practice of coaching increasingly appealing to academics. As a result they, too, became progressively involved in part-time coaching work, alongside their core academic activities.

Competencies: Practitioner Researcher vs. Academic Researcher

COMENSA 2011

- Practitioner Researcher
- Achieving impact: commercial value, dissemination, use within practice, contribution to professions
- Research knowledge: research methodology knowledge, research design, listening and observing skills, maintaining credibility, adhering to process, discipline
- Self-management: Self-awareness, leadership, process management, stakeholder engagement, maintaining practice focus.
- Project management

VITAE UK 2010

- Academic Researcher
- Knowledge and intellectual ability: competencies, knowledge, creativity
- Personal effectiveness: self-management, personal effectiveness, CPPD.
- Research governance and organization: professional conduct, research management, finance, funding and resourcing
- Engagement, influence an impact: communication, dissemination, engagement and impact, working with others.

Figure 0.1

Career coaching is particularly suited to convergent academic and experiential scrutiny which – combined – supports the proposition of a practitioner–researcher role in coaching.

Unlike other types of coaching, career coaching has clear directive aspects plus rigorous steps similar to the scientific approach, such as: methods, tools, performance indicators, a critical path to goal attainment, transparent goal-setting and defined success outcomes, contracted and objectively measured. At the same time, the nature of the process work between coach and coachee is individualised, emergent, subjectively experienced and amplified by the quality of the relationship. The value of the practioner's personal experience when exercised against a set of criteria, and with the deployment of certain skills and capabilities, meets a way of scientific thinking that makes room for positioning oneself as a practitioner–researcher or scholar-practitioner, with a credible voice in the scientific world (Passmore & Fillery-Travis, 2011).

It slowly but surely treads the path that leads from surveys and case studies to theory development and qualitative techniques, to quantitative randomised controlled trials, and finally to meta-analysis and outside-the-norm findings. This process reveals the acting factors, prerequisites and specific context, and expects a result that can be generalised and it is the way of "formal" research. But the complementary and mutually enhancing role of practitioners as inside researchers and academics as outside thinkers, both in the pursuit of the same purpose of finding answers, is rarely explored or realised even when it comes to long and old established professions. It is obvious that a dialogue between the two groups can only be meaningful and beneficial to both, plus the other potential users of those findings. However they are also separated by different values and thinking paradigms.

The differences reside not only in resources, time scales, issues and enquiry methods, but also a difference between the questions each group is interested in. In this light, raising questions about the respective competencies that may be needed for researchers and practitioners, as well as how those sets of competencies may be similar or different, is topical and pertinent (Armsby & Fillery-Travis, 2009).

Coaching practitioners, organised in professional groups such as The Global Coaching Community or local professional associations, such as the South African Coaching Professional Association (COMENSA), have come together with academics on the matter of competencies, and good progress has been made since 2010. Now there is a framework that identifies the clusters of competencies for practitioner–researchers, compared to academic researchers:

Practitioner–researcher

a   Achieving impact: commercial value, dissemination, use within practice, contribution to professions;
b   Research knowledge: research methodology knowledge, research design, listening and observing skills, maintaining credibility, adhering to process, discipline;

c   Self-management: self-awareness, leadership, process management, stakeholder engagement, maintaining practice focus;
d   Project management.

Academic researcher

a   Knowledge and intellectual ability: competencies, knowledge, creativity;
b   Personal effectiveness: self-management, personal effectiveness, CPPD;
c   Research governance and organisation: professional conduct, research management, finance, funding and resourcing;
d   Engagement, influence and impact: communication, dissemination, engagement and impact, working with others.

The overlap areas are quite clear, even if the language may be different (points a. and d.), (c. and b.), (b. and a.), for example. The points of difference relate mainly to:

- *Source of funding*: external versus within practice itself;
- *Stakeholder engagement*: to raise funds (at the beginning of the process) or throughout the research process (in the case of the "insider" position of the practitioner);
- *Explicit sharing of the research back to the profession*: publishing is mandatory in academia but not a regular activity in the practitioner community.

The practitioner–researcher model applied

I hold a strong belief in the value of backing up practice with science, and experience with formal training. I also believe that our opinions and perspectives benefit from being informed and supported by what the wider circle of academic and practitioner peers may have to offer as credible and robust; a common body of professional references.

And this is how I related my own activity to the practitioner–researcher model when reflecting on my competencies and overall professional capability. My career took me from an extensive international business practice back to my earlier interest in and study of psychology, having accumulated on the way significant cross-cultural savvy gained through life and work in six countries, which all led to me establishing an evidence-based belief that the critical factor of success in business and life relates to people factors.

My point of access into management consulting happened to be career coaching, in an associate role. This setting provided structure and rigour to the process of working with individual career coaching clients. This enabled me to track and map my own body of experiential evidence, against the practitioner–researcher competencies listed previously. And here are some highlights of that match:

On the subjects of research knowledge, methodology and discipline, in career coaching there is specific knowledge supported by:

- Specific selection/recruitment process to this profession;
- Specific career coaching training;
- Experienced peer environment;
- Continued professional development (CPD) and supervision.

The operational set-up included:

- Use of specific systems;
- Data recording and reporting against key performance indicators;
- Client and sponsor satisfaction tracking and reporting;
- Process improvement;
- Multi-contracting between service providers, corporate sponsors and individual coachees;
- Integration of the career coaching function within the wider remit of talent management.

The packages offered to clients enabled for me a fast learning curve and exposure to high client diversity and visibility of the outcomes – hard to otherwise achieve in private practice in such a short period of time and within a regulated and formalised set-up, at the beginning of my own coaching career. This satisfied my own standards gained in my previous years with exceptionally good companies, which required a highly professionalised context for practice, and to which I had long been accustomed.

Self-management – evidenced in:

- Process management: as required by the packages on offer and the goals and targets that were pre-set;
- Stakeholder engagement: by the communication and reporting that linked targets, goals and results through the "four-way contracting" (sponsor, individual coachee, coach and service delivery organisation);
- Maintaining practice focus: my main task as a coach was to deliver career coaching services, directly and indirectly, to individual coachees, sponsors and the delivery organisation. In this dynamic process I have been able to gather my own sample of data by meeting hundreds of individuals who found themselves at that point in time in a moment of transition, change and need for decision-making and decisive, focused action to further their professional lives.

In parallel I also developed my own private practice of clients, which added another set of contracting and working principles that I developed myself.

Knowledge and intellectual ability – including competencies, knowledge and creativity, as follows:

- Psychology: also psychophysiology and psychopathology, therapy, pharmacology, psychiatry, experimental psychology – all providing scientific underpinning to my thinking and work;
- Sociology: group dynamics, social group, anthropology, enculturation and acculturation, which provide models on thinking and behaviour of groups;
- Psychometric assessments: for occupational assessments of abilities and personality (known in the UK as levels A/B) plus, StressScan, Thinking Style, Myers-Briggs Type Indicator (MBTI), Jung Type Indicator (JTI), Birkman, Values & Motives, Fifteen Factor Questionnaire Plus (15FQ), Belbin, Mayer-Salovey-Caruso Emotional Intelligence Test (MSCEIT), The Bar-On Emotional Quotient Inventory, Minnesota Multiphasic Personality Inventory–2 (MMPI-2), Occupational Stress Inventory (OSI), and so on – all useful ways to map and articulate ideas about individual preferences in mental processes and behaviours;
- Neuroscience: MRI-driven knowledge on the workings of the amygdalae and the limbic system, to regulate subcortical emotions and related behaviour – provided specific science related to processes of the mind and behaviours;
- Executive and team coaching: variety of models as stated previously also own models – the Unified Coaching Model and the Onion Model, the multilayers of culture;
- Philosophy: dialectic materialist principles, history of philosophy, formal logic and ethics – these gave me useful frameworks for my thinking and work;
- Science: chaos theory, complex evolving systems theory, quantum physics – constantly informed my thinking and practice;
- Extensive business experience: with IBM, Alcatel, Johnson & Johnson, Bristol-Myers Squibb, etc. across functional expertise in quality management, audit and process improvement (ISO 9000, CMM) operations, manufacturing, supply chain, international trade, project and operational resources management, which enabled me to work with the widest range of clients knowing their work environment so well;
- Extensive multicultural exposure: lived/worked in London, Paris, Bucharest, New York, Johannesburg and Sydney and also travelled extensively; multilingual: fluent in English, French, Romanian and German, and some Italian and Russian – this gave me an advantage in my work with international clients;
- Martial arts and Eastern philosophy: the practice of tai chi, chi gong, yoga and aikido have enabled me to develop unprecedented states of awareness and focus (distributed or simultaneous) over my mind and body. This new

learning has developed my ability to be "present and open to the other" in my coaching practice;

- Academic experience and research methodologies: as a visiting lecturer, with UK and European institutions, teaching business psychology and strategic HR management subjects, which kept me up to date with the latest thinking and research;
- Speaking and publishing: on subjects related to people, psychology and work/life balance; to peer, academic and business audiences, which enabled me to share knowledge with others;
- International education: in business and psychology (MSc, London; MBA, Paris; BA, Bucharest), which has given me access to and experience of the diversity of education systems, policies and politics, and the possibility to analyse how they impact working adults' self-awareness and positioning in the labour market.

Significantly, my life in London – arguably a most influential centre in coaching with a mature coaching market – has provided an exceptional opportunity for immediate access to primary sources of learning through talks and presentations given by thought leaders, such as Sir John Whitmore, Prof. David Lane, Prof. Stephen Palmer, Prof. David Clutterbuck, Prof. Daniel Goleman, Prof. Philip Zimbardo, researchers Dr. Paul Babiak and Dr. Robert Hare, Jonathan Passmore, Meredith Belbin, Sir Richard Branson and many others. I had the chance to meet some of them and with some I have worked on specific projects or collaborated in pro bono professional settings.

I also embraced over time multiple professional memberships and accreditation standards: Accredited Member of the Association for Professional Executive Coaching and Supervision (APECS); Accredited Member of Association for Coaching (AC); Principal Member of the Association of Business Psychologists (ABP); Member of International Coach Federation (ICF); Member of the Special Group in Coaching Psychology (SGCP); Life Member of The Coaching Academy; Affiliate Member of the Chartered Institute of Personnel and Development (CIPD); and Graduate Member of the British Psychological Society (BPS).

My continued professional development (CPD) log is in the public domain and this direct access to and enjoyment of primary sources has informed my opinions and professional views. Over time, I have accumulated a sufficient body of knowledge and experience to be able, in turn, to share it with others. And I do so through pro bono work and various forms of knowledge exchange, such as this book.

Chapter 1

Valuing experience and the power of past practice

A brief introduction to coaching

> Reality emerges and exists everywhere, all the time and all at once, like an endless web of changing content through which we constantly create our unique corridor of action and meaning.
>
> Adina Tarry

The history of humankind reflects the fact that since the dawn of time individuals and groups have strived to survive, achieve, improve and find meaning to life. But the environment in which human society has expressed itself has also changed greatly, not only naturally – due to vast climatic shifts and natural disasters, such as volcanic activity, creation of continents, movement of tectonic plates, and severe weather pattern disruptions – but also as the result of the individual and social activity itself. The successive industrial revolutions notwithstanding, the advent of the internet and mobile telephony has pretty much singlehandedly caused the most dramatic overall change and, more importantly, the fastest pace of change ever known to us. But human drivers have been and remain largely the same, and range from survival and basic hygiene factors of life to higher aspirations and achievements expressed in the arts, science, technology and a relentless appetite for discovery. Our brain and psychology have also remained the same for many thousands of years. This is why reading literature from 1,000 BC or staging plays dated 300 AD still resonate with us today in terms of the emotions, ambitions, behaviours and conflicts that they depict about an individual or a group. In addition, ancient values and beliefs still prevail alongside new ones that would have been unthinkable only twenty years ago.

The landscape we live in is mixed and filled with contradictions, but our individual mission, apart from what we do for society, is to cope, survive and ideally thrive in our lives and turn our existence into as good and positive an experience as possible within the given parameters of our circumstances, potential and duration of life. And this objective goes back to the dawn of time and has been facilitated through learning, shared experience and development. Over time, educators, philosophers, researchers and scientists have all pondered and contributed to the establishment of methods, systems and approaches to achieve human aspirations.

Alongside general knowledge, some schools of thought were specifically promoting ways of developing critical thinking and reflection. And one way to gain such higher capability was linked to the "person to person" interaction, either from master to apprentice or between peers or under the patronage of a third party. The concept of enhancing the performance of "one" through the presence and influence of "another" is ancient and to this day we have all benefited from such encounters that may have impacted our present, or past, or even completely changed the path of our future.

In the last forty years or so, "coaching" as a developmental method has gained traction as an activity distinct from sports coaching, where the practice has been used for a very long time. And its purpose is to take a person from where they are at the time to another place – mental, spiritual or physical – where they would like to be. Coaching is about that journey and the changes that come with it. Coaching, as we understand it today, was born in the 1970s, and there are many definitions of coaching; but in essence, coaching serves development, transformation and the attainment of a fulfilling life and personal expression of potential, within various contexts. The coaching journey takes place in the real world, as we define our identity and spark the light that shines the path we create for ourselves, through this intricate, infinite, multidimensional fabric that holds us, to fulfil our destiny. In doing so we also use the experiential wealth that others may have created before and for us.

And if we deconstruct reality into its components, we find environment and society, values and beliefs, economics, nations, organisations, personal and professional identities, social roles, institutions, political, religious and ideological contexts, education and skills as some of the many key facets of our interactive engagement with reality.

Reality is complex and changing, intricate, layered and interconnected. It requires awareness of and attention to its many aspects. This mandates the development of awareness – of self, others and of context – sound judgement, the ability to improvise when things are uncertain, and a strong self-belief to navigate decisions, actions and outcomes. And coaching is one way to enhance such capabilities, by working with "another".

Overview of career coaching

> We must have perseverance and above all confidence in ourselves. We must
> believe that we are gifted for something and that this thing must be attained.
> Marie Curie

Career coaching is defined by a specific scope and clear objectives. It also has a good number of aspects that are directive and as such may be aided by training as a complement to coaching. There are prescribed activities and outputs – such as how to write a CV, how to answer difficult questions, how to research the job market, etc. – which are about method, and can be learned by those who need this knowledge in order to secure a job. Many of these questions have good and free answers on the internet, or are very well covered by practical career focused books.

The pragmatic side of job search is important, and looking for a job is indeed a process where, once engaged, things tend to flow in a certain way for most people, most of the time. This is why in career coaching, instead of people spending most of the time looking at underlying causes that may impact outcomes, most attention goes to the method and the process. This is understandable since the "what" and "how" require great effort and energy, and as we all know, looking for a job is a job in itself! Career management certainly benefits from planning and from directive advice and counselling, which deal with what is rational, planned, linear and predictable in known, stable contexts.

But career coaching also needs to achieve another objective and refocus a person on another level – that of the unknown, of the unpredictable, of the developmental, where the irrational, the emergent, the strategic and the meaning and purpose emerge from the shade into the light – increasingly important as we attempt to project from a known present into an unknown future.

Because the world of work has changed and we can now work 24/7 from any location – in all ways from "gig jobs", to self-employment in "start-ups", to working for corporations that pretty much own the lives of their employees by skilfully blurring boundaries and blending the private-public-corporate spaces. Such variety of options is both exciting and confusing and, more importantly, needed to meet our aspirations, values and purpose, which raise the deeper "why?" questions.

This emergent dynamic world and our renewed perspectives on career and life bring to the fore the need to constantly reshape our higher selves and galvanise the unexpected resources that we may have in addition to a necessary strong but fluid core, so that we can meet randomness and chance with flexibility, hope and self-belief. This new environment requires human beings, who have not changed for millennia, to respond immediately to and make sense of this brave new world – in the making since the 1980s and now on the cusp of the fourth industrial revolution – and adjust to it very, very quickly.

This is why the coaching conversation is now increasingly about the wider world of others and context, be it the job market, the planet, new industries, changed personal circumstances, financial stability considerations, etc. Work, life, technology and the state of the world now form a vast context with a set of interconnected systems and subsystems, each at various stages of development, more or less aligned.

It is only when we achieve an integrated view of self-other-context that we can act adaptively and behave in an effective way, which will serve well across the entire system. It is also true that people can behave with great impact when they are aware of others or of context, but may not be highly self-aware. The importance of self-awareness remains, however, critical, in that it is a foundation ingredient necessary in building a sense of self-worth, finding direction, meaning-making and achievement of personal fulfilment and happiness.

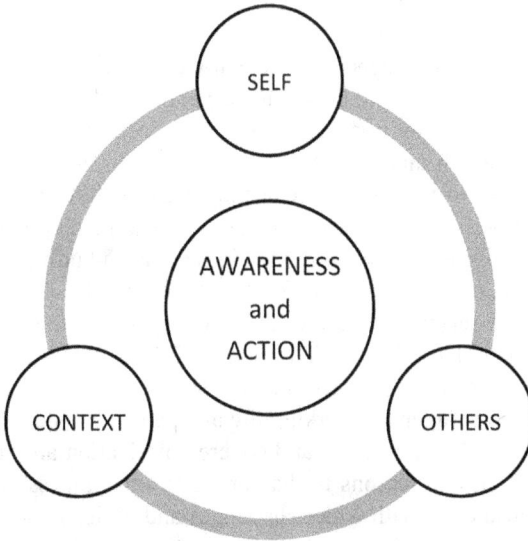

Figure 1.1 Awareness and action

With this in mind, this chapter explores to a sufficient degree – but not exhaustively – salient aspects of career coaching that relate to the "why" rather than the "how" and the "what" of the career coaching content.

Each topic includes an overview and definition of the theme, a brief presentation of the supporting formal reference (model/framework/research findings) if applicable, a presentation of group findings with some examples, a case study, practical suggestions and a summary. This structure is in place to enable all readers to find some value. The accessible language conveys contents that are based in research, theory, current scientific models and experiential findings.

Learning from practice: coaching themes and patterns

> We are all different. There is no such thing as a standard or run-of-the-mill human being, but we share the same human spirit.
>
> Stephen Hawking

My new career in management consulting focused on people development. It was built on the strength of my extensive international business experience and my formal qualifications in psychology. This opportunity came after due selection, induction and specific training in career management methodology and related questionnaires, tools, tests and models; many of which, I found, over-lapped with my pre-existing knowledge acquired from psychology or business methodology.

Career coaching holds a special place in my coaching experience because it is one of the most complex and interesting types of coaching. This goes against the general perception that it is mainly a service, instrumental in the practical preparation for the job market (CVs, market research, marketing documents, etc.). It is true that most clients seek coaching because they just want to update their CVs, do a bit of interview practice and have some help with job market research. Such services are also provided in schools and universities for those who finish education and often look for their first real job.

No doubt such services have merit, but in my work, the focus has been on those questions that fall outside the immediacy of CV reviews and inter-view practice. Instead, it has been, more often than not, an unexpected and unplanned review of an entire working life and personal history. With conver-sations that, before long, changed and covered motivation and invisible driv-ers, true aspirations and reasons for happiness or unhappiness in work. These conversations also dealt with wider challenges and options, including consid-erations about finance, health, family, dependents, one's place in the world and one's past, present and future in life and in work. This much less explored side of personal identity and evolution as a human being, engaged in society, often leads to profound transformative outcomes and unexpected insights and deci-sions, and initiates moments of important evolutionary step changes. It also empowers people to find clarity, discover the language to articulate findings about themselves, to understand and own moments and encounters that have been significant in their evolution. It takes them across all the inner structures and subsystems that make them who they are; from personality and age to the outer systems of obliquity and transitions.

CV templates, test-answering practice, letter samples and interview ques-tions to prepare for assessment are all available online and could easily be enabled by machines, which is the way things will happen in the future.

But what follows are findings that have been gathered by real interactions involving two human beings who have brought to the conversations two com-plex, aware, intelligent, empathic, creative, meaning-making human beings; and my work of almost two decades has provided a unique opportunity to meet a significant number of individuals. In 2015 I logged 2,872 hours of coaching (and stopped counting after that), and whilst I have not kept a log of the num-ber of clients, using a number of say four hours of coaching per person, this results in approximately 700 individuals.

And this is what the client group profile looked like:

- Educated to degree level and often postgraduate level;
- Middle or senior management, often executives with profit and loss responsibility or high potential individuals;

- Technical specialists, with inputs that have been mainly knowledge-based;
- Aged between 25 and 55+;
- Covering all industries, from media and arts to manufacturing, research, public, private and NGO sectors, and across all functions from factory managers, to researchers, accountants, HR specialists, stockbrokers and auditors.

Without fully extrapolating from this group to a general population, and based on an informed evaluation of the themes and patterns that have emerged working with these individuals, it is likely that such themes may also resonate with and benefit many other individuals looking to map and manage their career in a more effective way, whilst self developing in the process.

The themes covered in this section are: personality, invisible drivers and values, age, personal branding, assessment centres, polymaths, working internationally, obliquity and transitions.

Personality and individual differences: when all things are equal there is always one that is not quite the same

It is rather amazing to contemplate that with so many billions of humans inhabiting the earth, no two people have the same personality, not even identical twins, just as our fingerprints or earlobes are unique. Keeping such great differentiation in mind, it is also amazing to see that people are able to communicate and collaborate, acting together in social structures, instead of the world being just a cacophony of individuals living at their own pace in their own space. In fact, the achievements of people when they get together are most extraordinary. And whilst each individual is an exception to the rule, we all share the same rules and descriptors that define humanity and human beings.

There are hundreds of definitions of personality, but a few common elements are found in all of them: personality is about characteristic patterns of thoughts, feelings, attitudes, values, aspirations and behaviours arising from within, which make a person unique. Personality is something that makes us distinguishable and remains stable over time, even if some of its facets may change. This is a construct that retains an inner congruence whilst it manifests itself in emergent states, as we evolve through stages of life, over time. Personality involves emotions, feelings, free will, inner drivers such as values, beliefs and attitudes, learning, motivation, reaction to external influences, and response to genetic heritage . . . pretty much everything that relates to a person and the way they act or react to the environment and the way they appear to us. Defining something as being "many things" is problematic but sufficient to identify and work with this construct, with clients and in reflective practice.

Personality is about uniqueness, and individual differences are essential whenever we wish to explain how individuals differ in their behaviour. In any study, significant variation exists between individuals. And it is possible to study narrow or specific factors such as reaction time, emotional range, defined preferences or behaviours, values, intelligence, memory and so on. And the results are helpful in building and understanding a common baseline for individual variance. Importantly, individuals also differ when it comes to ways and magnitude of responses to external circumstances. Individual differences are the variations from one person to another on variables such as self-esteem, rate of cognitive development, being outgoing or reserved, preference for the big picture or detail, being assertive or pleasing, being anxious or relaxed, seeing the glass half full or half empty. All in all, the study of individual differences helps us to understand not only what makes humans similar to one another, but also what makes them different. By considering the variations that can occur from one person to another, we can best understand the full range of human behaviour.

And models to explain personality have been many over time, in an attempt to find causal links for aspects such as physical attributes, heredity, nurture, culture, range of needs (from survival to higher needs for education, knowledge, creativity and spirituality) and behaviour, to name just a few. What is interesting to note with all these contributions – some of which have been abandoned and others still utilised today – is that they all build upon each other or open a new approach that is later taken further, and the timeline of contributions clearly indicates these interconnections. The evolution of thinking on personality presents an interesting mix of biology, psychology and sociology, which focuses on heredity or learning and, to a degree, broadly places theories in the nature vs. nurture dichotomy.

Looking at various generations, for instance, it is clear that personality is not a factor that can create generational differences, but the system of values and beliefs and the collective life experiences of a generation (war, prosperity, rapid change, etc.) all have their say in groups of people sharing common characteristics, whilst their personality remains individually distinct.

Another example is how some people believe the labels and the "truths" that others tell them, whilst others, quite the contrary, become even more determined to be themselves; they experience the same external stimuli but have different individual reactions. Or how some people feel "old" because society tells them so about their biological age, others do not. Modern research on neuroscience, socio-psychology, team dynamics, learning and development, individual differences, genetics and epigenetics seem to make room for all pre-existing thinking, with appropriate modern corrections. The emerging outcome is a complex dynamic picture of non-linear impact, where the power of the unconscious, the genes, the epigenetics, the developmental learning and experiential socio-economic context are equally important and equally represented in what one can observe in people and their personality, in action and in real time. Specific aspects of personality are further explored in the subsections that follow, to complement this introductory overview.

Reflecting on group findings

In my work, I have encountered all personality types, traits and combinations of nature, nurture and epigenetics. The people I have worked with were unique in appearance, behaviour and thinking. They had different and specific aspirations, motivations and ambitions. Individuality was prevalent. And whilst what we did and the way we did our work may have used common methods and a partly pre-charted path in a process, in all cases, each encounter and each coaching programme was different. It was always a case of meeting someone new and being forever surprised and alerted to the fact that every person demanded focused and specific attention to who they were.

In my experience I have also worked with people that knew each other, either related or partners, pursuing the next job. Although our work together (just like with many hundreds) covered similar process steps, the way the actual process unfolded was unique, and I cannot remember any two clients that have been in any way similar, let alone identical, not even when working with couples that lived together and engaged me to deliver the same thing – coach them on the way to their next job. Their individuality always came to the fore in spite of similarity of methods used across the board or their goal being the same.

My case study

Even before I became aware (at the age of fourteen or so) of psychology and its object of study, I described myself as being quiet, observant, happy in my own company, enjoying a small number of close friends, not very happy in crowded, noisy places, and very interested in noticing and reflecting on my observations of the world around me. I was also drawn to academic pursuits and the arts. In the words of a school friend that has known me since I was ten, I have never changed and I am today exactly like I was that many years ago.

Such a comment, on the one hand, has surprised me, since my life experience of a few decades has definitely made me evolve into a different person, but, on the other hand, it is clear that, indeed, all the attributes that I described previously are still true today. So what am I to make of this mixture of change and stability that are both true about me? My own training as a psychologist provided me with a vocabulary and understanding that helps me mitigate the two apparently opposite poles. And it has also given me clarity of the many aspects of my personality that are at play in my normal everyday life. In this light I have been able to differentiate what is specific about the way I think (thinking style) and about the way I learn (different learning style); what types of risk I am happy to take and which not (risk appetite); what is my best communication style (one to many, one to one, in writing, verbally, public, private); how I behave and how others perceive me; how I react under stress and what I look like at my best; what are my weaknesses and what are my strengths; and what is my level of resilience and what replenishes my energy.

The combination of all this information about me did not happen at once and there has been a progressive collection and then "assembling" of the pieces of the puzzle that make up my personality. Some I have gathered by self-reflection, others as a result of using psychometric assessment, others by listening to what people say, and some by reflecting on what I inherited from my parents (physically and psychologically) and how in some ways I remain like them or developed independently from that heritage. All this eventually came together into one coherent picture that informs me, in a self-reflective way, of who I am and enables me to identify at various point in time and in different circumstances why I behaved and communicated in a certain way, as well as what aspects of my personality are more or less engaged and more or less in flow with the people and activities of my work life and my life amongst other people, close or not.

By creating that connection between my personal reality and the reality of the world of work and life, I am better able to manage choices and achievements, chances for success, and opportunities for gratification, growth and learning. To give some examples: I have always moved on from a job the moment I had nothing new to learn, because I have an appetite for learning and get bored with repetition of things that are known. I have always preferred jobs where I was left to get things done independently but offered a mentoring support as and when required, because this was a model and expectation that I have built as a result of my historic collaborative relationship with my father. I have avoided jobs that required physical stamina and physical risk, because this is one risk that I am averse to, whereas I have taken social risks in terms of being an independent thinker and maintain my position in spite of group pressures. I have been drawn to work that involves the mind and problem solving rather than actively engaging physically. I also preferred jobs that required me to embrace the big picture and look at possibilities; monitoring, evaluating and improving existing systems, to support a vision for the future which is always better than the present reality. This self-awareness is invaluable, as it informs me on how happy and productive I am likely to be, when I need to evaluate a potential new role and work or collaborate in a new environment. As a result I can make an informed decision, or create and exercise work-related choices.

A useful exercise

In the internet age there are numerous free access questionnaires and tests that you can do to explore aspects of your personality, and even if you have never been tested in a formal setting (such as recruitment processes, or job-related opportunities for promotion, or talent fast tracking) you can do so on the internet. What is important is to understand that personality is a construct and therefore you can test different aspects (such as thinking style, personality type, personality traits, emotional intelligence, risk appetite, etc.) individually. But what you need to do next with these individual results is most important. You need to apply an integrative and critical perspective on these results. Because they are not an exact mapping of who you are, but a close approximation, and there are many factors and dynamic variables that need to be taken into consideration, including aspects of nurture, such as socio-economic influences, significant others in your life, skills and work environments that impact who we "become", how we perceive ourselves, and how others perceive us.

The process of reflecting on results, in itself, is very empowering, and owning one's identity is a useful developmental step. From this new position of awareness and ownership, everything becomes possible because this enables developmental work to be done on weakness and is an immediate and effective utilisation of strength. This builds a strong base around which one can engage with controlled forays of discovery, thought change and experimentation. It opens up a wider field of possibilities and options as well as the ability to aim for success and plan future steps, based on what can be built today, followed by a next step tomorrow, and to build a path for aspirations to come to fruition into an increasingly more distant future.

In professional terms, you will be able to better discern what jobs and work are better for you at the present, what you could aim for in the future – if you close gaps that you may have found in skills or experience – and step forward into the future fully aware and prepared. It is hard to be all things to all people, so understanding complementarities of strengths and weaknesses, compared to others, will also enable complementarities within groups and teams, to deliver that complete package. If you want to be successful you need to appreciate and value others who are successful in other ways and who, in turn, may well need what you have and can bring to the table.

Critically reflecting on the various aspects of your personality will highlight that they are never quite developed all at the same level and at the same time. This opens up the possibility for you to work on harmonising those levels by matching your intelligence to your emotional intelligence, for example, or your skills to your motivation, or your thinking style to your personality trait, or your emotional development to your cognitive, and so on.

So the individual tests that you can take to receive a psychometric profile that covers various aspects of your personality (values or personality traits or types, emotional intelligence, etc.) need to be integrated and made sense of, in light of your personal history, specific circumstances, real life relevance and context of your development. This active integration of information and applied meaning-making is more important than the sum of the various parts of data that you collect about yourself.

In practical terms, here are some simple steps to achieve the personality assessment:

- Gather from various sources (controlled or open) as many results on aspects of your personality as you can (thinking, values and beliefs, emotional intelligence, team contribution, personality type and traits,

leadership capability, etc. to broadly cover cognitive, emotional and relational aspects);
- Look at the results and check how close or not they are to what you think about yourself;
- Try and identify other variations that may enhance or reduce some of those aspects (for example, you may be quite engaging and open in one-to-one situations but more reserved in group settings, so number of people matters in the way you behave or come across . . .);
- Integrate them to create a whole picture;
- Reflect on how and which aspects have changed over time and what were the circumstances (for example, one can become very assertive, directive and pragmatic when working in an environment that is more practical and results-driven, when in fact the person may be, in other circumstances, quite sensitive, warm and considerate towards others; nursing vs. manufacturing);
- Reflect on what jobs would best suit your default nature, or develop those aspects that you wish to change in your nature, and opt for such choices.

There is nothing more empowering than knowing who you are, who you would like to be and what choices to make to get there. In the knowledge that the work environment impacts us all, making the right choices guided by awareness of the self is the best option that is likely to keep you balanced, motivated and gratified by what you do, whilst becoming and being the best version of who you can be, at any point in time!

Summary

Individual differences and personality represent one of the most important, if not THE most important factor that impacts a person's choices and life journey. As such, it is also a complex construct made of multiple complex facets. Knowing all that self-awareness enables us to know about ourselves, our personality and the way we typically are and react in the world will provide the best possible start that we can have when analysing our options. This also impacts the way we set objectives – be they in our career or in our private life, since both are closely interlinked. Knowing one's personality enables each individual to work with oneself to mitigate setbacks and utilise all untapped potential.

Invisible drivers of behaviour: values, motivation, attitudes and more, and why similar outcomes do not evidence similar intentions

Picture an unknown person coming towards you in the street with a big smile. What would you think? And why do you think they smile? It could indeed be that they are a friendly person, an extrovert that just wants to say hello, and they could equally be bipolar and in a state of excitement, or someone who needs to get close to you with an intention to harm you. So the same behaviour can be motivated by different intentions, and we usually translate what we see into an explanation that often relies on conventions or our own view of the world, and so we may be surprised or puzzled or may reciprocate and smile back, or may steer clear and avoid that person, thinking something is not quite right. But the interesting thing is that none of these judgements or reactions brings us any closer to knowing exactly and for sure what is going on. Superficially, we see something and react to it, but at a deeper level and from the perspective of the other we remain in the dark. The truth is that it is really hard, if at all possible, to know another person's mind, unless they tell us and they tell the truth. Behaviour can be deceptive and not reflect the truth. There is no linear connection between behaviour and motivation.

But how strong is the causality that can be established between communication and actions, on the one hand, and invisible drivers, on the other? Again there is little certainty in this link. Because the same words and deeds can be expressions of a completely different set of values and beliefs, for example. And we can only hypothesise what is behind what we see. In fact, in many ways, what we see is not how things are and this has been amply proven by both illusionists and scientists alike.

There is no straight and readymade path available to knowing ourselves or knowing others. We have to actively engage, be curious and explore deeper to find our answers. This is how links and options become apparent together with potential outcomes and choices that we can evaluate and use to serve the purpose that we pursue. Whether we pursue change and transformation or a better relationship with others and the world around us, finding and understanding the deeper links between the invisible drivers and actual behaviours is always a useful way to go about achieving that purpose.

The list of invisible drivers is quite long and covers words that we use in our everyday life: motivation, values, beliefs, attitudes, aspiration, expectations, feelings, emotions and culture. All words that do not indicate a direct connection to thinking but are linked to another aspect of our human nature, a deeper level of being and interacting that is in many ways unconscious and subcortical. In terms of neuroscience they are also linked to the workings of the older part of the brain, the limbic system, and what is known as the reptilian brain. This is because its function is, simply put, to keep us alive and in a state of readiness to self-defend against stressors and threats, in order to survive. This activity is expressed through emotions, which are quite embodied and very much involved in our physiology and trigger changes in pulse, breathing, blood flow, skin conductivity, etc. They are deeply connected to our primitive brain and the parasympathetic nervous system.

Emotions range between positive and negative, and link directly to the way we respond to stimuli, which cause us to react and move one way or another. If the stimuli are perceived as negative, we distance ourselves and look after ourselves by experiencing fear, anger, disgust, shame and sadness. This defensive reaction can be significant to the point of complete system shutdown, causing us to faint, as an ultimate way of avoiding and escaping the negative or threatening situation. And I can think of a close friend of mine who was so afraid of forthcoming surgery that on the morning she was about to go to the operating theatre, she simply fainted before anything happened, and only came to after it was all over. She just shut down and was not "present" during the traumatic except in body.

On the positive side, we gravitate towards and attach to stimuli perceived as positive, by experiencing excitement, joy, trust and love. Emotions consolidate into more personal, subjective, longer-lasting feelings, which with development become expressed in language, gain meaning and inform our behaviours. An endless pallet of emotions can be created as a result of a blend and variations in intensity and mix of the nine emotions listed previously.

Emotions have not been widely researched and there are variations on what scientists consider as the definitive list of emotions. But there is agreement that they provide the fuel for all the structures that are built on top of this biological foundation that resides very much in our primitive survival brain. So this subconscious force is what drives our visible and conscious behaviour and informs in direct or mediated ways what out cortical brain decides and how it deals with information coming from all sources. The prefrontal cortex, also known as the executive centre because it makes judgements and moderates impulses and rash reactions, has to deal with the information coming from the level below. What follows is a list of these invisible drivers, with related simple definitions, as a reminder of the role they play in our lives.

A belief is an internal feeling that something is true, even though that belief may be unproven or irrational. It is about a mental conviction and acceptance that something is valid, and actual. Accepted as such by a person or a group, beliefs provide a sense of certainty that something exists or is good, a feeling of being certain about something. A value is something that we hold dear, a measure of importance attached to something; qualities and things that we hold dear. A value is formed by a belief that an individual or group holds, related to the worth that we attach to something – be it object, behaviour, thought, quality or standard. Values influence attitudes, aspirations, behaviours, judgements, the decisions we make and the way we conduct ourselves. They are considered important to live by because they are useful or appreciated. Initially based on a tendency to naturally react in a certain way, and linked to a positive or negative experience (instincts), they give rise to emotions that a person "feels" rather than "thinks". They manifest a spontaneous experiential reading/reaction that can also lead to sentiments (more embedded and long lasting) that determine behaviour, which in turn involves a mixture of emotions, reason, feelings and attitudes.

An attitude is the way a person expresses or applies their beliefs and values and is expressed through words and behaviour. Attitudes are the way one thinks and feels about something, not visible except as expressed in language or actions.

Aspirations are a strong desire, wish or hope to achieve something great or important. Aspirations are about aiming for a positive outcome and having the ambition to achieve it. Expectations are beliefs and hopes about what might happen, that something will happen or is about to happen, a good feeling about the future. Also in times of uncertainty, it is about what is most likely to happen.

Hope is the feeling that what is wanted will come to pass; that something positive will happen and things will turn out for the best. Hope is about a positive attitude and an expectation for positive outcomes for oneself and for the world at large. Hope is about wishing for something to occur. Behaviour is a typical or particular way a person usually acts, especially in relation to the people they are with and the circumstances they find themselves in. Behaviour is about acting in a specific way, in relation to others and oneself.

And the collection of all such behaviours, ideas, feelings, values, beliefs, customs and artefacts that define a group of people at a point in time come together to form what we know as culture.

What is blatantly obvious once we consider an overview of all these drivers and their definition is that they define each other, in circular dependencies, are terribly entangled, and converge under either the individual umbrella of personality or the larger tent for social groups, known as culture.

And so every time we consider one of them, we are in fact including all the others in an impossible to disentangle mix. What they all have in common is the fact that they can only be made visible when mediated by communication and behaviour, yet none of them create a linear causal link, to fully explain either one. Dealing with one, it seems, is to deal with them all at once. And if we look for specifics, we can artificially focus on any one at a time, for research purposes, but not because this singular way is the way they actually work in reality. There is no wonder, therefore, that the study of the deeper aspects of personality and the invisible drivers of behaviour have been hampered by difficulty.

The same challenge is presented to us in terms of individual levels of self-awareness about our drivers. Unless we specifically make the time to focus on this aspect of our personality and understand how, when and why they have become such a force in our lives, we remain at their mercy whilst they stay hidden from our scrutiny. It is important to note that whilst awareness is rightly considered our main path to self-understanding, awareness itself is equally difficult to define and remains one other somewhat intangible aspect of our psyche. It is true that in neuroscience we may be able to see how the brain is activated by focused thinking, but we still cannot answer the questions about how those regions link and why we get that specific landscape of activity as we see it, and not another.

Neatly separating and grasping the specific invisible object of our study, to dissect, monitor, categorise, classify and subject it to scientific scrutiny, has proven rather challenging, not least because we have difficulties in specifically defining it. Like with other aspects of individual psychology and anthropology, the definition of one will involve the mention of other invisible aspects.

Values are defined by beliefs, beliefs are supported by attitudes, in turn fuelled by emotions, which all lead to behaviours, and are also connected to culture, which in turn is a result of accumulated artefacts, beliefs, practices, values and so on. We are faced with great interconnectedness between the individual terms we try to define as stand-alone concepts – as a consequence of one thing being defined by another, in turn defined by the next – and so face little success when trying to untangle such interdependencies in the pursuit of a clear stand-alone definition of a single concept. As a result the only practical ways left to verify or interrogate people on their invisible drivers (values, beliefs, attitudes, emotions) are to either use self-reporting questionnaires, or observe behaviour and infer the invisible drivers from that. Both methods lack accuracy for a number of reasons, such as bias or absence of strong correlations between factors, for example. This is why since the 1950s the "black box" approach to behaviour – where values and beliefs were left out and research focused on that which it could capture, measure and evaluate – has taken precedence and led to many applications, including in management and recruitment, through, for example, competencies frameworks and situational interviews or the collecting of historic information.

There is, however, some certainty about the origin of our values and beliefs, which is to be found within the environment we have been born into and the initial observations we have made from a very young age of what our carers, parents, other relatives, friends, colleagues and all social groups were signalling in their interaction with us, and amongst themselves, expressed in behaviours and communication, including specific messages about values, beliefs, aspirations, motivations and so on. The do's and don'ts of our first years of life, embodied by the most influential people that we had around us, often leave a profound and permanent legacy that may be hard to undo.

Around this inner core of invisible drivers that remain stable over time, there is an outer ring of values, beliefs, aspirations, attitudes and emotions that do change over time. Such changes occur under the influence of many factors, such as: personal experience that proves to us if what we believed was in fact the case, or not; or the influence of significant others, who bring into the exchange their own values and beliefs, which we may explore under their guidance and end up embracing; or aspects of culture (values, beliefs, attitudes, etc.) that society at large presents to us, some of which are also changing and which inform our own as part of that social group.

If we reflect back to society as it was, say ten, twenty or forty years ago, we clearly see how far some things have changed and how conservative or incompatible or backward some other things have remained in the context of our twenty-first century society. Today we may be shocked by some aspects of the past, captured by documents of social history and anthropology, which at the time were widely acceptable and accepted by most. Fortunately agents of change are at work in every society and this is how history presents us with both new and old aspects of culture, at any point in time. But we also know that culture takes a very long time to change, holding within it the old, the new and the transitional aspects of its dynamic evolution; and this is why we look at decades rather than months or years for culture to move on. The cautionary lesson here is that we have to have patience and maintain momentum, instead of hoping that things will change overnight, which is not a realistic expectation but understandable wishful thinking. On the other hand there could be extreme events that may cause an overnight change due to their significance or shocking nature. This can indeed be so impactful that it will shock the world into an overnight change. But otherwise the element of significant length of time is always present when we talk about changes in people, society and culture, because they are all systems of a high level of complexity.

Back to hidden drivers, the recruitment and work-related profiling and assessments try and capture hidden drivers and attempt to predict behaviour or explain behaviour by looking at values, beliefs and attitudes. This remains an approach that is not precise, because it is dependent on probabilities and patterns that may be true (statistically) for large numbers but do not necessarily and accurately hold predictable value when it comes to the behaviour of a specific individual. But psychology uses statistical analysis and this is why communication in psychology often uses words such as: typically, very likely, may, maybe and probably, to signal this uncertainty and set the correct expectations; that we may get it right one time out of three. Or that we "get it wrong" two times out of three.

Behaviours and communication (verbal or not) enable us to navigate our social contexts, make sense of what we see and hear, and in so doing "sense" potential dangers or opportunities. What this reveals to us is how important our human hardwiring is when it comes to our ability to adapt, read and decode the signals that our social interactions give out. We develop an intuitive way of making decisions that short-circuits linear judgement (heuristic thinking) and can often tell us that "something is not right", or "there is something wrong with this picture", or we just "know" something is going to work or not.

Navigating the social human landscape is extremely complicated; this is why children – who are still developing such skills – can be vulnerable and gullible, for example. But at one point in time or another we can all be "fooled" by others, and such ability to deceive also has a place in evolutionary psychology, and is expressed in activities such as "pranks", "practical jokes", flattery, and manipulation, as commonly manifested in social interaction. This make-belief is also elevated to an art and entertainment form by magicians and illusionists, who enchant us, puzzle us, but also scare us a little, when reminded of how complex and shifting the interplay is between what we see and what is real or what we believe is true, but is not. Society is the place where the mystery of the invisible and the science of the visible come together, endlessly and dynamically manifesting themselves through the human condition.

The advantage of unravelling the mystery of our own behaviours, through self- awareness and awareness of others (both aspects of what we also call emotional intelligence), not only clarifies and directs our decisions better but also increases our ability to understand and better predict what goes on in the minds of our fellow human beings and specifically of those who really matter to us, whether colleagues at work or friends and family. Emotional intelligences, and the specific aspect of being empathic and being able to be in "other people's minds", is a very useful capability to have as social beings, considering that our entire life is essentially unfolding with and in the presence of other human beings with whom, ideally, we need to develop harmonious and successful exchanges and relationships. As perennial students of life, we all stand a good chance of understanding others and pursuing harmony with them, if we only have the motivation to do so, a positive attitude to this pursuit, an aspiration for happiness, and we value enough the positive emotions and reactions that result from our good behaviour towards them. It is all about what we value and how we express this belief through our words and actions!

Reflecting on group findings

Most if not all of my coaching clients had some difficulty in articulating where they stood in relation to invisible drivers. It was even more difficult to work with such notions once articulated and connect them with the rest of the career conversation. Related questions typically stopped us in our tracks, by reactions of surprise or some doubt as to the relevance of such explorations. The focus being, typically, of a pragmatic nature (let us update the CV or talk about the market or recruitment). The other challenge was that only a few could actually articulate clearly individual values and beliefs let alone categorise them in clusters. Although words designating values and beliefs are commonly used in language and my clients may have used them often too, this did not ensure that the meaning of those words had been fully and deeply understood or personally owned, but rather that those words were used as attributes to define something or someone else. For example, clients may have said that they like a person because they are very nice; but if asked where "nice" ranks on their list of values and beliefs, the reaction was often a surprised look and possibly the comment, "A good question, I don't know, let me think . . ." Their own inventory of values and beliefs was somewhat limited.

Another pattern highlighted that a link between actions and motivators in regards to one's behaviours, was missing. To the question: Why would you do that? Or, what would make you act in this way? The answer usually came as: "I am not quite sure, this is an interesting question; let me think about this." Further down the process, however, once this awareness set in and they started questioning and probing deeper, my clients responded with excitement and curiosity to the information that had been opened up to them about themselves, which they were ready and happy to embrace and continue to discover.

Typically they enjoyed this process and found it very useful. Now they under-stood connections and interdependencies, discovered a new world of explana-tions and opportunities to change, experienced renewed clarity, energy and hope. Knowing what may have been the values and attitudes that had nega-tively impacted their choices and actions for far too long, this was a time to be rid of those hidden blockers and enjoy a new start. Maybe explore a completely new direction!

But big changes and new choices, that have little connection with past expe-rience, are more easily articulated than implemented. Typically, changes for something really different are processes and not events, and involve transi-tions. During transitions there is a continuous evaluation and re-evaluation of motivation, options, possible outcomes and ways to achieve them. Due to con-scious or unconscious reasons, there is a journey that needs to be completed, to connect decision and action. In the world of work such changes may involve changing priorities. For example, favouring freedom over money; or individ-ual contribution over collective identity and co-branding as part of a company; or a new perspective on what really matters most in one's life – achievement at any cost or relatedness and people – or the revival of an old dream left on standby for some time, because of the heavy demands of a career, and so on.

There is also correlation with age and what is important at different points in time in our lives, as part of our process of individuation and self-expression. In addition, there are considerations of the impact our decisions (values and beliefs included) have on those around us – family, friends, colleagues – plus consid-eration of our obligations and commitments. In this light some options may be timely, whilst some may need to be postponed or discarded, to protect those who may suffer an adverse impact. Typically, financial obligations or family responsibilities weigh quite heavily when deciding over choices around work.

However, the more I reflected on my coaching work, the more I found that in the end, the most important aspect of people's working lives remains linked to invisible drivers, even when they may be on hold for a while and manifest sometime later. The key questions that people grapple with and their anxiety or uncertainty are not really linked to how good their CV is or how up to date their skills are, but something quite different and more profound, linked to a sense of personal identity and meaning. With this in mind, I make sure that my coaching journey with my clients, starts well away from CVs and the job market. Instead it begins by a facilitated reflective enquiry on their level of self-awareness, their history including significant others, the forces that inspired and shaped them, their aspirations, beliefs, achievements and what puts them at their best.

Contemplating one's history is exceptionally useful and significant. Not only does it enable the person to become aware – by clearly articulating and describing their value system, role models, and significant events – but it also traces the evolving line of continuity over time, from past to present and into the future. In doing so, it enables clarity on choices, in personal and profes-sional lives. Together, historicity and time provide a solid frame to a person's journey. Reflection on that journey, brings rich information about situations of failure, disappointment or disconnection, often explained after careful scrutiny, by a misalignment between personal values and organisational or other outside systems' values. Having to cope with the resulting tension leads to burn-out, disengagement, stress and unhappiness, which may often be diagnosed incorrectly but can be addressed correctly at the source, once the real reasons have become clear. Often clients can explain why their work or their career is not going well by describing specific conflicting relationships with bosses or colleagues, etc. But soon enough it becomes clear that behind it all the issue has been caused by an impossible conflict between their "conscience" and identity, and the compulsory and expected behaviour (activity) that they may need to display at work; compromises that eventually become unsustainable. Conversely, analysing examples of success, happiness and achievement, can highlight the necessary factors that enable a person to be at their best, including the alignment of clearly articulated drivers with the context of their work and life.

Values, beliefs, attitudes and emotions are all at the very core of our personality and our lives. This is why it is useful to get into a healthy habit of regularly taking an inventory of our drivers (above and beyond trigger events, such as looking for a new job) as a matter of "wellbeing hygiene" and remain constantly aware of and in tune with our inner selves.

My case study

I have reflected on the origins of my own values and beliefs and I found that many of them, which have not changed over time, come directly from my parents and the way I have seen them lead their lives. For example, my mother was a formable, practical woman who had enormous energy and could "move mountains" without even pausing to reflect on the magnitude of the task. She simply had a natural "can do" attitude. This was passed on to me as a capability for pragmatism and implementation, with the belief that actions speak louder than words. Nothing is impossible within reason and there is always room to do things better and improve on what is there. In my working life this translated into me being good at project management and manufacturing and supply chain management. My mother was also an extrovert and very good at connecting with people, who created around her a significant network helpful when it came to mutual assistance. With me this worked out in a slightly modified way. I am not such an exceptional networker, but I do know people on a more selective basis and I help a lot, although I am reluctant to ask for help myself.

My father was the opposite; mainly creative, shy and softly spoken, except when he came alive with the people he knew and liked. He focused his cognitive energy on the arts, reflection and creativity. He was also a natural and competent mentor and looked out for others, particularly in their desire to better themselves spiritually and intellectually. Significantly, he treated me as an equal from childhood and so I embraced the principle: "I am ok, you are ok and together we can do even greater things" and also the joy of learning though collaboration. I also value creativity and knowledge and believe in self-development and helping others to develop.

Both my parents had great integrity and were very honest. It would have been unthinkable in my childhood to get away with skipping school, aided in the deceit by my parents, and I remember clearly how puzzled I was when I saw this happening with some of my colleagues, who were doing so with their parents' blessing. Neither parent placed great importance on financial gain, apart from what was necessary for a comfortable, simple life with no ambition for riches. They both valued principles, aspirations and personal achievement above material possessions or rank and high formal status. As a result I have always been impressed by people as individuals and made judgements based on their human qualities or their cognitive or creative capabilities. And I have met remarkable people across the entire socio-economic spectrum. Personally, I have not pursued hierarchical power and status but rather the path of knowledge and self-actualisation.

These are just a few examples of how I have traced back the invisible drivers – now made visible through reflection – that influenced me. And alongside my parents I can name a few significant other influencers, such as my grandparents, some teachers and professors, and a few of my school and university colleagues, who have all contributed to helping me structure and internalise my own core references. I have also reflected on which and how some have changed and others not. But the most important outcome of this process for me was to clearly see the path of development, the factors at play, and the way history and time have transformed or consolidated my invisible drivers. I have noticed how influences, both external and internal, came to rest in the middle, harmoniously synthesised to accommodate my personality and nature with nurture and the outer experiential context.

My values and beliefs also manifested very clearly and strongly in my career choices and I always looked for jobs that held something new, where I could learn, that I enjoyed and which I changed as soon as I lost interest and had nothing more to learn or to improve upon. I also liked to work in industries driven by science, research and innovation, fast-paced and under pressure to constantly produce something at the cutting edge. In this light the juxtaposition of fashion, telecommunications, cosmetics, IT and pharmaceutical sectors, for example, no longer appears eclectic or outlandish. In the same way, jobs that related to manufacturing or marketing or audit or HR or supply chain management or consulting no longer seem strange, since they all enable both implementation, with its satisfaction of action, and tangible achievement, but also the reflective future-oriented side of the strategy and the big picture. In all these jobs, good work was immediately visible and one's contribution could get positive feedback and act as a reward and motivation to continue, under my "I am ok, you are ok and together we can do even greater things" paradigm that I embraced early in my childhood.

In light of my history and my drivers, my choice of jobs suddenly made sense and revealed a career congruent with my deeper self, instead of being random and unrelated, even though as a young developing adult, I made those choices in spite of an inability to clearly articulate why and how, just as many of my coaching clients did, before we opened up this line of reflection. For half of the course of my own career I have lacked clarity and articulation of what drove me. Yet those same drivers have remained at work over time, across geographies, industries and jobs, and are still unbroken to this day. With hindsight this is of course quite predictable because they are part of who I am. But this continuity also provides a visible testimony to the power of their influence and the fact that in my case, allowing this undercurrent to naturally follow its course, did bring me joy, a sense of achievement and self-actualisation.

A useful exercise

Embracing a regular review of your invisible drivers, at regular times and specifically at times of change – whether planned or unplanned – is a reflective exercise that can map the way forward and define a good landing place as a meaningful and happy outcome of that change. Answering questions such as: Being valued is like what? What motivates me? What makes me feel happy? When was the last time I felt valued? What holds meaning for me? What is that like? What has previously inspired me? When was the last time I felt amazing? What was I doing? helps generate the words that describe what is of importance to you.

You can also reverse the process and use word cards or word lists: choose and rank those that resonate, create shortlists of, say, ten words, then the top three words, finally link those words to practical applications; set goals and plan actions and situations to bring those invisible drivers to life and so aim for an actual best outcome for you at that point in time as it has been identified "from inside, out". Such explorations provide an exceptionally interesting and revealing insight into what goes on, who, and what course of action may be best. Career management is about finding fulfilment and happiness and these are hard to come by if one is not aware of one's vulnerabilities, gratifiers and preferences. If you align your deep identity with what you do in your everyday life, including work, where we all spend most of our time, this is likely to result in fulfilment and energising connections with both the self and society at large. Follow a path of identifying all your invisible drivers by starting from a visible behaviour; for example, a job or activity that you currently do and ask yourself the following:

- What emotions or feelings do you experience when you think about the work you do?
- What value does your role provide?
- What motivates you in your work?
- What attitudes do you apply to your work?

By pursuing such a line of self-enquiry you may clearly see when and if all these elements are aligned to your actual behaviour as well as being internally congruent or not. And this type of investigation will help you identify what is there and what is missing, or out of balance, within the landscape of your inner drivers. The next step may be that you then link those findings with external events and actions, such as behaviour and communication, around your work.

Summary

Values, beliefs, attitudes, aspirations, expectations, motivations and feelings are all factors that create our personality as something bigger than a sum of such parts. But they also hold a specific place and evolve as distinct drivers, from our early childhood into adulthood, throughout our lives. They provide the foundation of our behaviour, the direction and strength of energy that supports our actions, albeit in a non-linear way. They are hard to discern and not always flexible or transparent. And one cannot emphasise enough – for example – the exceptional influence that a person's aspirations, expectations and attitudes have on the scope and intensity of their ambition and achievements. Or how instrumental hope can be at the hardest of times, in dealing with randomness, change, chance and uncertainty. High aspirations, ambitions and expectations for oneself bring about exceptional resilience and creativity in finding solutions for the unexpected. They enable a return to a positive view of life and restores one's place in the world.

This is why having a regular review of our drivers should be a hygiene factor and ideally exercised with someone who can take an external, uninvolved view, in the process. Friends and family can play a great role in the day-to-day management of our lives but they are directly involved, partial and potentially unskilled in the talking or dialogical practices. Ideally, having a coach alongside us on our reflective journey, to "check in" from time to time – either at a moment of transition and change or just as a matter of verifying that we are on the right track – could be invaluable. After all, we do use the help of skilled outsiders, such as GPs, hairdressers, dentists, real estate agents, solicitors and accountants to assist us impartially and competently in our everyday lives. Why not extend the same consideration to the invisible forces that relentlessly influence our minds?

Age: some freedom from the tyranny of time

Age is an aspect that often comes into the career coaching conversations, usually for two reasons. Sometimes (and in my experience not that often due to the demographics of the groups) it is about people looking "a bit too young" and therefore having some difficulty in convincing the interviewers that they are in fact experienced, mature, responsible and reliable in spite of their youthful looks. But more often it is about people feeling anxious because they are

"a bit too old" for the market and fear competition or discrimination. Not deny-
ing that the variety of age-related reactions are real and affect people, what
we can do is choose to focus on our own position about age, and decide how
we wish to play the age card, in our own minds and in the interactions with
others, particularly in the job search exercise. This is about understanding and
accepting what one can or cannot change, clearly planning to make the best of
what we can control and aim for the best possible outcome. Easily said but not
so easily done. Because one's relationship with one's own age is multidimensional and depends on many personal and external factors.

Age could be defined as a span of years during which something has been
alive or in existence, or during which events occurred. Or the time of life at
which some particular qualification, power, or capacity arises or rests. A lot
has been said about age, covering many aspects from equal opportunity and
discrimination to legal considerations, various rights and socio-anthropologi-
cal perceptions, mores and memes. In addition, the term "age" has often been
used interchangeably with the term "maturity" and they are not the same thing.
Statements such as "age does not matter" and "anything is possible regardless
of age" or "never too late" and "better late than never" all carry some truth
and some wishful thinking. In my view there is such a thing as "too late" and
"age does matter", because I believe that all things can be true, depending on
circumstance and points of view. Context really matters. Which makes statements of absolute validity somewhat difficult because depending on circumstance and perspective, for someone with a sense of adventure and risk, who
is unattached for example, moving from one country to another at the drop of
a hat is feasible, regardless of age, whereas for someone else who has family,
commitments and a low appetite for risk, moving from one country to another
may be very hard, even in their thirties, which is arguably the prime of life. I
have taken the example of moving abroad, since many people can understand
this event even if they have never experienced it themselves; but popular culture and TV programmes, for example, analyse such events in detail and for the
education and entertainment of viewers. Not necessarily because it is difficult
to move, per se, but because it is a very complex undertaking. It involves a full
range of deliberations and considerations from financial to emotional and from
personal to family and other groups of important people.

Another example may be that of starting careers or even hobbies that involve
physical prowess and stamina at a more advanced age, which quite frankly is
almost impossible. Ballet dancers, for example, spend their lives training hard
and working daily to keep in top physical condition. Such people do recognise
publicly that they lose faculties by the day and typically retire early (in their
forties), acknowledging that for some things age matters. Wishing to become
a ballet dancer at fifty may indeed be somewhat unrealistic. A similar impact
can be found with mature singers, who with age and changes in vocal cords
and lung and muscle capacity lose the edge on the top register and the ability
to project their voice. The unsettling truth is that from a biological perspective,

we start "ageing" around the age of twelve, when the first signs of "defects" in the reproduction of live tissues appear, as a result of metabolism. As we know, our entire body is not the same, even if it appears the same, because all our cells are regularly replaced by billions of new copies, over and over again for many decades, in our lifetime. Eventually these copies become corrupt and imperfect. But even without this knowledge, people just exercise common sense when making judgements about when it is or is not reasonable to say that age matters. But when talking about work or the mind, it is also true to say that it is never too late to learn something as long as we set realistic expectations about outputs and performance in relation to that change or learning.

In my experience I was once rather discouraged by someone's comment that my desire to improve my touch typing is misplaced because it is a bit late to learn this mechanical skill. Upon reflection I then thought that perhaps he was right, perhaps learning automated movements later in life may be more challenging. But I also thought that in my youth I may have learned faster to type better, but also had less to write about. Whereas now, my typing may not be very efficient, but I have plenty of experience and thoughts that I can write about.

What I have noticed and learned from and about my clients is that age changes priorities and ambitions. In the earlier career, people do not care so much about money or status, but a lot about the opportunity to learn, to build a reputation, to associate with a good company and to find opportunities for a wide variety of interesting work that they seek to experience. Later, in their thirties, people tend to wish more for acknowledgement, professional status and better pay. By now, generally they also have some personal obligations (family, partners, mortgages, etc.). And so their choices are driven by gains of different kinds, status and stability.

After the age of fifty people tend to want to do something different and often wish to give back to society. Typically by now they have put behind them financial and personal obligations (children have grown, most of the debts and mortgages have been paid, they have achieved status and recognition) and so this becomes increasingly a time for personal fulfilment of those values and aspirations that have been put on hold. This will see them reconnect with the wider society and make contributions of a pro bono nature or for lower salaries, provided they get the right job with the right company, to align with their new values and beliefs, or attitude to work and society.

People over fifty tend to be choosy and need recognition of their accumulated experience and knowledge, which they are keen to share. But they also become more and more independent and do not "tolerate fools gladly", which includes anything from working with bosses they do not respect to sticking to a rigid schedule or not having flexibility to make their own arrangements and working patterns. This is because the ageing process brings about increased individuation and differentiation. People become less similar to their peer group than in earlier years and increasingly dissimilar (as an individual) because with time they know more and more who they are, what they like or dislike, and what they have to offer.

In this context one needs to introduce the concept of maturity, because indeed this is not about age (not the same as being older) but nonetheless related to age, because maturity requires time and time therefore translates into a more advanced age. It is not to say that someone older is also necessarily more mature – there are young people that mature very quickly under special and sometimes really hard circumstances, but overall maturity and age go hand in hand. We increase our emotional and social intelligence as part of the natural process of maturing and better understanding and relating to the world around us and this fact about ageing and maturing is really encouraging.

Age is indeed a reality experienced subjectively and individually as well as collectively and socially. At an individual level, the perception of age is volatile, because it involves some contradictions and tensions. There is no doubt about the fact that no matter what age, people feel the same feelings, desires, hopes and aspirations. They want to be connected, to be loved and appreciated, they want to be visible and useful, they want to carry on as always doing what they do best – working, or appreciating leisure time or doing what they did not have time to do when they were dealing with the responsibility of family, partners, finances and social duties of all kinds. They do not want to be lonely, isolated and invisible. And this is due, amongst other things, to the fact that with age, indeed, most people become more self-aware of their likes and dislikes and of their strengths and weaknesses, more insightful, more choosy and more succinct, and possibly less patient with trivia, the mundane and idle pursuits. They understand what really matters. They get straight to the chase and often tell things as they are. In effect they become more confident and streamlined in thinking and action. In addition, they need less to live, they consume less food or clothes or household goods and in all respects embrace a more frugal and sustainable existence. This combination of increased clarity and personal effectiveness with decreased consumption is a positive one, without a doubt.

Yet in parallel there is another indicator, which is increasingly a negative one. The one related to biology. The system is simply deteriorating constantly and without possibility of reversing that biological entropy. This process is slower or faster and different from one person to another, due to many factors: genes, lifestyle, socio-economics, type of work, place of birth and residence. Still, the overall name for this direction of travel and bothersome transformation is entropy; meaning progressive and irreversible unravelling and decay of the system. And so the bitter irony is that the two aspects antagonise each other, and the way people experience this antagonism is different.

Some accept this "gracefully" and some do not. And it is easy to understand the frustration of those that just cannot accept the inevitable when in their hearts and minds they feel just as "young" and even better in their skin than when they were thirty years old, except that the skin itself is deteriorating by the day. The shell that carries the person and their mind, experience, emotions, vitality and identity is fragile and beyond a certain point cannot be repaired and will unavoidably perish sooner or later. As they say, it becomes just a matter of . . . time!

Yes, it would be ideal to have in one's twenties the money, the wisdom and the confidence that one might acquire in their fifties, and be then able to combine peak physical health with financial stability, emotional maturity, professional skill and the energy of the age, to fully live a life of adventure, value-creation and outstanding contribution. And thereafter, over time, slow down and fade away as the systems progressively fail and so achieve synchronicity between biology and psychology. But things do not happen that way. And so we are left, indeed, with the task of trying to reconcile the best we can this unfair but inevitable misalignment between our socio-psychological golden age and our biological sunset. As always, the human spirit does not take defeats lying down and science is on a permanent lookout for the magic solution that can put an end to this unfair succession of events. There is research around the possibility of capturing the human self and placing it into a non-biological form that could potentially live forever. But to achieve this, we still have some way to go.

Meanwhile, dealing with the matter here and now, beyond biology and physical changes at an individual subjective level, age is also a notion that has its roots deep in society and social culture. There are societies where age is very respected, and the fact of being older and more mature brings enhanced credibility and respect. It also places that person at the centre of the family, whilst communities positioning such "elders" as trusted advisors and decision makers, particularly at times of crises when there is a need for greater wisdom and thoughtful direction. The older people take a leadership role based on their age and acquired experience, which is valued and welcomed to bear on current and future circumstances that affect others.

On the other hand there are also societies where age is an enemy and the obsession with eternal youth and the pursuit of it at all costs (literally) is prevalent. It is notable to say that whilst the Western civilisations have been somewhat enchanted by youth and the modern use of science to manipulate consumers' minds and seduce them through advertising has a lot to answer for. Presenting the unreachable dream as a possibility and firmly setting it as a horizon line to aspire for – forever slipping away – in front of the masses, only added to the wind beneath the wings of fantasy and wishful thinking.

The result is a renewed preoccupation with youth that is fuelled by increasingly lucrative businesses – started in the 1950s and more prevalent since the 1980s – and shows no signs of abating. America and the 1980s are specifically responsible for this dream machine that has seduced millions around the globe, and the money spinning from diets, fitness regimes and cosmetic surgery keep rising, whilst in practice, public and less public cases of age discrimination keep reminding us that no matter what, the state of being "old" remains a present and controversial reality. But how does this fact play out in the real world of work and recruitment for ordinary people in an out of employment? By and large it is a real and not so real challenge; and again it all depends on a multitude of factors.

What is immediately clear and needs no arguing is that employers prefer people who are well presented, appropriately dressed and mannered, with good articulation, who take care of their appearance and show an overall positive disposition. Going to interviews poorly dressed and looking tired and rather depressed does not make for a good picture. Picturing yourself as an employer, if honest, and asked the question: who would you choose – someone looking happy, healthy and well presented or someone looking down, poorly dressed, and rather depressed? The answer is obvious, unless you are in the actual business of rescuing and supporting people in need or crises.

This is why instead of engaging in a defeatist position along the thoughts of "I am too old, they will not take me, my chances are limited by my age", etc. people are better served by making the best of themselves and doing simple things like getting nice, contemporary, good-fitting clothes, being well groomed, polishing those shoes, getting a nice tie or a flattering pair of earrings, getting a good night's rest, feeling good about the opportunity, feeling hopeful and well prepared, and just putting one's best foot forward in that interview and letting the forces that be do their work, on the foundation of this personal effort.

When people like us, they do not ask questions about age; they just relate to who we are and what we present to them . . . by the time it comes, the question of age will not matter, because they would have already "bought" into thinking that we are going to be a good addition to their team. Any boss would prefer to work with likeable people, a person who gives them confidence and who will not be "hard work" to manage. The fact is that people that are liked by others are welcomed everywhere, regardless of age.

One's presence, individuality and positive impact can very well obscure the issue of age. Beyond trivialising reality and focusing on appearance – well captured by popular culture and TV programmes such as "10 years younger" or how to dress better – there is the undeniable message that appearance and perceptions do matter. Great transformations "from the outside in" can be achieved just with a bit of care for colour, style and an interest in the way we look. Combined with experience and skills, this personalised package may well be a winning recipe, including for those over forty, fifty and sixty, that go to interviews. A more holistic consideration of all circumstances may in the end yield a result whereby – I could summarise based on my experience with so many candidates – age actually matters both very much and not so much, because the presence of the individual is what in the end makes or breaks the deal. Just ignore age and work with the person that one is, both in presentation and substance, to make the best of what one has. There are a lot of "grey heads" in the public domain, from actors to scientists to politicians, who are well beyond sixty and seventy and yet are respected, influential and fully active, making a significant impact.

Neuroscience tells us that our vision is our most important source of information, whilst our limbic system crudely and very quickly sorts stimuli in a simple binary "friend or foe" model and then triggers the "fight-flight" response, which in fact translates into: move away (fly), go forth and confront (fight), freeze (no reaction, being stunned), and faint (removing oneself from the situation). So first impressions matter even if they may be the wrong impressions that get corrected later. But interviews are a "one shot opportunity"; if you look tired on that day and the image you project is not positive and reassuring to the employer, you will lose an opportunity, and not due to lack of competence. So why not increase your chances instead?

Personal branding, including the way we relate to and "display" our age is important. We do make judgements on appearance and usually within seconds of a first encounter, so make those seconds count in your favour; look fresh and smart, and smile – this "will take years off you . . .", not actually but in the way you project the image of someone they will want to have around them. If people want to be around you, your actual age will matter much less, if at all . . . this is a fact, and either juniors or peers and elders, will welcome your company and wisdom, in work and life.

Reflecting on group findings

My clients ranged in age from 25 to 55+, but most were distributed between 35 and 50 years of age, with the highest number in the middle at 40 to 45 years of age, overall reflecting a balanced bell curve. Age was more frequently discussed in cases of transitions, where there was some anxiety about trying to break into a new industry or company or role. They felt that everything could be held against them, including age, because to begin with, they did not offer an exact match to the job brief, but an alternative of transferable skills instead. Which for recruiters – age not withstanding – is already a riskier proposition. Interestingly, the perception held was that this is the way society is; it discriminates against people over forty and there was little they could do about this.

The problem was 100% owned outside, by society, which caused a sense of fatalism and powerlessness in the face of what prevailed. Both men and women felt quite defeated by this status quo and hoped for the best, in the sense of possibly being lucky in a process that was in any event skewed against them. And this is where the conversation became interesting for me, in terms of verifying their level of self-awareness about the image they projected and the level of care that they took regarding that image.

Conversations about clothes, style, colours, fashion and appropriate dress for various occasions came into play. And I found that there had been little prior focus on this topic. This led to us also discussing such details prior to interviews –first impressions and how to dress from top to toe, in detail. Overall, the importance of this discussion was well understood, even if not always translating into a more permanent change of habits or a new way of thinking about themselves. And it is fine to respect the fact that some people naturally take more care and pride in their appearance than others. But in the end, wearing something that complements one's appearance and personality, rather than not or spending the same amount of money on clothes that match and flatter, rather than not, offers a simple choice that should be easy to make for most people to achieve a potentially better way of turning up in the company of others. A little effort can go a very long way and lead to a much better outcome. This situation-specific truism was accepted by most of my clients, who indeed took my suggestions on board and modified the way they "showed up" for those important and potentially destiny changing meetings.

My case study

My perception of age has admittedly been somewhat blurred, maybe because I have been used to mixing, from my early years, with people of all ages and did not quite understand what the difference was, except for physical appearance and the way children and adults went about things. Beyond that I was never specifically interested in how old the people I met in my life were; and this worked very well for me, as typically I mixed with people close to my own age group, just by chance and because this is the way generational peer groups are established. I was lucky enough to know both sets of grandparents, but, again, the significant age difference was not an aspect I lingered on, perhaps because of their own youthful way of being with me. And so, in my twenties I had very good friends in their forties for example, but the age gap did not register for me. In my forties I had friends who were in their twenties, and again this did not register as a significant difference. With the passing of time, however, I became increasingly aware that the other people around me were in fact age sensitive and to a degree judgemental about it. They were presenting me with question marks and interdictions around age suitability and who should relate to whom, based on age, or how was one supposed to dress, according to age. So my first awareness of age differences and the socially enforced prejudices that come with it arrived quite late in my life and only because my age peers were raising their eyebrows at transgressions. This, I admit, surprised and saddened me but also made me take a position and argue against age-related prejudices in whatever form they come. This brought to me a new awareness about age pressures, when society forced me to consider the aspects of age and appearance, about me and about others.

The influence of my parents in my life has been – as for many of us – quite strong and neither of my parents were sensitive to age but both were careful with appearance. In addition I had an early education in arts and a natural love of colour, which became a strong part of my visual brand. And one may think that having such a strong individual image is a good thing, but not quite so, because as always, it depends on context. I had to learn to curtail my creative exuberance and adjust my look to what my work environment demanded.

I love colours and the positive energy that they provide and a black and white world would be unthinkable to me. Yet there are entire industries where the colour code for the "organisational look" ranges from black to navy, to grey and white, with shirts, skirts, jackets and trousers, in any combination of the above. All of which I find rather impersonal, rather dull and dark, and would not represent me at all. But clearly me turning up for interviews as my authentic self, colourful and accessorised, would have meant a career non-starter. So I invented an in-between style; a suit but in deep, rich dark shades of burgundy, purple, brown or charcoal, with a simple round-neck top and never a shirt. And I reduced the size and number of accessories, to a maximum of three small items. This created a look that was aligned but not quite standardised, which on the one hand made me acceptable within that culture, but, on the other, set me apart. So I managed to stick to my identity, but also adhere to external norms and expectation. Once "in" I progressively softened the look and slowly moved closer to the genuine me whilst keeping my appearance toned down a level or two, compared to the way I looked in my private life. Whether we like it or not, image and the way we turn up does matter. Let us make the best of this understanding and use it to our advantage!

As to age, I retain and uphold my "age blindness" as a value and belief that I am not prepared to change because others say so. Today, as always, I have friends who are thirty years younger or twenty years older, and I enjoy these interactions where my experience accumulated over decades is useful to them, just as their energy and inspiration is useful to me. In this exchange of complementarities, the combination of all ages offers an exceptional balanced mix and bringing together children, young adults, mature adults and older people is the best combination that we can enjoy and value, in work and society at large. Age inclusion and the diversity it brings to the common table are exceptionally precious and needs to be celebrated and encouraged! And this is a stance where my emotions, values, beliefs, attitudes, aspirations, behaviour and communication are firmly, unequivocally and happily aligned!

A useful exercise

It may help you to reflect on your view on age; how and when did you first form an opinion about it? What are the elements that you have drawn from your experience? And what are those that you may have inherited from your family and early social circles? Also question those beliefs today, based on what you think, not what you have been told to think either at home or by society at large.

Ask yourself how your views have evolved or changed. Ask yourself to what degree your judgements on age have been blockers or catalysts for your work-related choices and the way you "inhabited and embodied" your age, at various points in time. How did this reflect in your appearance, manners, choices, aspirations, successes and state of mind? And if your appearance is not at the top of your daily agenda, just consider if and how clothes may help you get where you want to go, or fit in, or help in making a memorable positive impression when you need it, regardless of how old you may be.

Also reflect on where you are within the norms of what is expected in the work environment that you belong to. Because the expectations on the way you dress if working in marketing or the arts or creative industries (colourful, trendy, flamboyant or minimalist) or in IT (relaxed, casual) or in a banking (formal and monochrome) will vary. With this in mind it is also useful to have some basic understanding and ownership of your unique body shape, features and colours so that what you wear complements your personal attributes and creates a flattering, appropriate, self-affirming and enhancing image that supports your skills and experience. It is not hard to achieve this and here are a few tips that everyone regardless of age or gender can follow:

- Keep your clothes and style simple and make sure it matches the culture of the industry or country or type of work that you are hoping for;
- Be well rested, relaxed and open when you meet people; think that you are happy to be there and this will show;
- Be engaged, curious and attentive;
- Observe the others and mirror the general tone and pace of the exchange;
- Whatever happens, remain polite, calm and articulate; stick to good manners;
- Think well of yourself and this will show and command respect.

All of these are things that can be done regardless of age but have the desired impact to make you come across at your best, whether you are thirty or sixty. Try to come across just like a person you would like to hire yourself. Would you have something in favour or against a person's age? And if asked, would you not in all honesty prefer to have around you at work – for eight or so hours a day – someone who looks after themselves, has a positive attitude, with stable mood and manners, is engaging, competent and contributes to the effort and work of others, regardless of whether they are twenty-five of fifty-five? Quite likely the answer of most people will be "yes", and therefore, precisely why you should come across in this way too, when interacting with potential future employers.

Prejudices do exist and time will hopefully continue to change the culture around age, as it is the case already, but in the meantime, in our own right, we can take ownership of the way we put ourselves across and be the best that we are at that specific time in our lives whether in our twenties or sixties.

Summary

Age is implacable because it represents forces of nature: time and biology. Age is also defined by society and our subjective state, personality and beliefs. We have little control over many of the complex forces at work, and therefore wisdom should prevail in the choice of not fighting losing wars and instead focusing on those battles that we can influence or control or win. Making the best of what we have, at a personal level (direct control), and doing our part in informing or correcting social perceptions and ideological norms, at a socio-political level (influence and limited control), is the best we can do.

The fact remains that older people hold the majority of the future. People live longer and many are expected to reach 100 and beyond. Pension age is moving and people are likely to work into their seventies. Increasingly and predictably, businesses and organisations will have to accommodate amongst its workforce people aged between twenty and seventy. Sixty is the new forty, and eighty is the new sixty. The HR function, the government, businesses and society at large will have to eventually notice and adapt to this reality and this may be a slow process, since changes of values, beliefs and culture are typically lagging behind all the other changes, particularly fast-moving technological ones. And whilst we may make our own small contribution to the bigger picture of cultural change, what we can definitely do is what we have control over. Much more can be achieved by us focusing on factors that we can control and change. Being aware of the difference between what we can or cannot change is the first step that we all need to take to yield benefits, in both our career and personal lives. Whatever age you are, live to the fullest. Do everything that your physical capability allows you to do and make sure you also stretch that capability just a little bit more!

Personal branding: knowing yourself enables others to know you too

To judge or not to judge a book by its cover? This is the question. But is it not the cover where a lot of thought, money and effort are being spent on? Because it is that cover that draws the readers to the content inside; it is the cover that informs the potential buyers of what is to come; it is that cover that helps, more than anything, the book to sell. Designing the right cover for a book is a key part of its marketing and commercial success. It helps those who have written and published it to achieve their objective: namely to turn that book into a success, even a bestseller.

So what about us, when we present ourselves to the world and the future potential employers? Should we not put in an equal amount of effort to make the promise and signal what we may bring to the table? Should we not aim to impress at first sight and create the appetite in people to want to know more, engage with us, be curious, ask about ourselves and so give us the opportunity to reveal the assets and advantages that our knowledge and skills can bring to a potential employer?

It is true that we could spend time arguing why one should not be hindered by one's appearance, since it is the essence that matters, no matter the wrapping, or one could choose to spend an equal amount of time polishing one's appearance and looking good, not only for the others but for ourselves too, by creating an image and a promise of professionalism and competence that the interviewers cannot resist.

In commercial marketing, the brand is about creating a unique image and name for a product or service, in the minds of the consumers, by way of advertising a consistent theme, which establishes a differentiated presence in the market, to attract and retain customer loyalty. The American Marketing Association definition of a brand is "A name, term, design, symbol, or any other feature that identifies one seller's goods or service as distinct from those of other sellers". The legal term for brand is trademark. Branding is about pull and not push, about expressing the true essence of the value of a process or organisation or service. It is about a concentrated communication bite that captures what the brand is or is not about.

A brand explicitly communicates about identity, talking about "what I am, why I exist", with an invitation to be embraced, if the consumers agree and wish to align themselves with what the brand stands for. Branding is for the long game . . . it is forever . . . marketing is about now; it tactically supports the brand, but the brand is above all and any marketing effort. When marketing has finished its task, branding is there to stay. It sticks in our minds and associates to the organisations, products or services, whether in the moment we buy into it, as users, or not.

A brand is resilient and stands on its own merit. For example, I do not drink soft drinks, but I certainly know of Coca Cola. I do not wear jeans, but I certainly know Levi's; and so I could go on and name many brands for products I do not buy or recommend to others to buy at all. The brand is built from many things and amongst them is the lived experience of the brand. This is why brands are often linked to actual lifestyles, aspirational stories or narratives of future possibilities.

The essence of a brand is multifold. A brand is about certain qualities that are specific and also in a very specific distinctive combination. It is also about a promise of something – durability, loyalty, quality, authenticity, longevity, transferability – which makes it desirable in our lives. It is also about aspirations for something that we do not have but could obtain by association with the brand. Finally it is about being more reassured and happier as a result of the brand becoming a part of our lives.

The history of marketing indeed involves psychology and the psychologists who in the 1950s were involved in advising big business on how to sell their products better, by appealing to the market's unconscious, to their dreams, and unsurfaced needs and wants.

At an individual level, in essence, a brand is a symbol of values, beliefs, aspirations and positive reassuring emotions. Brands speak to our reptilian brain, the same brain that is at work when we develop our personal moral compass, indivisible drivers – the inner structures whereby we can feel reassured that the environment is friendly and we need not fight or fly but we are ok and the rest of the world is also ok. It is about our own place in the world and our mission and vision for ourselves, which becomes embodied and expressed in our behaviours and the way we communicate.

So branding is about our deepest self and the way we display this unique identity through our presence. It is also about our history and the sources of our individuality, whether inherited or nurtured or self-directed, as we progress and develop with age and experience.

Reflecting on the definition of branding will stimulate anyone to think of their own impact on others, and factors such as age, values and beliefs, aspirations, personal qualities and strengths will all resonate with the branding note.

Our professional brand is never far behind our personal brand and ideally both should have a significant overlap. The fact is that whether we know it or not, we do have an impact on others and they are left with impressions that sometimes can be lasting, or not, depending on the relationship. If this is the case, perhaps we all need to pay attention and decide whether it is useful for us to understand, refine and manage the message that we send out around us, in order to make that message work for us and ensure it is an authentic representation of who we really are and what we stand for.

Reflecting on group findings

I have often reflected on the following scenario, which I have encountered with many of my coachees. When asked "what do you do?" – one of the predictable first questions asked in social circumstances – the typical answer is: "I work for X company". If that company is well-known, the next question is likely to be: "Ah! So what do you do at X company?". "I am a resource investigator" may be the answer, or possibly an acronym of a job title that may make sense in that organisation, but not to outsiders. So another question follows: "So what does a resource investigator do?". Followed by more explanations, which eventually lead to another "Aha! So you are in sales . . .".

Now this succession of exchanges that slowly lead by ever smaller circles to the essence of what one does, demonstrates how people often talk about "something or someone else" when answering questions about themselves. In the initial exchange, the person has been "selling" another brand – the company's and not their own. They define themselves by "proxy" in connection with another identifiable brand; a company name or a job title, and so bypassing the identification of their area of expertise that they – in their own right – own, in favour of describing their employment circumstances.

But an accountant is an accountant regardless of where they work, and so this is who in fact they are, in terms of individual professional identity and branding. And this is the first thing that people should state about themselves. From experience I can say that the most complex aspect of my career coaching work was with people transitioning from one job to the next, particularly as a result of restructuring, because they had to define and rebrand themselves as stand-alone professionals and sever the umbilical cord that linked them to the company they just left. All people identify themselves with their work groups, in one way or another, particularly when the organisation is a well-established brand that everybody recognises.

For people that have been with the same organisation a long time, it is often the case that they become "institutionalised", meaning that their identity is so very closely merged with that of the company that they may well lose themselves in that collective identifier. Obviously if that deep connection is brutally and unexpectedly severed by, say, restructuring, such a loss of identity is traumatic and a person needs time – weeks and months – to re-form and emerge again as a whole individual. Replacing one's identity is not an easy thing to do. This is also the case when one transitions by choice from one profession to another, or from one industry to another that are very different. An example that comes to mind is that of an accountant in her mid-forties that wanted to become an interior designer. Two professional identities that are quite different not only as such, but in the perception and expectation of people generally. Again, reconstructing one's identity is challenging.

My case study

When I moved from being a corporate employee to an independent management consultant the words failed me when I had to tell people what I did. This was due to many factors including that I was not sure what I wanted to do and be. Whilst trying to find out, I kept changing the descriptors of my professional self for a good while, sometimes using words that related to my past activity (auditor, quality analyst, supply chain specialist) other times to a possible future activity (management consultant, psychologist, coach) or even work that I would have liked to do but I knew I could not realistically turn into a full time job (designer, film director, script writer, poet). To this day I have kept the successive business cards of the last twenty years, printed over and over again, each a new version of the previous one, as evidence of how they changed with words slowly disappearing, to make room for new words until eventually I stood quite firmly within my new professional brand.

That process continued even when I got a grip on the "management consultant" descriptor, but then a new set of words appeared to define more specifically what I was doing under that umbrella. Eventually I rediscovered the "label" psychologist and so went full circle back to my original passion and formal training in a field where I had a degree and a lifelong interest but limited work experience. I was surprised by the joy this return to a label earned and abandoned so many years ago brought me, and I embraced it fully.

However, my love for the arts and my activity as a writer, remain confusing. In some circles I am known as a writer and people have no idea about my "real job". But this is also in line with what is known as "multiple identities" and it is the normal face of the complexity of who we are. As individuals we may engage throughout our life in numerous roles and each demands of us a level of competence to fulfil it properly. There is enough time in a lifetime, if there is motivation and a personal drive for it, for a person to be a polymath; a highly satisfying status, that is not without its challenges when it comes to explaining oneself in the job market, or even social circles. Multidimensionality, apart from a fleeting interest in "oddity", generally confuses people; instead, a clear, simple label usually serves better in general encounters and communication. As a result we develop these multiple presences and different people may see us in different circumstances, with different faces, even though they are all served by the same core beliefs, values, attitudes and emotions.

Whilst our behaviour may change to adapt to circumstantial needs, our drivers, most of the time, remain stable, and apart from some beliefs and values that change over time, due to self-development and experience, they pretty much stay the same around the core we developed early in our lives. Historicity and time play a fundamental part in what is stable and what is variable about us. This is why knowing our inner self and being able to articulate that knowledge, own it and work in harmony with it, provides a much needed individual congruence that guarantees a firmer centre from where we can manage almost any challenge and change, aiming to achieve the best possible outcome within the context. A strong core for all potential personae that we may become over time is fundamental, not only for managing our career effectively but for being generally successful in life.

I always had a flair for marketing but no formal or structured understanding of the process or methodologies, and when I wanted to learn more about my brand I asked a professional friend for advice. As a result, in 2009 I conducted a short survey of friends and colleagues, and key words such as style, colour, good taste and inclination for aesthetics emerging as common attributes coming from all the participants made me realise that these specific elements were part of the "look of my brand". Whereas key words like knowledge, reliability, honesty, achievement etc. came to define the "essence of my brand". I also found out that my professional and personal brand overlapped, capturing the stable core of my identity as perceived by others from my behaviours and communication. All valuable knowledge that helped surface and articulate fleeting self-perceptions that finally consolidated in a self-awareness about the contents of my essence as reflected in my brand.

A useful exercise

The following is an exercise likely to be useful and hopefully enjoyable. Choose three to five people from the three categories of family, friends and work colleagues. Then:

- Create a number of questions (at least five and no more than ten) about you, and send them to the three sets of participants;
- Analyse the responses and look for key words and descriptors that may be common across their replies;
- Compare those key words from the friends group with those coming from your work- related connections;

- Check for similarities or differences;
- The key words that result at the end of this process define your brand!;
- Use them subsequently in all written messages across all platforms (social media, biographies and CV, advertising, fliers, etc.), obviously adapting the message by ranking and blending those words with other attributes, as appropriate for the specific purpose of that marketing and sales communication.

Reflect on how the key attributes that define your brand link into your motivation, attitudes, values and beliefs, and your personal history. Check how they compare to what you know about yourself, and look for matches and areas for improvement or opportunities to clarify, for your own developmental benefit and the perception of others. Also reflect on how your brand matches or not your work environment and what you can do to make that alignment stronger. For example, if your brand is that of being dynamic and communicative but your work environment is of a more quiet nature, you may wish to moderate your perceived presence accordingly but exercise your energy in the type of activity and the quality of outputs that you deliver to that work environment and achievements, which will soon become another descriptor of your brand. Once you have understood, articulated and communicated your brand, ensure that you manage it properly.

In an age of structured and commercialised or personal and unbridled exhibitionism – the number of reality TV shows and the culture of selfies, as opposite examples of the same range – there is no stone left unturned, anything goes and nothing is off limits when it comes to humans. Social media have set up huge platforms that are constantly looking for new contents and are luring people to freely offer their lives and histories as fodder for the permanently hungry technology. What this also means is that whilst social media may lure people to all sorts of personal exhibitionism, the normative dimensions of the world of work and organisational cultures will also curate what is desirable and what not. Therefore a brand that is tarnished is not desirable, and an individual's opportunity of employment can be jeopardised by careless displays of aspects that do not resonate with professionalism and credibility.

In this light, a few suggestions on brand management:

- Choose your social platforms carefully and separate the personal from the professional
- Think clearly before putting content out, because once this information is out, it is very hard to undo its impact
- If possible influence what others post about you and avoid antagonising people
- Be generous in your "likes" but remain careful about what you "like", since this will influence judgements about you
- Think that potential employers will be interested in your brand, with consequences

- Demonstrate interests in matters beyond just yourself and be a part of the wider community of people, around interest groups, think tanks, and hobbies.

Summary

Your personal brand is the visible essence of who you are. Your brand sends out information about you, which is instantly perceived and interpreted by people around you. Great brands stand for something. And so should you. Display the "essence of you" to enable others to immediately recognise who you are and what you stand for. Be authentic, be yourself, have opinions and an attitude. Make yourself liked or needed by showing what you have to offer in minimalist and symbolic ways. Use visual and verbal cues carefully to protect your brand and its reputation.

Being able to package and market your "offering" is just as important as having an excellent content to offer in your work and personal life. People do notice and do remember others, if and when they make an impact. Make this count. Make that impact work for you. Keep in mind that today most, if not all of us, have left an electronic footprint on the internet and social media platforms.

Remember that in this new age of technology, many related aspects are simply not monitored, regulated or legislated and it is an open field for all and anything goes. The moral, ethical and regulatory aspects of the modern virtual world are just about playing catch up with reality and information; placed in a world connected at an incomprehensible level this has become now – and for some time to come – just a runway train that no one knows how to stop. Do not allow this to take you on a ride. You have no idea where it may lead. Instead, control your electronically documented journey and make it positive and value-adding for yourself and your clear objectives! Above all develop, nurture and protect your brand and respect it as the valuable asset that it is!

Assessment centres: capturing and labelling the intangible

The assessment centres have become quite popular in the last twenty or so years, at the same time as the introduction of the constructs of competence-based selection and evaluation of candidates and staff, in recruitment and human resources (HR) management. This was mainly driven by the idea that what mattered in all things related to work and life was behaviours, that is to say, visible outputs. And that one could create a matrix of competencies and related behaviours that mapped back to job roles and the pre-prepared job role analysis.

This approach reflects the dichotomy of views between "certainty-uncertainty" that has divided psychologists, scientists and philosophers, polarising positivism and relativism, with the "black box" model at one end, where all that matters is what can be observed – namely behaviour, whilst the more complex and uncertain aspects of individual, invisible inner life are simply left out of the equation, because admittedly they are too complex and hard to track within a linear causality frame.

In fact, the pendulum of psychological paradigms has been swinging a few times in the last 200 years between apparently opposing aspects of the human condition; the "inner, unconscious, emotional, instinctual, feelings-driven" side – on the one hand – and the "objective, evidenced, measurable, visible, controlled factors-driven" side, on the other hand. A neat and convenient binary split that we can trace back to the Cartesian dualism of the immaterial mind and the material body, for example. In practice, psychology seldom, if ever, talks in terms of absolutes, and every self-respecting psychologist will only use language such as "it is likely", "it is possible", "it may be", "it seems that", "it looks likely", "perhaps" to precede or follow almost every statement that they make, particularly in writing and in the public domain, in diagnosis and reporting. Because psychologists agree that predicting behaviours and outcomes related to people, correctly and consistently, is in fact quite difficult and there are too many unseen and unpredictable factors at work. A human being is a complex evolving system and as such inhabited by the known and the unknown, by intended and unintended outcomes, hosting a process of transformation and renewal that changes the game of possibilities all the time.

Psychology is a science of probabilities, statistical analysis and correlations, and a good score for correlations between factors, typically starts at 30% or 0.30, which in absolute terms is not very high, meaning that psychological certainty is 1 in 3, on a good day! Hence, the need for caution in language, when making statements that could be interpreted as definitive.

But the assessment centre was hailed to solve all this by introducing a balanced score card of multiple objective perspectives. Designed by trained people and run by assessors who apply and monitor the process that the candidates go though, the assessment centre includes a number of "sampling points" that may cover: CV submission, one-to-one interview, panel interview, a presentation on a given topic, a teamwork exercise, an "in-tray" exercise (simulating a day at work filled with incoming requirements), reference gathering, sometimes security clearances, and occupational psychometric tests. In the mix, the tests are meant to capture work-related aptitude, performance, cognition, skills, values and potential for development.

An assessment centre will usually last from half a day to two full days, depending on the level of the position you are applying for and how many activities one needs to complete, and it is likely to be located at the employers' offices or those of the external consultancy that is hired to design and conduct the assessment process. Occupational psychometric tests (as opposed to clinical instruments) fall broadly into two categories: one is related to aptitudes and skills – which are normed and carry the implication that respondents can fail or pass them. They have been calibrated around an expectation that the majority of people taking them will perform to a certain middle level, fewer will perform better, and another small number will perform worse, compared to the middle range majority. Usually they measure a narrow and specific capability (numeracy, literacy, manual ability, perceptual ability, etc.).

The other category falls into what is called personality tests and they simply map the individual in their own right; they map the personal profile of the candidate. Personality is a construct and, as such, covers many aspects (traits, type, values and beliefs, integrity, emotional intelligence, etc.) that can be mapped whether individually or in some combinations, depending on the design of the test. There is no fail or pass in these tests, but there it is a way whereby one can be found to be more or less suitable for a job. For example, if a job role requires a person to be organised, attentive to detail, and structured, a candidate that views the world as a big picture, gets bored with detail and has no patience for meticulous activity will obviously be less suitable than someone whose preferences and natural attributes better match the role demands. Taking this into consideration does not discriminate against the person but rather avoids the common scenario of having the wrong person in the wrong job. Such a mismatch quickly leads to stress, lack of morale, low productivity and eventual separation, one way or the other. A lose-lose for both employer and employee. The purpose here is that the right job will fit a person's strengths and not lead them to inadequacy and failure.

The important usefulness of tests is to enable people to know themselves and use that knowledge for personal development as well as contributing to organisations. In a well-managed process, no one tool provides sufficient information to support decisions and action plans, therefore two or more tools should be used in combination, together with interviews and other methods of assessment, to provide a balanced and complete picture of a person's profile and preferences. Ideally, all individuals should receive the first feedback, and with their agreement the same feedback is given to business (management, HR or team).

Various related professional bodies have set out some best practice guidelines around ethics and regulation in regards to data confidentiality and access to feedback, to protect the candidates' position. But feedback is arguably the most difficult and demanding aspect of testing. Trainees can learn about the instrument and result interpretation relatively easily compared to the feedback skill, which is much more than reading results. It involves tact, emotional intelligence, swift profiling of the client's communication and thinking preferences, and being able to appreciate micro-reactions and adapt the feedback style in real time, almost from one sentence to another, to turn it into a developmental experience rather that a confidence-destroying one. Unfortunately poor skill in feedback combined with inappropriate use of those results by "labelling" the candidates and deciding that they are not suitable during the recruitment process, do trigger a lasting and counterproductive "fear of tests", which some of my clients experienced.

In the UK, access to training in the use of psychometrics is open to all who wish to learn and have the possibility to fund this training; unlike in Europe and the US, where only professional psychologists, formally trained at degree and postgraduate level, are allowed to use psychometric testing. This makes the access to psychometric instruments and the whole process around their use quite open in the UK, with quite different levels of control and barriers to practice. As a result there is variability in the skill that test administrators and users have when providing feedback.

Enabled to a degree by technology and increasingly used since the mid-1990s, assessment centres have been hailed as a universal panacea, providing objective evidence-based evaluation and equal opportunity for all, by a standardised and repeatable process and context that was thought to best serve the purpose of hiring the best people for the job – away from subjective considerations – based on hard data gathered from several perspectives. This also meant a "one size fits all" approach, with little interest in variance and the famous individual differences, which carry diversity, the factor that on the other hand has also been hailed as supporting creativity, increased performance and effectiveness in organisations. The variability of individual talent, learning styles, strengths, motivators, attitudes, levels of maturity, history and complexity were all put aside to allow the reassuring power of the "process" and pre-set "metrics" to prevail. Now, some twenty years later, there is an increased awareness that this one approach for different people and different levels of professional maturity or job complexity is not exactly all that it was hoped and hailed to be. And that assessment centres work very well sometimes, less well other times, and therefore not all the time! As always the answer sits in the middle and typically the middle ground is hard to reach and may emerge eventually after the pendulum has swung a few times, from one extreme to the other and back, until by decreased motion and energy brings it to rest in a balanced middle.

Reflecting on group findings

In my coaching work I have often met clients who had a limited understanding of assessment centres and my priority was to encourage them to take control and empower themselves by being informed, and as a result prepared mentally and emotionally, and gather information by asking simple but useful question such as: How many and what are the steps of the assessment process? How long is each step? Who is going to be in the room during each step and why? How is the feedback – if any – going to be given? How is this information used in the final decision? Are there any go/no go gates and at what points? Did they need to prepare; if yes, in what way? How do these steps of the assessment process relate to the actual job content and predictability to perform?

This was designed to shift attitude and perception from the belief that the assessment was something that was going to happen "to them" to the belief that this was something that will happen "with and for them". We also discussed practical tips such as: having a good night's sleep the night before, wearing appropriate but comfortable clothes, making sure they arrived with plenty of time to acclimatise to the environment, being well nourished and having a small sugar "pick up" in the pocket just in case they suddenly felt tired or hungry, and staying with the process with the understanding that it is not "against" them but in favour of getting the right people in the right job. Most importantly, I advised them to focus on the "here and now" to achieve their best performance at every step and not to lose energy on the more distanced goal of getting the job, since that outcome was not entirely under their control, whereas how they performed at every step was! I also used the simple analogy of trying to sell products in a market; displaying a carefully chosen and well-presented offer, so that those who walk around looking see an obvious choice before them. Because when such buyers of skills have to pick three people out of ten, who have been selected from thirty, who have been shortlisted from three hundred, it is best that they work for this as little as possible.

With some of my clients being parents, this was immediately understood, because they had been supporting their own children, from pre-school all the way to university, through a similar process, which also included them being interviewed alongside their children for suitability by those institutions, in the ruthless race for the one scarce and coveted place in a "good school". And this was a case of transferring experience and adapting it to their job search agenda. But these conversations also shed a light on the wider picture – the culture of results-based testing and the educational approach that in some countries is utterly fixated on correct outputs that little, if at all, affords importance to the significant information about the path and critical thinking, for example, that leads to answers; a more subtle and qualitative analysis necessary to balance and compliment the formulaic outputs-oriented one.

In any event, my approach alongside the strong, empowering, motivational and positive perspective that became the focus of conversations did instil strength and confidence in most and positioned them with a better chance of winning. I was gratified to meet some of my clients many years after working with them and be told that every time they went to interviews and assessments for a new job, over the years, they remembered and applied my suggestions.

Across the group, in terms of subjective and emotional experience, some were quite relaxed about it, understanding that if they wanted to get to their objective they just had to put up with the method; others were anxious and disliked the process, based on previous experiences, and had to work harder for it. Finally, others were quite confident, because they knew the tricks and really regarded it as a role play situation, where over time they became better and better at dissimulating and being in the role with a degree of artistry and were often almost guaranteed a positive outcome. But also interesting was that longitudinally, those who were successful in trumping the process – whilst offering genuine high skills and professional competence – were also those who were rather less easy to control once inside the company and often left after short periods of employment (less than two years) to move on. Whilst many of those who felt intimidated and of an average level in skills were also those who, once in, tended to be more loyal and dedicated workers who did provide "return on investment" (ROI) on the costly assessment process.

In my experience, the weakest link of assessment with negative impact on candidates' experience and often self-confidence and self-belief is that of psychometric tests. This is due to poor administration, poor feedback – if any – and lack of clarity as to what they are and how they play a role in the decision-making process to hire or not. But overall, most of my clients were aware or experienced with assessment centres, even when they did not understand the deeper or detailed aspects of that process, because there was no getting away from it. A positive aspect to note is that when and if the assessment centres were properly managed and the feedback was professional across all the steps, it became a rich source of new experience, increased self-awareness, an opportunity for reflection and learning, and a step closer to change and self-development, alongside an opportunity to ask and answer the question: "Do I really want to join this organisation?" With experience and a positive mindset, they became increasingly self-aware and more skilled and therefore in any event benefited from this experience as a developmental opportunity along the way.

My case study

My experience of recruitment covers two rather opposite ways of hiring: the simple one, where the hiring manager received my CV and then had a conversation with me to decide whether I should get the job, when I always succeeded. Then the complicated one, where I have been put through an assessment centre and often failed. An intriguing binary outcome that makes little sense if not contextualised across age and time and the wider system of the world of work.

The days when I experienced the simple recruitment process were also the days when as a young professional I had a limited experience and range of skills to offer. As a result, there was a simple, linear connection between what the employer asked and what I had to offer, an easier match to achieve. In addition I did not have a lot of demands or preferences, my objectives being that of learning, gaining experience, working for a good reputable company, making a living and positioning myself on a good career path. On my side of the recruitment interview, I was a young adult, with moderate self-awareness, finding my way in the world, not quite sure what my real strengths and weaknesses or my preferences were; I was a work in progress. On the other side of the recruitment table, the future mangers were assessing my specific limited range of skills and more importantly my character, my presence and the level of trust that they could project on me, as a result of how I turned up in the room and what I was saying in reply to their questions, which offered a window into my thinking and values and confirmed my behaviour and my CV statements. For a skilled manager this is more than enough to assess risk and potential, and it is amazing – as I have found later in life – how able a good manager is to correctly assess people, simply by observation, hunches, common sense and general wisdom (also known as emotional intelligence, empathy and instinct).

In those days there was also some scarcity of occupational tests on the market, and technology had not yet been democratised. Selections of the more sophisticated kind mainly sat with large government institutions, due to size and the number of candidates; defence, civil service, and possibly a few global players, but not much else. The human resources function was unsophisticated and procurement had not yet gained the status that it has today, after being so much advanced by the use of computers.

So my early experience of recruitment was a direct reflection of the times. In addition, I also worked for smaller organisations, which, again, even when the more sophisticated assessment centres were gaining traction, did not represent the key buyers of such expensive services. And this is how for some twenty years I looked for job advertisements, applied for a job, sent my CV, got an interview, and got the job, every single time; and this also with corporations that I happened to access thought a smaller business division that could exercise a simplified approach to hiring. Based on feedback, I performed in my roles to my employers' expectations but more often than not well above it, and so in my experience this type of recruitment proved to be an uncomplicated process leading to a win-win for both parties.

But in 2002, when I transitioned to management consulting and self-employment, my life became an ongoing succession of applications for contracts and associate work. By now the personnel function had renamed itself Human Resources (HR) and the assessment centres had become the way to hire and the latest fashion in recruitment best practice. The newly elevated procurement function was mandated to save money at all cost and empowered to buy everything on the principle of scale; from soft skills and strategic consultancy to cleaning services, food and beverages, and facilities management. The world had changed! And so had the dynamics around the recruitment conversation as far as I was concerned.

On my side of the recruitment interview, I was no longer a debutante in the world of work, but an experienced professional with an equal amount of international life experience and a clear view of my identity, strengths and weaknesses. I was embarking on yet another stage of professional expression with a fully formed view of the world, values, opinions and attitudes, and was strongly self-directed and clear about what I was interested in and prepared to do and with whom, and therefore asking as many questions as I was answering.

On the other side of the recruitment table, the future mangers were assessing a portfolio of capabilities that typically exceeded the job brief, and were being met in conversation by someone who had views, ethics and certain demands, and who was checking them out in the same way they did. The window into my mind was offering thinking landscapes that were rather wide and complex. And so, predictably, this conversation was flagging risks coming from a person that was interesting but perhaps not so much in their own image.

And again the skilled managers could see risk and potential in the way I turned up for interviews, the way I answered their questions, and the fact that I was clearly intriguing, substantial, strategic and quite unconventional in my reflections. And risk typically prevailed over potential, raising unspoken questions about me being easy to direct and whether I could be told what to do without me answering back to ask why. A high potential to contribute maybe, but too independent, too far from a safe pair of hands, not pliant enough to be managed and therefore not quite aligned to what most prefer to hire. Recruiters and managers are risk averse, no matter what they say, and familiarity is reassuring; uniqueness and individuality are not.

Other conversations turned out to be enchanting meetings of the mind and led to a clear acknowledgement of the value of what I had to offer, but again, there was a misalignment between the way I was prepared to work and their internal structure of work delivery (for example, full employment as opposed to part-time or contract work), which did not match what I was looking for, which effectively was delivery of expertise and no involvement in organisational hierarchies or politics.

But it is with hindsight that I understood what was going on and there are a few key findings and open questions that I have gathered along the way. For example, about the so-called teamwork exercises. They consist of a group of candidates being observed by assessors whilst asked to complete a task together. This is a highly demonstrative setting where the floor is naturally set for extroverts or those who are good at exhibiting skills. I have seen actors doing well in these situations because they are professionally trained to skilfully make a visible positive impact in such public improvisation settings. I admit I was surprised to see how many actors work as facilitators, team coaches and trainers in between or in the absence of actual acting jobs. Their confidence in dealing with what effectively is a piece of theatre – normalised under the name of "team exercise" – is to a degree predictable.

On the other hand, I could never quite work out how the actual knowledge, common sense, emotional intelligence, experience, individual preferences, and even the pre-existent ability of the candidates in the group, and the group as a whole to be a functional team, were being assessed by those "observers", who sat there with pads and pens in their hands, watching and busily making notes. Obviously it was a box-ticking exercise; and I did ask the question but got no proper answer. In fact it became clear that more sophisticated questions and perspectives beyond such a simplistic and mechanistic set up has simply not entered their consideration, in the first place, meaning at the point of assessment exercise design.

There were also issues of confidentiality, ethics and boundaries that concerned me even more. I did raise such issues with the assessors only to conclude that they were simply not aware of the weaknesses of the process design or perhaps understood the questions but were not competent enough to give an answer. I found these situations concerning and they raised for me a lot of questions about professionalism.

Another example is that of what I see as a mismatch between the qualifications and level of seniority of the interviewers compared with the more skilled candidates, particularly in the middle section of assessments, where the objective is often that of significantly cutting down the number of applicants. As a result, a conversation with someone who is less experienced and more junior than the candidate is a wasted opportunity, since the assessors are out of their depth and unable to appreciate the information coming their way from a more experienced candidate. As a result they gravitate to the lowest common denominator that they understand.

The use of psychometric test results to label people and use clichés to categorise them was another concern. Western society seems to be biased in favour of extroverts not introverts, pragmatists not idealists, specialists not generalists and so on. In addition, the instruments are placed in the hands of people that may not be very experienced, in an overall UK national context where controls over who is allowed to train and use psychometrics and who not, is weaker compared to the US and Europe, for example.

Another concerning factor relates to the baffling contradiction between the pressure to hire a person for that vacancy as soon as possible, whilst – incomprehensibly – there is seldom time for the hiring managers and interviewers to schedule those interviews in their busy day, even when candidates are found. There is huge pressure on HR, recruiters and assessors to get candidates to interviews with hiring managers. But very often they cannot find the time to read CVs or schedule the interviews, and when they turn up they are in a rush and tired and take the easy option of just asking "tell me about yourself . . ." to catch up. I have often been in this situation (just like my clients) and some interviewers have had the decency to recognise this openly. Which helped me to set my expectation for the next time and have that "broken record" statement about myself, ready from the start. But I could never abandon the thought that I was being disrespected by this lack of preparedness on their part.

I have also experienced – just like my clients – situations where after a long effort – sometimes lasting weeks – I was successful at the end of that recruitment process, only to find out that there was in fact no job available. Either because the internal process had not approved the "headcount" or because the intention behind the process was to research skills in the market; or to "crowdsource" ideas during the presentation exercises that were in fact real situations that needed a solution; or because this was a "zero hours contract" for highly skilled workers, where the successful candidates became quantitative assets for databases of the hiring organisation (usually a consultancy firm), which enhanced their status with clients by showcasing an impressive cadre of specialist on standby, and where only 30% of those recruited ever got work.

But my practice also enabled me to be on the other side of the table as an assessor myself, part of the recruitment process, by way of administering individual sets of psychometric assessment, giving feedback and also contributing my view to the collective inputs gathered from the various sources. In this role I went to great lengths to defend the right of the candidates to get sensitive and constructive feedback and be treated with respect and dignity. Every person, no matter who they are, has the capability to develop if they can find that point of rapport and level of humanity that enables honest, constructive and fair exchanges on both sides of the recruitment and assessment process. This resulted in positive feedback from candidates that were happy to have gained a lot from psychometrics and related feedback session, even when they did not get the job; and they felt stronger and more prepared for the future. My objective was to treat them with respect and in a way I would have liked to have been treated and respected myself, in a similar situation.

A useful exercise

Imperfect as assessment centres may have been and still are today – not all as well designed as they could be and not all, necessarily fit for purpose, all the time – they do offer candidates an opportunity to better know themselves, to assess how they react and perform under circumstances that are new and possibly unpredictable, and where maintaining self-direction, self-belief and asserting their right to feedback and access to information are all good learning opportunities that can only strengthen their core. Therefore my work as a coach was to get on with reality as it is and approach this selection process that my clients had to experience in a positive way, to empower them to take advantage of it, get as much information as possible, on the whole process and its individual steps, and prepare well by, for example:

- Asking whether they will get feedback and make sure they got it
- Reflecting after every such situation on what went well and what did not
- Reflecting on the reasons that may have caused them to underperform and how to address such blockers
- Taking their thoughts to our coaching conversation to use in self-development
- Using all the learning for the next similar assessment situation as well as future job choices
- Strengthening self-awareness and being realistic in choosing jobs that really motivated them and played to their strengths, rather than jobs that seemed glamorous or financially rewarding but where, if honest, compromises were needed, which in the long run would have impacted them one way or another
- Being aware that what worked for them in the past may not work in the future, as individual deeper drivers and priorities are likely to change over time.

Summary

Assessment centres work sometimes but not all of the time. And they become increasingly unfit for purpose as the seniority of the candidate or the complexity or nature of the job increases or is different. The merit of assessment centres is that they try to set up an objective process-driven set of steps and gather information from a more rounded perspective, to increase for employers the chance of predicting future work behaviour and obtaining a positive match between the candidate and the job specification.

To achieve this, it uses a number of sampling steps (CV, interview, group activity, presentation, psychometric testing, etc.). All these sources have their value, but may or may not be used as decision-making criteria. In fact they need to be balanced and collectively integrated and evaluated. The potential use of test results as fail/pass tools remains a risk, particularly if existing guidelines and best practices are not properly monitored or enforced.

However assessments and tests remain an important step on the path to a new job. This is why it is important for candidates to accept this reality, be prepared and remain confident, whilst coaches need to support their clients as much as possible. It is also important that candidates claim their ground and enquire about the process, outcomes and feedback as well as voice their concerns, if any.

The more candidates/coachees learn about assessment centres and testing and can prepare for this process, the better they position themselves to turn this unavoidable situation into a positive exercise of increasing self-awareness.

We have no control on the final outcome of a full and complex recruitment process, but we do have control over our readiness to participate and engagement with its various steps, at our best.

Hopefully this controlled contribution in the pursuit of success will also lead to the less controllable win of the final prise . . . that much coveted new job!

Polymaths: "Jack of all trades and master of . . . all"

I am an avid learner and conferences or documentaries are part of my weekly diet. During this stimulating consumption I watched and listened to people who, at the forefront of their area of scientific specialism, had also been accumulating other surprising strands of knowledge, mixing – for example – degrees in biology and philosophy with a PhD in physics, or degrees in engineering and chemistry with a masters in genetics.

Such combinations excited and surprised even me, open minded as I am. But beyond surprise, this awareness led me to specifically reflect on the question of multiple talents and interests. Upon analysis, the deeper connections between sciences and apparently different areas of specialism became clear and in fact connected by underlying common denominators that enable such "stacking" of apparently disjointed disciplines, and offer amazing possibilities for cross-transfer and cross-fertilisation of methodologies and solutions that eventually lead to invention, innovation and overall knowledge advancement. But our every-day thinking is not very open or clear about such possibilities and advantages, and so it seems that the market and the typical employers remain challenged by people who are capable across disciplines, whilst also decrying that it is hard to find someone who can see the woods instead of the trees; and in so doing, contradict themselves! In my career coaching experience this disconnection between rhetoric and fact has been evidenced by my coachees' experiences, revealing the surprising reality that those clients who were polymaths encountered the greatest challenge in their search for a job, as opposed to narrow specialists.

A polymath is a person whose expertise spans a number of different subject areas; such a person is known to draw on complex bodies of knowledge to solve specific problems. A polymath is a thinker who is highly competent in several fields of science and the arts and embodies the principle that people should not limit their capacity and should embrace all knowledge and develop their capabilities as fully and widely as possible. It is true that the Western rationalism has encouraged the "specialist paradigm", a mindset busy with a linear, analytical and fragmenting approach to reality, thus discouraging our ability to venture away from what is obvious and in front of our eyes to see. To put it simply, the last few hundred years have bred excellent "tree watchers", who may have, in the process, all but lost sight of "the woods". In my personal experience, I met a senior consultant who told me that she was an expert in the medicine of arteries but she knew little about veins and an ophthalmologist who told me that he knew about the inside of the eye but not the outside. I found this strict and artificial differentiation between veins and arteries – which obviously work together as an integrated system, together with the heart and blood – so astonishing that I would not have believed this account, had someone else reported it to me. Equally I fail to see how the eyeball and vision are not related to the way the eye is held in place and moved by its external muscles which hold it in its socket. And the point here is that the Western positivism has pushed specialisation to such an extreme, that integration of fragmented and disjointed aspect of the same reality and object of study, has become a scarce capability, not entertained even in speculation.

In the Europe of only a few hundred years ago, Renaissance gave rise to a Renaissance culture, where individuals were encouraged to be well rounded and capable to excel in as many domains as possible. In antiquity, educated people were also knowledgeable in more areas than one and able to make, as such, a wider range of contributions. Philosophy, initially the science of all sciences, went hand in hand with mathematics, astronomy, chemistry and natural science. The same expectation applied to crafts and arts.

Michelangelo preferred to be called a sculptor, but when he had to raise money to pay for his very expensive and much loved blocks of marble, he reluctantly rolled up his sleeves and painted the Sistine Chapel as a means to an end. Lucky humankind . . . to be gifted such a masterpiece as a result of the mundane financial shortcomings of a creative genius!

The Eastern point of view has generally been more open to bigger pictures, even to this day. In old Japan, for instance, the three arts of calligraphy, music and poetry were inseparable, and a truly refined and educated artist had to be able to be good at all of them. To this day, the combination of arts, philosophy and belief systems is in Japan the true key to their culture, and to understand it one needs to observe how the people embody design, tradition, history and philosophy in ordinary life, from villages to mega-cities. Such sophisticated, integrated and applied view of the world is normalised in everyday gestures from gift-giving to the packaging of the most ordinary goods. There is ceremony and decorum everywhere with philosophy, spirituality, technology, modernity and meditation, all integrated to form a rich backdrop to the most humble of activities.

A similar collective expectation is not however reflected in the saying "A Jack of all trades and master of none", raising the question: why not embrace instead "A Jack of all trades and master of . . . ALL" that would encourage openness to a more rounded range of knowledge or appreciation of multiple competences and mastery of multi-specialism combined with extensive general knowledge, to contextualise and give depth to specific disciplines?

But in more recent times the light on the horizon has been brought by the introduction of the term "generalist" as a more acceptable and widely used descriptor in professions such as IT and Human Resources, which, as it happens, are also disciplines dealing with extremely complex environments and subjects: humans and software; both known for a degree of unpredictability, no matter how controlled the environments and the approaches in dealing with them may be. An acknowledgement of the fact that having a world full of specialists does not necessarily ensure faster or more accurate progress, neither in our endeavours nor in the way we are able to respond to complex challenges, increasingly coming in all shapes and from many unexpected directions, as unintended consequences.

In my experience, and to my surprise, I found that those who had the most difficulties in career changes and finding a job were the "polymaths" – those professionals who had a wide range of expertise in different categories and were indeed able to do a number of jobs very well. This in spite of the rhetoric that "in today's environment we must skill up, be flexible, embrace a lifelong adherence to Continued Professional Development (CPD)" and be able to flexibly create our job description and content, or undertake a variety of tasks and responsibilities that may be thrown at us at short notice by organisational needs, or widen our skills and capabilities. Because the actual situation in the job market is quite the opposite.

Recruiters and employers are quite risk averse and tend to hire for "safety", meaning: there has to be a clear label on one's skills and the person must have done in recent times, and consistently, that which is "written on the tin". What this means is that polymaths cannot honestly communicate to the market: "I am good at a number of things, and can do more than one job", even if this is true. Not a trivial matter, since this lack of opportunity to disclose one's true profile, be proud and authentic with one's professional identity, has a negative impact on the way such candidates experience the recruitment and selection process and the whole job search journey, which becomes an ordeal.

This reminds me of the time when I was qualifying in psychometrics and was using a team roles tool. One of my respondent's profiles distributed almost equally across all dimensions, with no significant loading for any of the roles. I was excited about this and thought that this was an ideal person who could fulfil several jobs and therefore be quite flexible and accommodating and, with good management, be a real resource for all needs. But my assessors held a rather different view. In their eyes this result looked suspicious and possibly not valid, because such a profile did not make sense; it did not allow the use of a clear "label" for that person. I stood my ground and stand it to this day. What remains interesting is our need for labelling and clear categorisation and our adverse reaction to what does not neatly "fit" a model that may be familiar and therefore reassuring to us.

Back to the candidate that can do more than one thing: well, this seems to me an unbeatable offer, because as an employer I can use one person to do several jobs instead of needing three people for the same (time and percentages of activity considered of course) and because one person can be flexible and almost certainly motivated and excited enough to embrace those changes of activity and use all of their skills as opposed to just one or a few. Unfortunately, this is not how things pan out. The typical reaction is scepticism; "surely you cannot possibly do all these things equally well . . . I am not sure; what are you?" And to avoid any risk I may just hire someone who has one professional label and has done that same job consistently in the last three to five years.

And this is the end for a polymath, because what they are forced now to do is deny the truth about their professional capabilities and artificially remove cross-references and evidence of multiple strands of work in order to pick, compartmentalise and pack sets of skills into easy to understand bundles of offerings, neatly labelled for the job market to select. These bundles need to be embodied by a candidate who IS "the label" – effort that involves a diminishing of the professional self down to the smaller representation of what the label says – then carry this persona into the interview room and maintain that altered presence all the way to the moment when the job is secured, through a deception that is sustained and convincing enough. This process is quite stressful for candidates, because it requires them to deny a part of their professional and personal identity and diminish the statement of their capabilities, in spite of their ambition, achievements and pride in their polymath capabilities. Being a polymath is a result of a journey led by a specific way of thinking, and the way information has been hardwired in their brain, alongside the aspirations and motivation that enabled related choices and individual evolution. This is about one's identity and it is not a trivial matter.

So the pressure to carve out and separate strands of offerings is difficult but not impossible. And often necessary. Otherwise the job market views polymaths who do not compromise on "packaging" their skills neatly, as "odd-ities", who provide an unusual, stimulating and intriguing experience for the interviewer, but otherwise finish with no job gain. Because people often hire "in their own image", and according to what they understand and perceive as "low risk".

Reflecting on group findings

The polymaths I have met in my work shared similar attributes and similar challenges in the job market. They typically had a great ability to connect "left and right brain" and hold an integrated creative and scientific view, with rich general knowledge to contextualise several areas of specialism; were able to work with the small picture as well as integrate specific findings in the wider perspective, were high achievers, got bored easily, and liked a challenge and the opportunity to get something done but also learn something new. They enjoyed complex problems and were able to hold multiple perspectives at the same time, with a balanced view across a number of potentially conflicting strands. Whilst similar in general ways, their skills, preferences, qualities, abilities and ambitions clustered in quite unique ways, which was reflected in the range of jobs, their career paths and their private lives. Everyone was dif-ferent and an individual. In the workplace, they seemed to either form strong relationships with bosses who left them the freedom to work according to their style, or they were perceived as triggering anxious, negative reactions from those who had a tendency to control and micro-manage what seemed to be a threatening and incomprehensible force.

They were also stunned into utter incompetence when having to deal with the formulaic and mechanistic demands of performance reviews and setting developmental goals, given that self-directed, multistranded, ongoing learning has been a way of life and a natural part of their cognitive DNA. And surpris-ing as this may seem, I have spent many hours with them just "holding their hand", with great empathy, in the mind-numbing process of splitting hairs over personal appraisal and development tasks needed to fill in the forms – all com-petency based, all goal focused, and all with measurable inputs and outputs – which drove me to destruction in my own corporate days.

Beyond a shared sense of exasperation – which I had to hold back – my job was to reassure them in the process, keep them on track with the require-ments of the forms, guide their steps from section to section, help them cross-reference the various documents involved, keep their anger at bay and project a sense of meaning over this process, to make it look like a worthwhile chance to pause and reflect over their natural inclinations and behaviours around think-ing and work. All things that we coaches have to do in our work. Personally, I found this whole exercise a sad reflection on the lack of space that organisa-tions and the world of work present to inclusion and diversity in high achievers and people who think outside the box.

I also reflected on the limitations of performance and assessment evolutions in the workplace as they have been institutionalised since 2000. Organisation are well equipped to develop people that need assistance to improve performance – through training, coaching and mentoring – but do not quite know what to do with those that over-deliver.

My thoughts about polymaths and their challenges reflect what I have covered in the section on assessment centres, as the two themes are closely intertwined. The fact remains that neither the market nor the assessment centres are designed for people that do not neatly fall into a preformatted set of expectations or do not satisfy a rigid process that does not allow room for individuality. In my view it is a great loss and a missed opportunity for organisations to acquire, nurture and fully use individuals that have a lot to offer but do not deliver that unusual output in an average standardised pre-set packaging.

My case study

I grew up reading short science fiction stories instead of fairy tales, then moved on to read the biographies of famous painters and the history of art. Later on I read the sci-fi classics but also the world classics of literature. At school I liked physics, biology, literature and languages but also economics and psychology. As a child I was exposed to life in different countries and have been looked after by nannies who spoke to me in their own language, not in mine. I was bilingual from the moment I could talk and, I am told, was quite liked by my nursery teachers. I liked school, reading and to learn, and I was quite serious in my outlook of the world quite early. I made a decision to study psychology and never changed my mind from the age of fourteen. Yet after graduation I promptly did an MBA in international trade.

Then I spent twenty years in international corporations working in supply chain management, manufacturing, operations, quality management and audit across the fashion, pharmaceutical, IT and telecommunications industries. As hobbies I always loved all the arts, and acquired an extensive knowledge of various cultures of the world from the Japanese Kabuki, to Indian Kathak and Kathakali, to Pina Bausch's modern choreography to the Bolshoi's classical ballet. I enjoy jazz, symphonies, blues, opera and prog rock. As a second career I returned to psychology and coaching, to work with people in business, and added an MSC in business psychology. But I also completed certificates in filmmaking, scriptwriting and in gamification, and published poetry and prose, and went to Cannes twice as part of my addiction to cinema. I remember walking down La Croisette and on to the red carpet of the Grand Palais des Festivals, for gala screenings, as one of the happiest moments of my life, alongside the launch of my first book.

I have friends who have been architects or dentists or engineers all their lives and pursued much fewer other interests. They clearly are specialists.

By comparison, my career has taken a different and more meandering path. But across all jobs, I always loved what I did and when that excitement faded, I moved on to something new and exciting, but in some way clearly related to my previous job. This scattered landscape makes complete sense to me, because it has a coherent inner thread that links all this apparent chaos. The industries I have worked in are all driven by innovation, fast pace, high risk, high reward and advanced technology. They also have a creative aspect in the way they use related communication, marketing and branding. In this context I have worked in functions that are related and together make the coherent end to end fabric of a full business process, which I always found highly exciting. The job changes have been driven by boredom with repetition, curiosity, a need to learn, a need to achieve something tangible, but also be stimulated mentally and stretch my imagination. I stepped into new jobs by offering general business skills and specialist skills, with the intention to learn new skills that I could stack on top of the others.

There are six managers in my entire working life that have been exceptional mentors and enablers of growth, starting with my first days in work. I am still in touch with five of them today, some thirty years later, and it gives me joy to be able to remind them how different and significant they have been for me. Significant and more skilled others have always played an important part in my evolution and I sought the company of those who knew more and better, so that I could learn from the best on a journey to achieve a better version of me, to understand who I was and what I was capable of doing and how I related to others, in the wider context of different cultures and countries that I embraced. And one thing remains true about my potential at work; I have never been fully utilised by any company I worked for, in spite of me asking for more and performing or over-performing in, and beyond, my roles!

And upon reflection and in hindsight, perhaps I, too, qualify in the end for just one clear label that says it all: Polymath.

A useful exercise

If you are a polymath you need to narrow down your various capabilities under the heading of a job title and then package the contents of your work experience according to that heading. As a result, you may need to have more than one CV, each demonstrating one specific set of skills or capability or job title that you wish to pursue. I always suggest having a concurrent pursuit of at least three objectives or jobs, given that obliquity and chance will have a hand, and we never know which one of the options will come up with a win. Once you have chosen the specific job title, prepare a CV that supports the chosen job from the beginning to the end, no more, no less. To support the document you need to prepare a narrative for the interview, which needs to – again – showcase a specific segregated rendition and prepared answers that relate to the job title, no more, no less.

During the interview, remain alert to signs indicating whether disclosing other skills and experience may be helpful or not. This is critical, since saying too much about other aspects of work may cloud the message and confuse the interviewers, who in the first half of the process are usually less skilled than you, and may become anxious or overwhelmed, which is not in your interest. It is also important that the hiring managers are reassured that you are not going to upstaged or threaten their competence or authority. Try not to express opinions or open complex and sophisticated lines of dialogue. You do not know where that may lead and this could end up being to your disadvantage. In a nutshell you need to cut yourself down to the size of that job and nothing more. Your other professional selves are for show and discussion in the other interviews for the other jobs where you turn up as a specific incarnation that matches the edited documents that you sent ahead of you.

Summary

Polymaths are people that have a wider range of capabilities than specialists and can draw from many sources when looking at problems and contemplating the world. There was a fashion for such ability during the Renaissance, but the increased quantity of information and the Western positivism have encouraged specialisation as a preferred option in learning and professionalisation. As a result, it is somewhat problematic to find the right place in the world of work to express and realise one's diverse offerings to the job market. On the other hand, with the new order of the fourth industrial revolution on our doorsteps, the time of polymaths may finally come. The new world of work will require people who are flexible, open-minded, and able to morph and adjust to changing situations and dynamic opportunities.

Polymaths have a good chance to meet these requirements. Alongside an ability to think with complexity in mind, the future of work is hungry for people who are open to change and continuously expanding the range of their professional and personal capabilities. Perhaps it is technology that will this time open the doors to make room for a new wave of Renaissance ideals about a multidimensional model of individual development, upgraded for a digital age. Time will tell!

Working internationally and cross-culturally: this may be our world, but my world is not quite the same as yours!

A personal international experience of several decades across six countries left me in no doubt that cultural differences are a powerful component of effectiveness in our working lives, in culturally rich environments. And we have all gathered anecdotal evidence from friends, work colleagues and popular jokes or stereotypes that relate to an international setting, in life, work or play, that there are indeed differences, joys and challenges when engaging with other peoples. The encounter with this difference, when it happens, is organic, "ad hoc". It can be frustrating and often gets – literally – lost in translation or can be full of joy and a sense of discovery. It all depends on many factors, from individual preferences and personality, to circumstances and the way the other side responds to us.

Such similarities and differences that define groups, large numbers of people or populations are known as culture and culture is a word that we all commonly use yet seldom stop to ponder about its deeper meaning. Definitions of culture are numerous – over one hundred – and the reason is that culture, whilst an omnipresent phenomenon and intrinsic part of our social life, is in fact a composite construct, made of many facets. But in spite of numerous definitions it is possible to identify a few attributes that cut across variations. These attributes of culture relate to: values and beliefs, symbols and rituals, artefacts, collective practices, "the way things are done around here", and shared and collectively recognised meanings.

This brief list could in itself be a subject of a book, since each attribute is in its own right a more complex concept. And indeed, culture has been a subject of research for psychologists, sociologists, psychiatrist and philosophers for quite some time. But staying with that which we all recognise and understand from our everyday use of terms, there is an agreement that most groups of people, or small and large nations, would have culture, as a sign of that group's identity. The most common notion around culture is that of national culture, which we all understand, as we know that are different nations on our planet. And there have been opinions and stereotypes that have gone with it, because since the history of human exchanges began, every continent has had their own leader board in terms of which nations hold what position for what prevailing attribute and why. For example: the Chinese are said to be ambitious and competitive; the Japanese structured and minimalist; the Italians are extroverted and unpredictable; the English are reserved and unfathomable; the Americans are brush and direct; and the Germans are precise and lack humour . . . and so on.

But diversity of gender and culture in a group, when properly utilised, brings about greater resourcefulness, creativity and innovation. Our job is therefore to capitalise on this resource to increase our cross-cultural savvy and ability to work with diversity. In the work environment of today, we are quite likely to interact with bosses, colleagues and clients who are originally from other countries. Our private relationships also have an international flavour and we meet people in our travels or visitors to our countries of residence with whom we make connections and establish long-lasting relationships. In practice, the cultural characteristics that manifest in the daily dynamics and alongside other conditions can become enhancers or detailers of our cross-cultural interaction. And we need to know how to rather capitalise on this opportunity and become comfortable with variations from our normal system of reference, by adding flexibility to it.

So beyond that initial comprehension – more or less sophisticated – that each nation appears to have its own values and beliefs, symbols, rituals and common practices – the rest of what we learn and know about cultures becomes indeed a matter of individually gained experience, driven by our curiosity for and openness to the other cultures and "the other".

In our modern times the affordability of travel and the movement of people across the planet for work (due to a globalised economy) or for leisure (following deregulation of air travel and the creation of affordable and structured holiday packages) means that the level of awareness that there are differences between nations has increased. But it is a matter of personal choices and the behaviour of those who travel that determines how deep, genuine and transformative that exposure may be. In the business world it is quite possible to spend one's time as an expatriate, working in a company that is familiar; living in a compound or neighbourhood for expatriates; using private transport; and patronising clubs, shops and schools designed and managed by expatriates, so much so that the contact with the local culture and the knowledge of the real host country remains quite superficial.

On any trip to the main points of interest, tourism has to ensure that one can have access to familiar surroundings, from food to accommodation and the company of other travellers, so much so that pretty much everywhere in Europe, for instance, or Australia and some parts of Asia one can find Irish pubs, English breakfast, French and Italian restaurants as well as all the cuisines of Asia, well represented. Becoming immersed and culturally savvy takes some effort, curiosity and most importantly the understanding of why this may be a useful capability to have, not only personally but also for business. Being able to meet other people in their cultural paradigm is undoubtedly an advantage, particularly when we need to get things done together with "the other" in business, work, or politics. There has been a trend of paying lip service to the advantage of being culturally competent and also the need to spend some time in training on this very subject. There has also been some progress made in establishing that working effectively across different cultures may well be more of an advantage than a disadvantage, and research in creative problem solving, cross-cultural think tanks and open collective platforms where people from all over the world contribute their ideas, imbued with the specific flavours of different cultural paradigms, did wonders for innovation and creativity, as well as speed of resolution and the novelty of the process that emerged as a result of this melting pot. Arguably most people agree that having a few minds looking at something together may be better than the judgement of just one person and the system of having advisors and counsellors, who assist individuals in positions of power, clearly make this point, just as in our private lives we often choose to discuss our thoughts with others and get some fresh additional perspectives.

These top level statements may by and large be quite obvious for many people and things would be relatively simple if the cultural complexity of our social lives stopped here. But what we have discussed so far only relates to one layer of culture. Indeed culture is not only a complex context but also sees this complexity multiplied a few folds, through its multilayers. If asked, most people would agree that the IT industry and the retail industry are not the same; they would also agree that marketing and manufacturing, as business functions, are quite different. Finally, there is also the agreement that a research team is quite different from a team working on an oil rig. We may also agree that the same research team, for example, may be different, depending on who the manager or leader is. We also quite easily agree that Virgin, Barclays and Ford are not exactly similar organisations. By agreeing to all these scenarios we have in fact acknowledged that there are different industries, business functions, and organisational and team cultures, in the context of, say, the wider national culture. And every one of those layers of culture would carry with it its symbols, values and beliefs, rituals, artefacts and a mindset about "how business is being done here". If we are to add to this the undeniable fact that, as individuals, we receive during our early years the cultural teachings of our environment represented by family, closest social group and the institutions we attend, we also acknowledge the existence of a personal and individual cultural paradigm. This, just like the others aspects of culture, may change over time, but the change is likely to be slow and based on the individual's ability and appetite to challenge and verify received ideas against their own life experience, and embrace some new values or stick to the old ones.

If we agree with the suggestion that cultures change, and I do believe this is the case, particularly based on what we can observe in our lifetime; if we contrast and compare behaviour between, say, the 1960s and today in relation to a number of aspects of ordinary life (the way we relate to smoking or recycling, or use of plastic bags, or fitness, etc.), it is obvious that attitudes, which reflect values and beliefs, which in turn are part of the cultural fabric, have indeed changed. More significantly is the fact that a change of culture, started in one country within its national culture, eventually travels across the planet and impacts other national cultures, creating a set of values, which is now overarching globally, and across all boundaries. Globalisation has made this transfer of cultural elements possible and has also increased the speed of first impact, by establishing early adopters as points of agency, in various places on the planet. However, how that travels across the entire national system and how long it takes to take a general hold, if that may be the case, is another matter. Cultural change does happen, but it is slow and sometimes needs entire generational renewals, to fully transform and become something entirely new, or more likely, a synthesis of what has been and what will be, a stable fabric for some time to come. So we are contemplating a combination of complexity and slow evolution, which indeed makes culture such a challenging reality of our lives.

For those who may think that culture is a bit of a "touchy-feely" subject, we have been made aware in recent times, in a rather brutal way, of the fact that a culture of risk, practiced and encouraged by people at the top, did drive financial institutions to behaviour that in the end impacted every individual on the planet and not favourably! The example was set at the top, permission was given, and a specific behaviour was encouraged and rewarded, for the systemic spread of an elitist, money-driven, risk-taking appetite that swept the world of finance for a number of years, all warped by a certain mindset (I am here to make money, the more the better, no matter how), value system (short-term gain with no vision or respect for future consequences), behaviours (reckless spending, alcohol consumption), symbols (of status and power), and artefacts (mansions, penthouses, real estate, fast cars). This was the case when the culture of a specific business activity impacted the world across national and international boundaries.

Acknowledging all the aspects described, we also agree and conclude that when talking about culture we need to keep in mind that we could be talking about: different global, or national, or industry, or organisational, or business, or team, or individual aspects of culture in fact interacting all at once. Hence the challenge of complexity and dynamics, which demand us to work with a moving target and hold this shifting paradigm steady in our mind. But there are some clear aspects that we can hold firm about culture: it is complex and evolving, has many facets and dimensions, has sociological and anthropological components, is created by a combination of individual psychology and social influences of nurturing and education brought about by our social lives. Cultural awareness and individual cultural competence enhance the ability to differentiate between subjective perceptions of culture relative to an objective framework that we can all share and rely on when talking about culture. There is no argument about the importance of being culturally savvy in the interconnected, interdependent world of the fourth technical revolution and globalised economy. In the business world, cultural incompetence can damage an individual's career and self-esteem, but with invisible psychological consequences that can go on un-noticed and unattended, until some other more visible and damaging breakdown, as personal or class action, manifests as a consequence. The reality is, as experienced by people and businesses, that just transferring skills and expertise to a country does not linearly work all the time, because the local dimensions and specific interplay of values, practices and behaviours do not match the ones of the country of origin. Various scenarios can play out; for example, an individual performing in one country and transferred to another to do the same great job may actually fail. Or an entire team being moved from one country to another may also fail, although, depending on the country, may succeed where the individual has failed. The previous winning recipe does not work. It needs to be adapted. In marketing there are examples where exporting a bestseller from one country to another, just like that, has proven a disaster for unexpected reason such as the product being of the wrong colour, or carrying an undesired symbolic meaning, or having a local association with bad luck, and so something successful in one geography does not necessarily work in another. Successful local recipes, in business and sales, do not automatically work globally. And today's world is highly globalised. Management as well as individual employees need to keep this in mind today, more than ever before. And the time is not too soon to actively engage in the process of acknowledging a reality that stares us in the face.

Today's workers and managers do not only need to be skilled and knowledgeable in their domain and also be good managers of people, but in addition become skilled and effective at working with valuable human resources and specialist contributors, scattered across the country or the planet. Technology is the only link, and, as we know, sometimes it works and when it does it is marvellous, but sometimes it just lets us down. Other factors such as culture, language, time zones and individual differences all combine to make the task of remote working and management, across cultures or with international and cross-cultural teams, both challenging and full of excitement and promise. So what exactly is this capability that we need to develop? The consensus today is that cultural competence refers to:

- A defined set of values, principles, attitudes, behaviours, policies and structures that enable individuals or agencies to work effectively cross-culturally
- Applied to businesses or clinical care and or any setting that serves racially and ethnically mixed groups of people
- Driven by an engagement to develop awareness, knowledge and skills, along the cultural competence continuum.

After all, developing cross-cultural competence is about an ongoing developmental process, the "kaizen" and the "do" the circle of development and the way that leads us along the cultural competence continuum or related awareness, knowledge and skills. And does so by policy, structured as a system adhered to and actively used by all agencies and professionals that work and wish to be really effective in cross-cultural situations.

Reflecting on group findings

In my coaching experience I have come across the entire range of life stories – from clients who have lived and worked all their lives in the same area, to those who have moved and changed within their own country, to those who enjoy going abroad for holidays to those who have come from a mixed heritage and have constantly moved around geographies with their original families or as a choice of lifestyle in their professional adult life.

Reflecting on those who have embraced or been born into a world of internationalism and cultural change, many of their personal stories and experiences have been similar to mine. I have found by and large that they enjoyed this lifestyle, were comfortable with change, had good resilience to deal with its sometimes taxing implications, and were multilingual, which increased their ability to think and communicate in different ways and with a greater degree of nuance and complexity. Cognitively, they were enriched by their curiosity and continued learning. They also developed strong opinions and value systems that reflected the way they processed differences and similarities as experienced. And it was also interesting to see how individual experience determined the opinions that they extrapolated over an entire "other" culture, that in turn could generate opposite opinions, if compared, about the same country or culture, if for instance asked "so what do you think about life in France or Australia?" Some would answer "great" and others would say "disappointing".

I found that my own international experience was very useful in the way I could engage with their paradigm and listen to their story, and also be able to help with adaptation.

I remember clients from the US and Australia who were finding it difficult to get a job in London, in spite of having excellent professional credentials, simply because of the way they spoke in interviews; the directness and tone of their statements was not quite landing well in London because of that open communication style. I also, at times, had to moderate the enthusiasm of some clients from Italy, who, in group settings, were so keen to participate that they pretty much silenced everybody else by their sheer energy, surrounded as they were by colleagues of a more subdued cultural background. In most instances, my clients used my feedback well and modified their behaviour and communication style as far as they could, short of not losing authenticity. And often their resilience and the skills and professional expertise that they had to offer in the job market prevailed in the end. I have also worked with people that eventually left the country, because they felt that the effort needed here was more than what they were prepared to invest and thought that other places offered a less taxing alternative for them to embrace.

My case study

My encounters with cultural differences have been interesting and developmental. For example, I became aware of my clearly European identity only when I lived in America and I could look back at what was the norm for me and what was new in that culture that was significantly different. This experience was profound and very personal indeed. I realised that I belonged to certain regions of Europe but not necessarily to a country, because my personality did not align with the general attributes of my original culture and found a better place for expression within the dimensions of another.

I also realised that many people need to connect to some roots, when I noticed how most Americans identified themselves as Italian-American or Irish-American, or Greek-American, naming a history that existed before theirs. I also noticed how apparently similar cultural and linguistic contexts have morphed into very different blended outcomes: for example in the US, UK and Australia where language and history are connected yet this common root gave rise to three rather different cultural identities including aspects that are opposite.

I noticed the degree to which I was experiencing the interplay of enculturation, acculturation and transculturation, manifest for example in the way I picked up accents and mannerisms or changes in tone of voice.

I remember moving from the UK to Australia and everyone being impatient with my acculturated "English" way of skirting around the subject and just alluding to what I wanted to say or achieve. And how a colleague at work just lost patience and urged "Just tell me, what do you want!?" And how in reverse, after a few years, I moved back to London and for some six months seemed to insult everyone as soon as I opened my mouth; I was too direct – Australian acculturation – and people here and now expected me to engage in that subtle dance of innuendos and allusion, purposely avoiding directness, to say what I wanted to say.

Culture and international life are a significant part of my identity and I have a lot of thoughts about it. But in a nutshell, my cross-cultural experience is quite rich and has been acquired organically, because I was ready to follow unexpected opportunities, when they arose.

I have also counted on my general ability to speak languages and communicate and the fact that my curiosity has been a positive and energising driver.

My general openness combined with enjoyment of change and renewal made my expatriate experience predominantly a positive one. In every new setting I started by finding a place to live as my own solid base, then a job to ensure financial independence and safety then made new connections and friends, and so adapt and appreciate what was on offer, without judging or comparing but simply evaluating if I was happy with things or not.

I remained observant, curious and appreciative, closely noticing details of culture and languages, and noting behaviours and the way I related to the "other" and the others to me.

In the absence of many, if any, prejudices to begin with – again thanks to my parents – I have developed my own views about the world and what I like, more or less, in what I see, places where I would like to live or not, and cultural practices that I agree or disagree with. And if curiosity takes me to places or draws me into situations that I do not appreciate for some reason – usually because of my values and beliefs, I step back from those situations and do not revisit them.

I actively create and review my own constructs about the new culture, which help me navigate the cultural changes, whilst using as my base, an inner core of my own, as a centre.

And regardless of where I am physically, I remain fascinated by the variety of artistic expressions and ways of life elsewhere around the world, from music and dance, to dress, rituals and protocols, local do's and don'ts. I am equally interested in the native cultures of Australia or Papua New Guinea or the tribes of the Amazon or the busy Japanese cities, as I am in the remote communities in Mongolia or the rapidly expanding mega-cities of the Far East.

My ability to acculturate is apparent to my friends who tease me by saying that I have become too English or too French or too Australian in accent and manner, if I spend a length of time in one country or another. This is because I respect the local mores, I adapt and integrate.

In a nutshell, cultures, languages and diversity are a great playground for learning and a puzzle that both challenges and teaches me something on top of what I already know. It is my normal place to be, and quite likely my international business exposure early in my life is an important component of normalising this context. I also know and understand that the same may not be normal for many other people, and I may in fact be on the outside of norms. But I was greatly and pleasantly surprised, when in London I met people from a couple of international organisations, to discover that my – "unusual" to some – experience had been modest and unadventurous compared to that of others. Such encounters have been a breath of fresh air.

And seeing so many people like me proved that whilst we may not be mainstream on the bell curve, there are thousands in the global community driven by the same curiosity and ability to explore, transition and adapt.

There is an entire terminology – in the domains of anthropology, sociology and psychology – around the relationship and interplay between individuals and society that is part of science and research. But the scientific terminology and definitions become quite fluid in the way they manifest in reality, in dynamically lived experiences, and in my case I suppose, I can conclude that there is openness to transculturation, with a synthesis between my original culture and the cultures I have encountered during my international life. I also think that behind all this fluidity there is a strong personal core and an unbroken connection to my own cultural identity, which I own with pride, and use as a gravitational pool for a steady coherent sense of self, within the transience of change and cultural diversity. And unsurprisingly, my own international experience in business was tremendously useful in my career coaching work with international clients.

A useful exercise

There is a full range of attributes that one can connect with the ability to work internationally and cross-culturally and they can range from personality traits to personal drivers and emotional intelligence, to one's ability to generally work with others and so on. But perhaps we could narrow them down to just a few: flexibility, open-mindedness and empathy alongside values, such as respect and curiosity. All revealed and developed through individual reflection, increased self-awareness and the predictable or non-predictable changes that this process triggers.

From a coaching perspective, the coaching methodology (client-focused, non-diagnostic, non-expert models) should open to international clients a space that is respectful, flexible and co-created, held by a coach who does not get stuck in their own cultural paradigms but remains alert to possibilities.

Whether self-directed reflection or reflection guided by a coach or a significant skilled other, the purpose and outcomes should enable learning and adaptation. And this can be helped by:

- Reflecting on your personal cultural identity as it is today
- Identifying and articulate aspects of your cultural individuality and their origins
- Finding out if and how your personal preferences align or to the culture you have been born into
- Comparing aspects of your home culture aspect (communications, behaviour, customs, body language, etc.) to the same in another or many other cultures
- Using values to frame cultural alignments or misalignments
- Understanding potential challenges and finding solutions to minimise the impact of surprise or shock.

Summary

Culture is a construct that has specifically been researched since the 1980s. Like all constructs, culture is hard to define and there are about 100 definitions of culture, with agreement on some common core descriptors. Culture has an anthropological and sociological dimension and relates to large numbers of people, but it is also forged by individuals and personally, by a combination of individual psychology and social influences of nurturing and education. Cultural awareness and individual cultural competence enhance the ability to differentiate between subjective perceptions of culture relative to an objective perspective, which we can share when talking about culture. The outcome of such an approach will mean the difference between being respectful, curious and flexible or being prejudiced and set in our own ways. Cultural competence benefits both individuals and groups (business, communities, society) in ways such as:

- Acknowledging the great opportunity for increased creativity and innovation that steams from cultural diversity
- Agreeing that this cultural advantage is something a smart nation or company or society wants to benefit from
- Providing thought leadership in educating the people at large of this reality and advantage
- Turning experiential and anecdotal evidence into proven facts that should support a structured intentional approach to developing cultural competence
- Using this education as a foundation for cross-cultural tolerance, respect and enjoyment of a pluralist work and life environment
- Cross-fertilising local wisdoms and practices for the benefit of a global agenda for ecological, social and economic growth and stability.

Obliquity and chaos: life and the roll of the dice

Chaos theory and obliquity have a lot in common: they both rely on the idea that the factors involved in complex systems are too interconnected and too numerous to be easily controlled or understood or be prevented from influencing outcomes in unforeseen ways. In addition there are many factors unknown to us that can play a critical role in future events. Therefore there is no way we can guarantee that pursuing a specific objective will actually yield the desired result when the outcome may be subject to forces that will only become apparent as events unfold, or perhaps never, yet still have a significant impact on results. With this in mind, the proposed approach is to pursue goals in a more open, generalised way, without rigid lines of action; to take a holistic perspective by considering all aspects of that purpose, since a positive consideration of all aspects may well converge to the same point and goal set in the first instance.

In career terms, obliquity means a non-linear approach to achieving career goals. Because our world today is complex and interconnected, change is permanent, and predictability of future events is low. The future is uncertain, problems are often ill-defined and unclear, and our world is now highly interconnected and interdependent due to globalisation and technology. In this environment small things can have huge consequences whilst also being hard to control.

The way we measure outcomes and predict future events lacks precision and is often based on statistics and approximations. In this world, probabilities of 50/50 and statistical correlations of just 0.30 are considered significant, even though this in fact means that we either do not know or we get it right only one in three times, if we are lucky! Hardly a precise and reassuring approach. We still use a linear thinking paradigm in environments that are utterly non-linear and where minor repetitive stressors can lead to major shifts.

There are people living on the eastern border of Europe who have lived in the USSR, Russia, Yugoslavia, Poland, Moldova, Ukraine and Romania without having once moved, just because of waves of territorial conflict and the variety of victors that have ruled over the territory and the people at points in time. The people of Alsace and Lorraine have successively been French and German over time. The people who happened to live in Algeria after the war survived only because the Americans dropped powdered milk there at that time. No pre-planning could have avoided or changed such realities. In my own case, it is ridiculous to see how, unintentionally, I have moved around countries exactly at the time of recessions, not that I planned it that way, but somehow, accidentally, I landed in the wrong place at the wrong time . . . quite consistently! Away from the global picture there is the matter of span of control; namely, what things do we have total control over, some control (influence) over, and no control at all. Can we control that the people we meet at interviews, whom we do not know at all, will give us the job? Certainly not. But can we control the way we dress, prepare, pursue and present ourselves in an interview? Certainly yes. Perhaps the most useful course of action is to concentrate on that which we can control and leave the rest to chance. Hopefully events and an accumulation of other factors – known and unknown – will play in our favour. We may remind the interviewers of an "important other" that they value and like . . . good for us! Or we may trigger just the opposite reaction . . . in which case no matter what we do, we will not be able to change that negative perception, because it has nothing to do with us., even if it will impact us.

We all make choices and exercise rejection on a daily basis. We accept or reject the invitation to relate and engage with some people and not others. Most of us have been in recruitment situations and have rejected many applicants in favour of others who got the job. So the way we ourselves react and make decisions in relation to others' demands is in itself not a linear "what you see is how things are" connection. Behind a behaviour that appears to make sense, there are values and beliefs at work that may or may not "make sense". What we say and do and what the interviewers see, do and say is determined by a multitude of causes, including the perceptions and expectations that all involved have and that are all quite subjective. A lot of this dynamic is not only driven by the cortex, but also by subconscious influences and the "primitive brain", which operates in a rather less sophisticated way than the executive prefrontal cortex. We react to "first impressions", body language, facial expressions, tone of voice and our personal maps of go/no go criteria to accept/reject, just like the other people, including those who interview us in assessment centres and make decisions as a result, do. But are we all equally aware of this type of "bias"? This is the questions and if the answer is no, there are implications. Clearly, the aspiration here is to develop such capability and engage with situations and people in a more conscious and balanced way.

Reflecting on group findings

It was interesting to see how in my client group, there was a variety of attitudes towards obliquity, depending on their personal experience, personality and way of approaching life. Some of them strongly believed in control, preparation and process and did not leave a lot to chance. And there is also merit in reminding ourselves that because the Western culture – particularly after the '80s with individualism and the belief in control and self-determination – has prevailed over other sets of beliefs and behaviour, such an approach was to be expected. The '80s brought about the individuality cult and the idea that whatever one wanted to achieve, one could; that striving for individual achievement and wealth was the ideal path to follow and that the individual will prevail over anything else. This attitude and approach to life and career is also more common in certain personality types and certain traits, where individuals are a bit more risk averse, a bit less tolerant of uncertainty, and pragmatism with active pursuit of clearly set goals, is the right way to get that job.

For others, the glass is always full and there is no need to worry about the future too much; what will be will be, and doing one's minimum best and then let things unfold is the way, because things always end up right in the end. And so I have worked with clients who never had a CV in their lives and got jobs by connections, recommendations and by just falling into a job that suited them; a case of just being in the right place at the right time, by chance. Whilst the number of such cases was not large, it was refreshing to observe their confidence in this approach that had yielded results for the best part of their working lives. I have also met people who did not have a business card because, I was told, they were just sufficiently well-known not to need one; not because they were in some way famous, but simply because they were known to those who mattered and could be instrumental to their objectives. As a result they were quite relaxed about the way they turned up and about work in general, as this typically just kept coming their way. And again such clients did not represent a large number. The conversations with them were always interesting, because some of the things I was supposed to focus on as part of the service were to prepare them for the market, which included relevant documents and interview preparation, for example. But I encountered some resistance, supported by statements that all they needed to do was talk to a few people they know to let them understand that they were looking for a job and then things were going to happen.

This contrasted greatly with my work with those clients who prepared in great detail, taking the process very seriously and putting the work into it. And it is also from my clients across the board of those who prepared and those who did not that I got stories about how "chance" and "serendipity" had their hand in the success that they sometimes achieved. They told me what one could think of as "clichéd" – yet true – stories; for example, about the hairdresser who acted as the "go between". Hearing one customer complaining about how hard it was to recruit the right person and another customer saying that they were looking for a job. The hairdresser got them connected and the rest became history.

Such stories, were indeed so simple, and to a degree common, that it was almost hard to believe, had it not been for the fact that I was getting them from the source. But here was the evidence that the most mundane activities and the small events of ordinary life could lead to extraordinary and significant outcomes for the people in those situations. What I have learned as I observed the behaviours, the motivation and the attitudes to job searching was that the variety and diversity of circumstances and ways in which career-related significant events occur is quite broad, and whilst the majority may have indeed clustered around the classic model of accessing a job, there were many other paths, quite unconventional, that equally led to the same outcome. This led me to ask questions and listen first, to allow my clients to focus on and identify the path that was the best for them, then work towards what they wanted to achieve and help them along that path, with an invitation to let other options in and remain open to the unexpected and the random.

My case study

In my own experience, obliquity with its quality of bringing changes, some-times for the better and sometimes not, may have been playing a part, but this did not register with me as such for a good part of my life. This is for reasons that have to do with personal history and values and beliefs developed early in my life; for example, that work and dedication bring rewards (meritocracy) and that we have control over our lives (free will); that a good plan prevents derailments and failure (linear causality); and if one keeps banging at that door it will eventually open (the value of persistence), all of which informed my actions for a good while, even when the contrary was staring me in the face. Thankfully this view has now evolved into a more balanced perspective on the dynamics of life.

With hindsight I have also identified the events and the times when obliquity really played its hand in my own journey. One example that was significant because of its timing and the change it brought about is that of finding a won-derful job quite by accident. I was, at the time, unhappy with my work and the industry I was in and looking for a change towards a different company size and sector. But of course, such transitions are always difficult, because typically most recruiters tend to box and label you for a quick sale and would not look outside that packaging, no matter what you tell them about your capa-bilities, transferable skills and personal wishes. Transitions are hard and I was really in need of a significant transition and quite discouraged by the lack of progress I was making in my search, yet unable to do anything more apart from what I was doing to achieve that goal. In a rather subdued mood I attended the birthday party of a close friend of mine. One of the guests was her boyfriend and we connected almost immediately, something not very usual for me, since typically I was rather withdrawn when around people I did not know. But this conversation was going somewhere and I found the mindset, the insightful comments and the big picture painted by him quite similar to mine. This made me comfortable and engaged and I became quite open about what I was doing at the time and what I was looking forward to work-wise.

He told me that in the past he had worked in recruitment and offered to help me review my CV and talk about my skills and what I had to offer in the market. We did so and I met him a few times in his corporate office. I paid little attention to the size of his office or the way others related to him. I remained relaxed and quite open, acting as myself, with no attempt to impress or to formalise the way I came across by minding how he or other people might judge me. I think I was, to a degree, quite naive and trusting in the way this conversation was going. But after a few such encounters, he took me by surprise when he told me that he was in fact recruiting for one of the departments under his leadership; that he was a senior board director with eight managers reporting to him and had personal and legal responsibility for one of the largest budgets in the organisation, which in the business world indicates (I now know!) that he was very powerful.

He also presented the job to me and then arranged a meeting with the hiring manager, who placed me on the formal hiring path. I was quite perplexed by this development and a little in a daze, since working for that company never crossed my mind. I was also not quite sure about the role description, but now curious and with a sense of gratitude I felt I had to pursue this opening. So I did get hired on a contract basis and eventually became a permanent employee.

This is one of the best things that happened in my life and it opened for me a whole new world of work, opportunities to learn and change roles – be in an environment that I discovered to be fascinating and a step change in my evolution as a business professional in my domain. My line manager also happened to be a person with whom I had a great connection and from whom I learned a lot. As a true mentor, he opened for me options for growth and increased responsibility. As to the person who I initially met as my girlfriend's boyfriend, I discovered that he was an exceptionally visionary individual, very successfully running one of the largest and most productive departments in the company. An inspirational leader, he was well ahead of his time, fully embodied his vision and enabled others to follow his example by adopting and making available to his team all that was helpful, progressive and enlightened in corporate methodology, technology and culture.

He was supportive and committed to his very large team, he pioneered for us advanced technology and ways of working and ensured we were well trained, recognised and rewarded.

He remains to this day, one of the brightest and most inspirational figures in my working life. And with such excellent first and second line management and colleagues, who were happy, engaged, competent and committed, this period of my working life has been one of the happiest ever. To this day I am still in touch with my business "significant others" managers and colleagues, and whenever we get the chance to meet, we fondly remember that exceptional environment of high performing teams, where we worked hard and played hard and had such an exceptional esprit de corps that bonded us all and produced excellent outcomes for individuals and the company alike.

So how did this significant event happen? It was a chance encounter that unknowingly I amplified by being open and myself, presenting myself in a way that elicited curiosity, trust and credibility. I was polite and engaged in that interaction and at my best, from the outset. And this represented the "under our control" aspect of obliquity. Being always prepared, responding in a positive way to circumstances, respecting people and being well spoken and well presented at all times are basic and positive attributes likely to catalyse whatever change is thrown our way. Without looking for anything specific we may well just fall into a situation that is exactly what we need. This was not a door I saw, let alone pounded on, yet this job happened to be all that I wished for and came at a time when I was really down and somewhat hopeless. The lesson here is that one should never underestimate the truth in the saying "you never know what is around the corner" but also be always prepared to spot a good thing when it comes along, as much as step away and keep clear of potential trouble.

A useful exercise

There may be, therefore, room for another take on how to pursue goals in a non-linear fashion and here are some thoughts to consider. You could reflect on this topic by asking yourself what is your belief: Is it that if you pursue something firmly enough you always get there? Or is it that you think there is no need to worry and work too hard for something because what is meant to happen, will? Or are you somewhere in between? You may also reflect on some examples for the various scenarios and see whether in your own experience one way has prevailed over the others. You may also reflect and become aware of a situation that you never quite considered carefully or classified but with hindsight you may now recognise falls into a category that is not that of your habitual beliefs, behaviour and way of pursuing objectives.

For example:

- Think of three situations when you did or did not do something almost trivial and of little significance that resulted in an unexpected serious outcome
- Think of a time when you really "knocked" hard at that door and . . . it did not open . . .
- Think of a time when you were simply "passing by" just smiling and someone opened the door for you . . .
- Think of a time when you applied yourself to open the door and . . . it did . . .

Can you analyse and say why these outcomes were different!? This process will illuminate for you the facts about what and why some event did take place in your life as well as the strength and orientation of your belief and related behaviour and possibly also the origins of that belief and habit of behaving. In this light you will then have had the opportunity to actually review and possibly correct your perceptions. In addition you may become more aware and able to control your general state of readiness and have hope in what is possible, and in doing so allow some hidden doors to unexpectedly open, when you do not expect but when you need them to open. We can either allow "chance" to act as "the spanner in the works" and undermine us, or we can be reactive, flexible, open-minded and positive, and try to use it to our advantage. Small, positive subroutines under our control, can make big differences over time.

- Take some care in your appearance (even if you go to the corner store); you do not know who you may meet
- Remain impartial or be positive in all situation and check your facial expression; it gives away things that are better left unseen, particularly under stress
- Do not tell others your worry or difficulty at the time; it may put them off and make them feel guilty if they cannot help
- Stay authentic but do not overwhelm others with your views

- Stay on track with your plans but also alert to what else may be happening around you that is not planned but could be helpful
- Accept that not all of your future is in your hands
- Stay in control and work with that which IS in your hands: appreciate degrees of control
- Accept that rejection and setbacks are part of normality
- Accept that in the big picture, which you cannot perceive, you may be going in a new direction altogether, which often proves to be much more interesting
- Trust and follow your instincts and gut feelings
- Accept that chance will always play a part in our lives with a 50% chance to be for the better

Going forward . . .

- Concentrate on the things that are under your control
- Stay flexible and embrace changes and unexpected opportunities that may come along
- Remain firmly anchored in your self-belief and your self-knowledge
- Go with the flow whilst upholding the essence of what is important
- Be alert and focused whilst remaining relaxed and confident
- Accept that your time frame and your path ahead as a straight line may not be what will actually happen
- Accept that hard-headed, single-minded planning and logic will not cover all the intricately connecting influences that may exist
- Listen to your intuition
- Be open for fast change
- Sense and stay with the general flow of events
- Allow "illogical" mindsets or motivators to help a logical desire (rational goal) to be fulfilled
- Use the pinball effect (hitting sideways targets or obstacles) or an alternative view on achieving your objectives.

The way we engage in a complex reality where many determining factors are not under our control is a matter of perspective and how we spend our energy. In order to enable the wider system to throw some unexpected opportunity your way, you can prime it by a number of simple but possibly consequential behaviours in social settings:

- Say something positive about yourself
- Offer a small piece of helpful information
- Listen carefully to the others and show interest in them
- Look for common ideas and interests and ask about them; engage in conversations that are mutually exciting and gratifying
- Offer a win-win, so that the interaction is meaningful to both sides

Summary

Obliquity is about allowing time and chance to play a hand rather than not, and remaining open to opportunities that a much focused approach may actually obscure. It is about the "roll of the dice" and how chance can, in the blink of an eye, change our path, for better or worse. There is little we can do about such unpredictable events and random circumstances, and we are surrounded by randomness all the time, in spite of our quite regulated, organised and structured lives and societies.

The daily news remind us of this volatile reality all the time and sadly mainly with negative examples. But what comes to mind is also the case of a British couple in their forties who won the lottery – a huge jackpot – twice, a few years apart, by playing the same lotto numbers. An unbelievable event and yet true! There are people whose lives were saved just because of the presence at the time of a medic or the proximity of a hospital or a new drug released a few days earlier. Such examples are numerous and maybe whilst not as numerous as the examples that fill the middle of the bell curve and what we call a statistical majority, they nonetheless do occur.

So why not allow such chances to come our way, in our favour? And how could we do that? Perhaps by doing the opposite or something different from what we always do, by allowing variety and a wider range of possibilities to cross our paths. In a nutshell, we could pull instead of push. Pushing hard often does not open that door. Appearing needy, insisting on an outcome, asking for help, is a push that may put people off more than motivate them to assist. Many aims – from finding the ideal job, to running a profitable business, to living a happy life – are more likely to be achieved when pursued indirectly, by setting less ambitious or intermediate milestones, especially in a difficult terrain. Deviating, reviewing the plan and changing our mind in synch with changes around us may also get us there indirectly. Successful sailing often involves going in strange directions. Happy people often focus on other activities than pursuing happiness itself. Driving up the mountain involves meandering on the way. Let us give ourselves permission to experiment, do "trial runs" and "rehearsals" and safely fail to enhance our chances to succeed when it really matters.

We can pursue flexible goals not necessarily through the efficient application of an ideal plan, but through a process of "constant adaptation" and "pragmatic improvisation", an acknowledgement that the complexity of reality is always going to outweigh our knowledge of it.

Transitions: changing direction to known and unknown destinations

Transition is a word that appears in our vocabulary almost constantly and refers to a multitude of domains and activities, from quantum physics and biology, to psychology, mathematics, the arts, culture, technology, computing, anthropology, to developmental psychology and our expectations of a normal life and work journey. Its omnipresence can easily be explained by the fact that the meaning of transition is that of a process that is dynamic and gradually moves something from a state to another. Synonyms for transitions are words such as passing, shift and change.

Change from one form, state, style or place to another usually involves a jump start. It is a point of inflection that changes a trajectory, to propel the previous state to a new different plane of being. Transitions occur without stop and start, but through a bridge that preserves an element of the previous state but also seeds new elements that will be a part of the next stable phase. Our life and work path is pretty much predetermined. There are stages and transitions that are predictable and firmly set by our biology and society. For example, as individuals we move from childhood to adolescence, then early adulthood, middle age and older age. We also travel through socially pre-set stages, from home nurture to early education, school and higher education, to employment and retirement. Linked to age and accumulation of skills and experience, we also transition from being financially dependent to being financially independent, then – in turn – financially responsible for others who are dependent on us.

On this pre-set individual path, there is the likelihood of known and predictable turbulence – even if we typically think "this won't happen to me" – related to health, accidents of all sorts, socio-economic and political upheavals, natural events, and manmade large-scale disasters or discoveries, which can change, from one second to another, what we may have perceived as a steady and pretty much uneventful trajectory to achieving personal fulfilment, happiness, a contribution to society, and higher levels of self-actualisation and spirituality, as pinnacles of aspirational and developmental states. Such events are typically showstoppers and cause startle and shock in most cases, as a first reaction. Thereafter, the way people deal with them becomes a unique and specific path, where the individual makeup from personality to invisible drivers, history, impact of significant others and the entire social and economic context of that person come into play.

After pausing – and depending on the answer to the question "Is this good or bad?" as a first assessment – some people become excited, or scared or just numb for a while. And this is generally the same whether it is about life or work. What follows are again different reactions across the entire range of emotions and thought from disbelief and denial to celebrations, confusion, depression, crises, to acceptance, exploration, letting go, recovery and constructive solution-finding followed by implementation. These reactions broadly follow phases from being ok to being shocked, then partial adjustment to deal with inner contradictions, and crises, to finally stepping into a recovery and reconstruction mode. The overarching process, as well as the bridges between the various stages, is all a matter of transition.

For a change to cause a transition, it is necessary that it imposes a major restructuring of a person's view of themselves and the world. In terms of resources to achieve this objective, there is notably the ability of a person to deal with stress – which is known to be a subjectively perceived element that can both stimulate activity as well as have a negative impact – alongside their resourcefulness, resilience, social connectivity and the ability to find opportunities no matter how destructive the situation seems to be initially. This process usually takes time – months or possibly years – and can equally affect positive as well as negative events, choices and changes. For example, marriage, children, expatriation, new jobs and promotions are, although positive, also demanding of significant changes for which a developed awareness of motivation, personal resources and strengths will be called upon, to reach that level of happy adaptation to the new normal. Individuals respond differently to transitions and have different vulnerabilities to stress, different recovery rates, different crisis points or relapses, and different ways of bouncing back.

Because we lead social lives, depending on circumstances, individual transitions also take others with it. For example a person's state of health, or job changes, or changes of location will involve and impact family, friends and partners, who will also need to adjust themselves to the new circumstances. As a result, transitions involve situational and interpersonal changes, learning and unlearning. Overall they involve a significant overall restructuring in emotional, cognitive, behavioural and even motivational and attitudinal aspects. It is a major redesigning of the complex personal landscape and the surrounding system that involves others. And again, the way people react to this major shift differs, with outcomes that can be more or less positive, depending on the many factors and combinations of factors involved.

In work, the famous first 100 days represent just a phase, the most critical, of a settling-in process that can take another six to twelve months to stabilise performance and get some return in the effort put into that specific transition. Organisations know that a newly hired person needs to stay with the organisation at least two years for them to recover the investment that has been placed in the recruitment, induction, training and mentoring that person into their new job. For both the organisation and the individual, the transition period is a time of uncertainty when things can go either way.

Reflecting on group findings

In my experience with clients, transitions have been a relatively frequent topic and triggered by a number of factors both internal and external; for example, external factors such as organisational restructuring, with or without direct redundancy, triggers concern and stress. This one point of inflection, which often raises the question: "What next for me?" within or outside this reshaped organisation, means a number of paths will emerge and will have to be evaluated and experienced by each person as a reflection of their individuality. Some become quite anxious and depending on their personality and personal circumstances find it hard to accept and to contemplate that change and adjustment are inevitable and that they will have to make that effort and move on to a reconfigured working life.

Others take it well and, in fact – particularly in the case of specialists – look for a working future similar to the past – same job in another similar company – where the differences to consider and negotiate are of a practical nature, such as distance to travel, salary, additional benefits and opportunities for progression. Others again, may be anxious but also sigh with relief, because this is a moment where the responsibility for making a drastic choice – which they have quietly contemplated for a while, but had no courage to act on, due to many responsibilities and circumstantial factors – can now finally be enacted. They are thankful for that decision to have been made for them and can now break free and do something that they have been dreaming of for a while. The disruption to them, but especially to others that are dependent on them, is in this case not optional and everyone just has to accept the events. This gives them a guilt-free path to a new and sometimes completely different professional path.

Such unexpected paths come to mind as examples; for instance, that of a client who in her forties, after a successful life as a corporate lawyer, decided to become an interior designer; a dream that seemed distant, given her obligations to family, but now became possible in the context of redundancy, but also with her family having grown up and some financial stability. She could afford that change and was ready to take the risk and get on with an implementation plan to get training and join design-related practitioner circles and professional associations, all of which she had "secretly" been thinking about for a while.

Another client, an accountant in mid career, opted to set up a small plumbing business. It was because he liked working with his hands and also because his current corporate career was increasingly expecting him to take on people management responsibilities, which he found quite stressful. Financially he was fine and had no obligations to a family of his own. Again, this was an ideal time for him to get on with his wish, get training and start work as a plumber; even if his siblings and parents were somewhat surprised by this unexpected choice.

At the other end of the spectrum I also remember a client who had been restructured out of her job and had been offered career coaching to plan her work-related future. But when I met her, the first thing she told me was that at that moment she was experiencing a serious illness and was undergoing chemotherapy, as well as having her husband also out of work, whilst they needed to pay the mortgage and school fees for the children, and that she was a significant contributor to their income. Her ability to meet her responsibilities had obviously been diminished not only by the loss of a job but also by her ill health, which was making her weak and vulnerable in the job market. This redundancy could not have come at a worse moment, for so many reasons. I remember distinctly how shocked I was by her circumstances, with so many things were going wrong at the same time, but I was also very impressed and moved by the incredible dignity with which she presented her situation, maintaining composure whilst being fully cognisant of the magnitude of the challenge and not at all in denial or full of self-pity. In such a situation I could not help feeling a great sense of empathy combined with a sense of powerlessness, where my modest support appeared to me rather inadequate in the face of such sheer bad luck that she was facing. And I am thankful that in my career I have been faced with very few such life stories, where no matter what I did, I felt out of my depth and faced with an impossible task, when listening to a personal story where all odds were clearly stacked against my client. Other aspects – apart from career – were not under my remit to affect, but I still had a duty of care and felt a sense of human responsibility that in practice, I could not fully meet.

On another occasion, a client that I had worked with on career matters developed a serious illness and again went through radical treatment and recovered. To celebrate her recovery and her birthday, she invited me to a party with friends and family, where she acknowledged my contribution to her overall sense of confidence in the future and readiness for a new start in life and work. But once again I felt awkward because I knew that her health battle was ongoing and I had no power to assist her in that. On reflection it is clear that clinically separating the "career" aspect from the client as a whole person is impossible. Whilst maintaining all the required boundaries in place, a sense of extended responsibility and a natural reactive desire to help remained strong.

And again, I have also met clients who had a way of life that involved significant and frequent changes and transitions, starting with a family history of diversity, with parents of a different nationality living in a third country, which resulted in them being very early in life exposed to travel, different languages, countries and cultures, then as young adults moving again to study and work in yet other countries, all of which had made them flexible, resilient and adaptive to change and transitions, as a norm. These meetings have been very exciting for me, since I could very easily identify with their view of the world and lived experience of transition and change. We could converse in different languages and share perceptions of what cross-cultural and social adaptation looks like and how it challenged each of us.

We could also identify the stress points, often related to the difference in references that people who travel have compared to those who do not, and the demand placed on such global citizens to explain themselves, to justify a way of life that is so "different" and not "fitting" with the mainstream expectations. A dialogue from such opposite poles can be difficult and frustrating at times, depending on the openness and flexibility of the listening party. And I have seen people in tears in my office, frustrated by the dialogue with other coaches, which was not going anywhere because – I was told – the coach could not relate to their multidimensional identity. But beyond such moments of fatigue, the choice of leading such a flexible life instead of another was never under question and they were determined to do whatever it took to be successful and enjoy their choices, even if they did not appear quite "normal" to others. There were no regrets and no complaints about the effort and energy required, just a search for methods and ways to be successful and reach as soon as possible the clear waters leading to the other shore.

My case study

Reflecting back on my own journey, my life had its average share of transition as I was growing up and getting an education. Whilst some aspects of my life have been changing, others remained stable, and overall I have coped with transitions quite well from an early age, which involved travel, being looked after by different people, and being exposed to different social groups and cultures. But the commitment of my parents to me and the education path remained firm and steady and possibly enabled me to find the ways to deal with the other changes in a good adaptive way. I am certain that I built early on a level of self-direction and personal resilience and independence that has served me well for the rest of my life. Most importantly, I was never in trouble, really enjoyed school and learning, and was doing well with high grades, without effort and virtually no micro-monitoring from my parents. In terms of developing self-belief, significant others played a critical part in this process, by inspiring me to think that I was capable, and whatever I wanted to achieve I had the resources to do it. Thankfully this self-belief did not inflate to delusion, and I was able to differentiate between what I realistically could or could not do, and so assess and mitigate risk. Later on, when I became an adult I opened myself to external influences and opportunities to explore and grow. I followed the lead of what was presented in front of me – without a plan – by being open and alert, listening to my instinct to decide on the yes/no response and to move in ever increasing circles of experience, relatively safely, using an ability to assess circumstances, people and risk. Without a plan, I ended up acquiring an experience that I could not have dreamed of. Taking calculated risks and believing that in partly controlled circumstances I will land on my feet, I was able to activate as needed, reliable personal resources.

The result is that my life has indeed been about a long succession of transitions that reflect my need and appreciation for change and continued renewal. My curiosity and thirst for discovery – which without a doubt I inherited from my father – and my ability to implement and pragmatically turn every idea or plan into a tangible outcome – which without a doubt I inherited from my mother – propelled me across an extraordinary succession of experiences mostly unplanned, yet mostly welcomed. This resulted in me living in many countries on three continents, working for four very exciting industries, exercising several related jobs across the entire business process and also coming back in some kind of a magic circle to my first personal and professional choice.

Experiencing transitions as an expatriate most of my life has been a defining feature for me whilst curiosity for cultures and languages have never ceased to excite and interest me. And so from smaller to larger aspects of life, my preferences are the same. I enjoy change, get bored by routine and the known and look for variations or improvements of the same theme, whether it is how many ways can I go from A to B to avoid the same repetitive journey, or how I can mix and match my clothes, or being happy to try different foods, or attend art events of every kind from music to poetry to theatre, to additional professional degrees, diplomas and certificates, to simply changing from time to time the colour of soft furnishings and wall pictures at home. I think that this also reflects a very strong creative drive that I have never fully used or cultivated in a focused professional manner. That energy gives me an appetite for small new creations of some kind, every day.

Understandably, this may seem like a lot of flux, but behind it, I realise, I have a few very firm and fixed points of reference that never change, provided by my core drivers and aspiration, as well as my stable codes of behaviour. In addition there is my personal space – configured in specific way that makes my use of it very personal – and my friends, who have been long-standing and important points of reference over time, even if indeed scattered across the planet. As a result, my openness and enjoyment of transitions and changes are firmly supported by solid and steady roots that sit within me, together with a few stable external points to which I always feel connected.

In my case, change, transitions and flux are the dynamic halo of a surprisingly solid and immovable core. This is why that which may seem to others an unusual life, full of anomalies and rather unconventional, is to me a journey that is congruent and makes sense; serving the purpose of self-actualisation and connectivity with others, observing and exploring the human condition – at home and away – through the artefacts and capabilities of cultures and civilisations.

Whilst some of my values and beliefs have changed with experience, others, such as curiosity, creativity, achievement, a positive "can do" outlook, empathy and honesty have remained unchanged and I know I have received from my parents.

Values and attitudes have guided my entire life, have helped me make sense of it, and also helped me in my work with others.

And yes, I have also implemented radical planned transitions that I appropriately consider "acts of madness" and I would not recommend to anyone. I have changed profession, employment, city, country and social circle in one swift move, leaving everything behind for an uncertain future where I had absolutely no idea what I wanted to do or how. But then I firmly knew that I was leaving behind a chapter that had run its course and I needed to move on, face a radical change and fully embrace the choice of opening up to entirely new possibilities. Such decisions were clearly influenced by both internal and external factors but remained fully self-directed including the radical way of implementing them. And yes, these were times when my friends around the world held their breath and got really concerned for me and, yes, these decisions did exhaust all my resources and pushed me to the edge. But months later – and "barely alive" – I landed on my feet and never looked back.

Perhaps I was lucky, perhaps I was exceptionally resilient or perhaps it was meant to be. I always took full responsibility, never blamed others and do not have many regrets.

Having said this, I would advise others against brutally disrupting the entire fabric of one's life and putting all reserves on the line, in one move. Instead I would recommend that we all plan successive steps and show kindness to ourselves, allowing time for recovery, particularly between significant step changes.

A useful exercise

A helpful exercise to do in transitions is to take a historic view at other transitions in the past, whether planned or not, and analyse how you coped with that change and stress. To achieve this, here are a few suggestions: first, go back down memory lane as far as you wish and identify transition periods on a timeline. Choose examples where you know you have coped well and also situations when things have been difficult, then analyse each transition in some detail to surface things such as:

- What caused that transition?
- How did it make you feel immediately after it became clear that change was imminent?
- What stressed you most?
- What coping mechanisms did you find?
- How quickly?
- How did they work for you?
- What outside resources did you need and where did you find them?
- How did you plan to use the skills and capabilities that you had?
- What have been your most effective recovery and coping mechanisms?
- How long did the process take?
- What external factors have hindered or helped the process and the recovery?
- What was the perception of that transition after things settled into the new order; how do you remember that situation?
- What, if anything, is the difference between stressors in work transitions and stressors in life transitions (similarities and differences)?
- How can you prepare to deal with aspects you know are difficult and set in place those resources that help, for the future?

In a nutshell, you need to use all the self-knowledge you have, from personality to invisible drivers, your inventory of strengths, skills, experience and your network of people (family, friends and others). This will help you tap into the positive energy of self-belief and resilience to activate all your available resources to use as needed in the process. What you are effectively doing is taking a holistic view of the entire system, including internal and external factors, whether events, people or specific circumstances that have or could have an impact and manage as many of those factors as you can, to get the best outcome.

Remember that time and randomness can also play a part either way, and whilst being well-planned and prepared helps, allow some energy and flexibility for unforeseen circumstances, good or otherwise, to ensure they will not derail your general direction of travel, so that eventually, and maybe after some meandering, you still get to a good finishing line.

Summary

Practitioners work with reality and individual situations that may or may not fall into models and techniques neatly, yet in an age of unprecedented pace and breadth of change, transition time is increasingly short and adaption is required without delay. We all need to normalise change, accept it as part of our lives, and deal with it as an additional layer of demand, on top of what is naturally expected, in our life and work. Transitions are demanding, even when planned and for a better outcome. They call upon our entire capability and all resources, both personal and external. They often involve not only ourselves but also others and take place in a context of systems and significant interconnections and interdependencies. The outcomes of transitions can realise pre-set goals but also trigger unintended consequences. Overall transitions impact us significantly and may take many months to complete. They require resilience and tolerance of ups and downs with swings from agony to ecstasy and from doubt to pure joy. When well managed they become an instrument of growth, progress and achievement.

As individuals we need to be prepared with increased resilience in the face of events and pressures that need to be dealt with effectively and rapidly, no matter how disruptive, unplanned and challenging they may be. Such events often trigger an entire review of a way of life as we have known it. Transition awareness and resilience are mandatory skills in a society where change has become the new normal.

Making sense of experiential findings

The themes and trends that cut across the client sample, combined with reflections on my own experience around the same themes, have provided an opportunity to take a closer look at what they meant and how we can all benefit from a deeper understanding of factors involved in our overall engagement with life and work. But whilst analysing each theme, in turn, it was impossible not to notice that every aspect was in fact connected to the others. And some reflections, thoughts and accounts may have been repeated across the entire section on trends and themes, not by chance but by design, as a constant reminder of how interconnected they actually are. It is also true that every topic covered is in fact a stand-alone area for research and a lot of information is available since they have been, individually, the objects of full focus for academics and practitioners alike. In addition many of us may have some prior knowledge of each subject, and there is always opportunity to further scrutinise and explore, at will. But the purpose of the exploration here, has not been to exhaustively cover each of them, but rather to gain an insight into the fascinating way in which they are all interconnected, interdependent and working as an integrated whole, in a dynamic way. In fact this is the way experiential findings present themselves to us; as an integrated and complex picture captured at a point in time. In real life there are no boundaries and distinctions between our thoughts, feelings, motivations, actions and communication. They all support each other and together contribute to the outcome that is the actual unfolding of our personal and working life, in flow, with congruence and connected to others, individuals, society at large, and the natural and artificial worlds that we find ourselves in. Our personal world is, in fact, just a fragment of the bigger worlds of business, society, the planet and our universe. But it is also made of the smaller but significant worlds of our body, heart and mind, which together make up our individual selves and map our very own journey through life.

Change and transitions are an integral part of it, and the dialectic thinking in philosophy also positions the idea of gradual changes and opposing forces that eventually lead to an accumulation of quantitative changes that result in a qualitative jump, to a new state of being. This theory also posits what we know from experience; that transitions are not smooth but a process that contains leaps, interruptions, U-turns and forth turns again, generally pointing to a state that is unique and not an identical repetition of a past. We live our lives by managing our actions across all the boundaries that delineate the various systems and subsystems that surround us. Indeed we know that "life is a state of flux" as Heraclitus, the pre-dialectics philosopher, put it. We also grow under the influence of significant others and role models that cross our paths at points in time, themselves a synthesis of a universe of reference that informs their own journeys. But the clarity of our vision is often fleeting and, as we know from coaching practice, we are all subjects to dilemmas and uncertainty. And as we often say, when it comes to truths, answers, making decisions and taking a moral or pragmatic stance, uncertainty comes in and "it all depends". The Jain dialectic philosophy beautifully articulates this relativity by a model of seven relative and conditional points of view (conditioned predication) to express the way in which something, "in some ways it is", "in some ways it is not", "in some ways it is and it is indescribable" and so on, to reflect the possibilities that exist in the pursuit of knowledge and the truth.

To help with this quest in the world of work there are coaches, educators, trainers and mentors who extend their knowledge within the formal set-ups of our individual, team or organisational lives, to contribute to our collective effort to make the world of work and the wider world, a better place for us all. They also help us to overcome what may be moments of difficulty, survive and strive to turn them into just stepping stones on the way to achieve something bigger. Because we all need to express the universal human desire to flourish and be happy, and use our potential to contribute in the wider transformation and development of the society at large, through our life and our work.

Chapter 2

Practice meets current science

Embracing theory and research to consolidate experiential findings

Why all roads lead to philosophy

One of the key missions of our human condition is to constantly try and find our place in the world, make sense of life and try to find the key to happiness. No matter what that answer may be. Who am I? Why am I here? asks Arthur Dent, the hero of *The Hitchhiker's Guide to the Galaxy*, as he travels across the universe in his quest to find answers about life, the universe and . . . everything. This is just an example of modern popular culture and the fact that since the dawn of time, in so many ways and at different levels, our collective consciousness has attempted answers by poetry, storytelling, music, and all artefacts of civilisation.

A formalised and educated pursuit of this line of questioning prevailed in European antiquity with the Greek civilisation, later embraced and further refined by the Romans. And so all roads leading to Greece and Rome also lead to the beginning of European philosophy, with the Greeks themselves thought to have been influenced by the Middle East, whilst in the Far East they all led to Buddhism, as a regional expression of philosophical thinking. Because philosophy – just as is the case in our own pursuits – looks for answers to the fundamental questions about life, death, happiness, truth, our place in this world and the cosmos, our purpose, the beginning and the end of time, the forces at play in our destiny and . . . everything in between. But it would be a mistake to think that philosophy is only for the elevated thinkers.

The exchange of knowledge and wisdom between people is part of our social dimension, and today, coaching in all its forms is also instrumental in finding the same answers in the work that coaches do, often guided by principles of questioning and answering, in the same way as the old philosophies of the East and West proceeded in their enquiry about life.

The current explosion of mindfulness in Western coaching and developmental practice may leave our Eastern colleagues somewhat baffled by such excitement, since meditating and being mindful are just ways of life in the Far East, part of a long history of cultural practice resulting from the local philosophy of life and Buddhism. Whilst for those in the West who practice yoga or martial arts or any Eastern form, mindfulness is just "warming up" for a still, but open body and mind, where an inner eye is primed to welcome flow and a different kind of experience and attainment. Simply a necessary foundation – and not an end in itself – to various physical and artistic expressions and forms such as yoga, tai chi, chi kung, aikido and all dance forms of India, Indonesia, Japan and so on – which are ways to embody the philosophical, spiritual and reflective dimensions of life.

Practice provides us with a very rich range of findings and it is possible to find themes and patterns that cut across wider information, on specific subjects of interest. But beyond that our purpose is also to make sense of it and find what else there is to illuminate our understanding of reality and to structure those findings into potential frameworks, principles and models that can be taught, understood and used by many others in their work, as part of our overall quest for professionalism, and to harmonise theory and practice. Coaching is a purposeful dialogue that creates an intended link between individuals and the world in which they manifest themselves and where they wish to do better with full awareness and pursue a higher quality of life and achievement, ideally to be happy and fulfil their potential. As such, coaching uses mainly the techniques of talking and interaction, based on questioning, reflecting back, and using the coach as a resources and silence as a catalyst, all within a safe, non-judgemental ethical space. Coaching aims to enable significant awareness and progress of clear thinking, emotional stability and focused motivation to take hold and become useful to the client. In this context, exploring the clients' own evolution to becoming what they are today, as well as gaining a better and more focused view and understanding of the world in which they operate (including the world of work), and finally linking this with their aspiration for what is next – in a general developmental or a specific goal-focused perspective – is enabled by increased knowledge but also clarity of the self and the world. This is why it is also useful to review what research and academic thinking has provided so far, in relation to findings drawn from extensive professional practice.

In career coaching, the main content providers to the coaching process are:

- The individual client, looking for a satisfying future career path
- The outside world, within which that individual will enact their work aspirations and contributions
- The coach, who facilitates a process of discovery and self-awareness at a deeper level that will inform the client's future choices, for the best outcome

And the interaction between the three spheres that interconnect in a dynamic way appears governed by dynamic forces that cover the entire scope of the career coaching, namely: change, growth and evolution. The knowledge available to us today is quite extensive and can be explored in relation to specific interests, but in relation to this exploration of coaching from the centre and projecting the core of our individuality as the main – if not the only – permanent

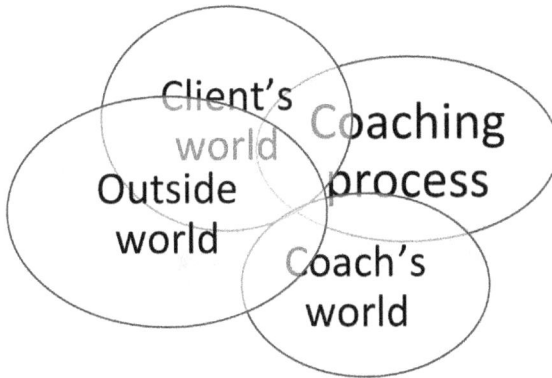

Figure 2.1 Coaching process

foundation that can support us going forward into an uncertain future there are three system of thinking that resonate quite closely with this enquiry:

- Dialectic thinking
- Complexity theory
- Individual developmental theory

The three reflect the wider philosophical perspective of the world (dialectics), the more specific point of view of science (complexity theory) and the unique and personal human inner world (individual developmental theory) all viewed as intricately connected, congruent and subject to an overarching principle of internal and external change and evolution.

Whilst the roots of dialectics go back to antiquity, the theories of complexity and individual levels of development are more modern. However, the link between past and present thinking is quite striking and there is no doubt about the value of the legacy that thinkers of a Middle Eastern, European and Far Eastern antiquity have handed down to the generation of the nineteenth, twentieth and twenty-first centuries. Many of those old fundamental principles continue to hold their value today, in light of advanced scientific research from physics to biology and mathematics. Whether under these names, or other, as human beings, we have always been curious to examine and refine our understanding of the way we manifest ourselves in the world over time and what could be the influencing factors that determine that history. In this regard, since antiquity until now, there have been models, principles and ideas put across, many still holding their value, which specific disciplines have picked up, to scrutinise in great detail, in search of increased understanding and ultimately the truth about our human destiny.

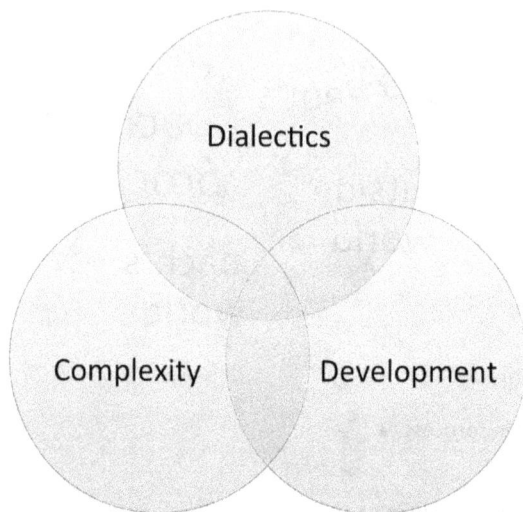

Figure 2.2 Scientific references

Some understanding of philosophy is therefore very helpful if we wish to exercise an increased degree of curiosity and go just a bit deeper to build a cognitive foundation for our contemporary thinking and our everyday experience of development and coaching with its manifold purposes, including that of achieving potential and making better choices in our life and work.

This is why there is value in reviewing knowledge made available to us by scientists, thinkers and philosophers, who have made it their life's work to study and propose explanations in addition to empirical or experiential information, in order to normalise, structure and further illuminate what we all experience in our daily lives. Chances are that such a synthesis of approach brings the best of both perspectives to create a more accurate and detailed personal view on our subjects of interest. And many answers and much knowledge can be gained by turning to philosophy as a source of enquiry.

Many of the scientists and thinkers that specialised in one domain of research or another were also at the same time, philosophers, cognoscenti of social sciences generally and above all curious about all the aspects of human nature and human society – polymath thinkers – over and beyond just one specific area of interest.

Science and philosophy relate like two sides of the same coin, both essential and yet so different that they can never face each other. Science is like an exploration ship, moved by a system of precision and made of structure and methodology. It sails the ocean of questions and stops from time to time, dropping anchor to explore everything within its radius, then it moves on and repeats the exercise.

As a result it can never quite enjoy an overview of all the oceans and seas, and how they fit on planet earth. Philosophy, on the other hand, just like a satellite orbiting the planet, can look from above and capture all the expanse of land and water that earth has to offer. This view registers and interprets this big picture, but exploration cannot happen from the air. Instead it raises new questions about specific regions, which are handed down to the detailed research conducted from the exploration ship, over and over again, to find specific answers.

Both science and philosophy feed each other and sometimes get really close to the point of merging, like in the case of philosophy and quantum physics. At the same time, sciences that research specific apparently unrelated subjects can also come together in unexpected way, as is the case of quantum physics and neuroscience in relation to the formation of memory in the spaces between neuronal structures.

Historically, philosophy has been known as the science of sciences because it is in philosophy that we found the inception of psychology, logic, ethics, aesthetics, medicine and mathematics, for example – all using the human capabilities of creativity, high cognitive functions, critical and symbolic reasoning – further expressed in individual and collective life by culture, social norms, morality and meaning-making.

And so, the main five branches of traditional philosophy include:

- Metaphysics: dealing with fundamental questions about life and reality through its two branches:

  1) ontology: the study of being, becoming, existence and entities
  2) cosmogony: the study of the origin, evolution and an eventual end of the universe

- Epistemology: dealing with our development of knowledge, how we learn, and the quality of our knowledge
- Logic: studying the rules of valid reasoning and argumentation
- Ethics: also known as moral philosophy, concerned with human values and how we should act as individuals
- Aesthetics or esthetics: dealing with the philosophy of art and the notion of beauty art.

But philosophy stretches out much further than this into other related branches such as:

- Philosophy of mind
- Philosophy of language
- Philosophy of education
- Philosophy of science
- Political philosophy
- Philosophy of religion

Figure 2.3 Main branches of philosophy

There are additional divisions into different philosophical traditions, such as idealist or materialist philosophy. There is also the division between Western philosophies (mainly based on the Greek philosophy in antiquity) and the Eastern philosophy (such as Arab philosophy, Asian philosophy, Indian philosophy, Hindu philosophy, Chinese philosophy and so on). Contemporary Western philosophy again divides into the "continental philosophy", based mainly in the subjective experience, and "analytic philosophy", which relies on applied logical, linguistic and scientific areas of philosophy.

Without wishing to present an exhaustive taxonomy of philosophy, the point being made here is that philosophy can be found in most of the areas that deal with the human mind, thinking and cognitive processes to say the least. It is important to understand the taxonomies of philosophy to contextualise the fact that specific aspects such as ethics, moral and cognitive development, development of thinking and language, and the process of learning – which are all part of self-development and coaching – are in fact, part of a much bigger and intricate landscape that has been crafted over millennia.

Therefore, some branches of philosophy are of particular interest in the topic of personal development and are likely to be more frequently mentioned, implicitly or explicitly:

- Ontology – which helps the study of being, becoming and identity
- Logic – which helps with the way we evaluate the validity of our reasoning
- Epistemology – which helps with understanding the way we acquire knowledge and learn
- Ethics – which helps us understand our values, and related actions and outcomes

Philosophical thinking: dialectics

Also called "systems-of-systems thinking", dialectic thinking is arguably the most complex, transformative and comprehensive way of thinking and in itself is a result of a dialectical process of thinking construction and evolution.

Dialectical thinking is an intellectual tradition that offers a third option against the two somewhat opposite traditions of thinking: one that is grounded in fixed, formal universal truths and the other that is grounded in relativistic thinking, assuming many relative orders and truths. Dialectic thinking is also more appropriate for open systems and significantly introduces concepts such as: the relationship between quantity and quality; the seeds of future evolution being present in the current state; transformation through processes that are non-linear but can be meandering and still leading to a set outcome; change is helical and not circular (no return to previous state); reality holds opposite forces that are drivers of change; hidden implicit contradictions that become explicit in an outcome that sees some elements of the past carried forth, some transformed and some eliminated; and the notion of "triads" in the presence of theses, antithesis and synthesis, as a non-binary cluster of activity.

All these aspects indeed offer an extremely flexible and coherent thinking system that can be applied to explain and reflect on dynamic reality in a more appropriate way than a rigid binary or positivist point of view.

Dialectic thinking in Europe

Heraclitus (c. 535–475, BC) represents what could be called the prehistory of European dialectic. His best-known statements are that "all is in a state of flux" and that "war is the father of all things". Heraclitus thus believed that, ultimately, all things could be reduced to a dynamic principle consisting of a contrasting or even a conflicting interaction between opposites. Plato (428–348 BC) was the original dialectic thinker who used dialectics to divide and create hierarchies across concepts and ideas, from the more general to the more particular. He presents dialectics as the art of logical thinking. Aristotle (384–322 BC) continued Plato's tradition by developing the systematic logic as the primary method for intellectual training, based on probable premises, whilst dialectics becomes contextual. Zeno of Elea (c. 490–430 BC) introduced later dialectics proper by using paradoxes, which, whilst counterintuitive and open to criticism, offered a perspective on the relativity of apparent or latent contradictions in perceptions. His best-known paradox relates to motion, by using the example of an arrow that may never reach the target because, conceptually, to get to the target it must first cover a half of the distance, and half of that half beforehand, and so on, ad infinitum, and therefore never leave. Zeno's attempts relate to questioning the use of quantitative conceptions applied to physical bodies and space, and he explores the use of mathematical notions in the natural world. Zeno's paradoxes, criticised for being sophistry, have indeed received in recent times recognition in relation to insights into the nature of mathematics. Socrates (c. 470–399 BC) later followed with a method of searching for the truth by asking questions and going back and forth to establish the truth of a statement and using the dialectic method in the process.

In the Middle Ages (mainly between 1000 and 1300 AD) a number of European thinkers such as Abelard, William of Sherwood, Garlandus Compotista, Walter Burley, Roger Swyneshed, William of Ockham and Thomas Aquinas employed dialectics and logic to a broad range of things, such as grammatical theory and intellectual activity. Dialectics dealt with the logical skills of analysis, the examination of theses and antitheses, and the use of syllogisms.

Kant (1724–1804 AD) proposes – in his critique of dogmatism – four sets of propositions (antinomies) related to an idea (for example, God) and then continues to prove that both the thesis and antithesis can be proven right, although they are mutually exclusive, therefore leading him to the conclusion that the exercise is futile and that the thesis and antithesis do not resolve in a synthesis but simply the realisation that such movement is impossible and cannot lead to a valid conclusion.

Fichte (1762–1818 AD) restarts the philosophical investigation by using theses, antitheses and synthesis as reflections of the dynamic between the Ego and the non-Ego (world), which becomes the object of the Ego's moral actions. The two come together by way of synthesis, which unifies them. Shelling (1775–1854 AD) builds on Fichte and introduces the Absolute as another, more universal notion.

But building on what has gone before them, it is Hegel (1770–1831 AD) and then Marx (1818–1883 AD) that truly develop dialectics to its highest form. Hegel captures and develops it into the idea of a universal dialectical movement towards a cosmic fulfilment in the Absolute and places it at the centre of his dialectic dynamic model of nature and history, as an essential aspect of reality (Hegel, 1967). Hegel's representation of the Idea manifesting itself in the world and history is that of a dynamic, changing, complex movement, with no static absolutes, full of complex processes and transformations, forever changing whilst coming into being and passing away, both in human thinking and also in reality, moving from lower to higher in an endless process of change, of forever becoming. He also introduces the idea of measure, a qualitative quantum as a measure of existence of quantity. The relationship between quantity and quality is very interesting in that each has a nature of its own but is also interrelated when a measure of quantity over a certain limit can transform into a quantum quality. This process where quantity appears for a time and then transforms in quality can be represented as a figure of a nodal (knotted) line.

Hegel positions the notion of "necessary" progression, where synthesis is a result not of conflict but of an internal potential, due to latent contradiction in all entities, mental and material. He extends this idea across everything from logic to history to world affairs. Each entity has within itself the seeds of its own negation, which resolves in sublation instead of destruction, which means a synthesis where some aspects are put aside and others are raised to another level in the synthesis outcome. Hegel also uses a number of triadic notions such as: affirmation, negation, negation of negation; in itself, for itself, in and for itself. He also uses the term speculation as a positive term to describe the process by which the invisible and implicit workings of the dialectic process are made visible and explicit in philosophy, and Hegel himself endeavours to make the implicit contradictions explicit, because the process involves the activity of implicit inherent contradictions that become explicit in the next stage and so on.

For Hegel, the dialectical tensions reside in reality itself and the history of humankind from slavery and alienation to a state of free and equal citizens is a result of the very dialectic process. Marx takes this idea and transfers it into materialist philosophy (Marx, 1932) by creating dialectical materialism, which he used to explain evolution and transformation in economics, society and history. His ideas are revisited today in regards to economics and the future evolution of a capital-market driven economy, in the light of globalisation and technological advancements. In the Marxist dialectic, the same dynamics take place in the world of the matter (not the idea) and contradictions are the engine of history and progress. Historical materialism sees history as a result of revolutionary clashes between social classes that are driven by opposing interests. Such conflict is the only real engine of progress.

Therefore Marx's dialectic is the same as Hegel's except that the original principle at work is Matter and not Idea. In Marxist theory the Idea is a result of the evolution of matter and the human mind. Human thoughts reflect the material world and not the other way around. These developments also relate to cumulative quantitative changes that at a point in time cause a qualitative jump and initiate a qualitative change. The process is not even, but may encompass interruptions, leaps, negations of the initial moment of advancement, and

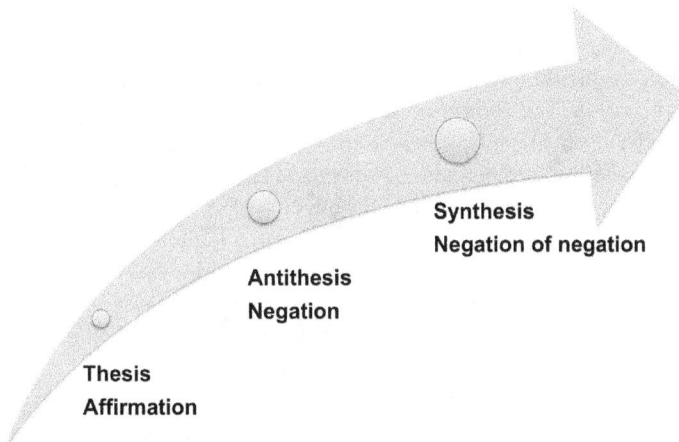

Synthesis
Negation of negation

Antithesis
Negation

Thesis
Affirmation

Figure 2.4 Dialectic process: Hegel and Marx

negation of the negation, and repetition at a higher level of aspects of a previous state; essentially, a non-linear progression, putting forward the aspect
of destructive opposition by antagonistic forces that leads to elimination of
some forces rather than harmonious reconciliation for a higher qualitative outcome, with nature being given as such an example. Marx fully appreciates and
embraces Hegel's thinking except that he places this dynamic in the real world,
which is reflected in human thought.

Dialectic thinking in Asia

Dialectic thinking also developed in the Far East and India is known as a place
where there is a long tradition of philosophical thinking.

Hindi philosophy has an ancient tradition of dialectic polemics, where the
two complements of "purusha", the active cause, and "prakriti", the passive
cause, bring everything into existence, by following the "rta", which is the universal law (dharma); within the Brahmana, Vedic and Hindu dialectic.

The long tradition of Buddhism has produced sophisticated and at times
institutionalised traditions of dialectics (for example, Nalanda University,
and Gelugpa Buddhism of Tibet). The clarifications of Buddhist polemics and doctrine thought, formal and dialectics debate is documented, and
Buddhist doctrine was rigorously critiqued in the second century by Nagar-
juna, whose logical approach to establishing the truth formed the basis of
a vital stream of Buddhist thought, to articulate an account of the cosmos
as it is and give rise to what is known as the Perfection of Wisdom, later
developed by thinkers such as Dignaga and Dharmakirti (between 500 and
700 AD). The traditions of Madhyamaka, Yogacara and Tantric Buddhism
evidence the dialectical method of truth-seeking. Later, Trisong Detsen and
Je Tsongkhapa in Tibet promoted the value of formalised training and dialectic in debate.

Of particular interest is the Jain philosophy on the problem of the Manifold Nature of Truth and the Theory of Manifold Predications (Teachings of
Mahāvīra, 599–527 BC, born into the royal family of King Siddartha of Kund-
graam and Queen Trishala, Bihar, India) which is expressed in the dialectic
concepts of the conditional point of view and the partial point of view. The Jain
dialectic is quite sophisticated and was developed to arrive at the truth.

The theory of conditional predications is also a logic in its own right whilst
providing substance to a subtle interplay between philosophy and logic, in the
Jain doctrine of epistemological relativism, doctrine of non-exclusivity or multiple viewpoints, a "could be" perspective which posits that all statement about
the truth are in fact limited, finite and contextual.

This is why it recommends that the term "syāt" – perhaps, perhaps, in some
way, maybe, from a certain perspective – should be prefixed before each proposition and so remove dogmatism and provide a conditional point of view for
every statement.

The Jain parable of the "blind men and an elephant", illustrates how reality is perceived differently from different points of view.

In this story the men were asked to describe an elephant based on how they sensed it and were each presented with a part of the elephant: head, ear, tusk, trunk, foot, back, tail and the tuft of the tail and asked to describe the elephant. Their opinions differed representing reality as they each saw it: the elephant is like a snake, a brush, a pillar, a plough etc., which obviously in fact did not represent the truth.

> To their disputations the Buddha replied:
> "O how they cling and wrangle, some who claim
> For preacher and monk the honoured name!
> For, quarrelling, each to his view they cling.
> Such folk see only one side of a thing."

Whilst they stuck to the truth of their individual findings, no one point of view was complete or true, because reality is so complex that no one statement can express the full truth about it: the essence of Jainism.

And this principle, the Jain doctrine also applies to itself – when it clings too much to its own tenants – by being in error precisely because it upholds just the one point of view.

On another level, this parable also urges life in harmony and acceptance of different beliefs, and the fact that the truth can be stated in different ways.

Unsurprisingly, this parable has transferred across many religions and lore from Jain to Hindu, Sufi and Buddhism.

Dialectic thinking in the Middle East

Ancient Assyria, Mesopotamia, Babylonia and Sumer were neighbouring regions in what is today known as the Middle East, and there are artefacts of sophisticated civilisations in the region dating back to 4000–1000 BC. This region had at the time a tumultuous history with various regions rising and falling as a result of the volatile and alternating dominance of various local socio-political structures. In spite of scarcity of written evidence we know that the region produced a rich expression of religious, artistic and philosophical thought. And dialectics is a part of that landscape.

Babylonian philosophy, for example, is traced back as part of the Mesopotamian literature – itself represented by poetry, lyrics, prose, folklore and proverbs – which was also imbued with a philosophy of life that particularly referred to ethics, dialectics and dialogue.

Significantly the Babylonian philosophy developed beyond rationality and pure reasoning into the realm of the non-empirical acquisition of thought and knowledge as well as contemplation and enquiry.

This supports the hypothesis that Babylonian philosophy influenced Greek philosophy and that the Babylonian "Dialogue of pessimism" (around 1000 BC in Mesopotamia) contain early statements that later can be traced to the Greek sophism, the Herraclitean doctrine of change and flux, and also to Plato's dialogues and the maieutic method of Socrates.

The "Dialogue of pessimism" is conducted between two people – which is typical for Middle Eastern wisdom tales, but not so for the later Socratic dialogues – a master and his slave valet about the validity or futility of a range of actions (dining, hunting, marriage, litigation, sacrifice, etc.) that the master proposes and then rejects, whilst the valet supports or refutes the master's statements, in a successive sets of stanzas.

There are several interpretations of the dialogues ranging from social satire to pessimism about the futility of life to an acknowledgement of the quandary of logical outcomes, to the fact that what is to be known for sure is only known by Gods, to our powerlessness in the face of destiny that is unknown, but ambiguity is a central theme alongside a range of possibilities that in turn may be sound but may not be what they seem.

Here there are aspects that relate to logic, ethics, ontology and epistemology, if we are to link the text to branches of philosophy.

This potential ancestry of the future Greek philosophy was founded at a time when the city of Babylon was at the centre of the rise and fall of the Babylonian empire, mainly between 2000 and 1000 BC.

There is no doubt that the activity on the trade routes around the Mediterranean basin between southern Europe and north Africa into the near and Middle East, on the land mass to the Caspian Sea and to the Persian Gulf, were also channels for cultural exchanges flourishing between thriving centres of ancient civilisations which undoubtedly provided foundations for the subsequent sophisticated thinking going forward in the Greece of 500 BC, onwards to the Middle Ages, and on to our modern times.

Examples of dialectic forms

Western dialectic reasoning aims to search for the truth and in the process resolve disagreements through rational discussions. One path to achieve this is the Socratic Method, where a hypothesis (and other statements) is shown to have contradictions and can therefore be dismissed as a credible path to the truth (reductio ad absurdum).

One other resolution of disagreement is to deny a presupposition of the theses and antitheses and move on to "sublation" and synthesis (transcendence), as a third thesis.

This type of process has been formalised in a number of concepts or principles of forms over time and here are some examples:

The Medieval Form was conceived as follows:

- The question to be determined
- The principal objections to the question

- An argument in favour of the question, traditionally a single argument ("on the contrary . . .")
- The determination of the question after weighing the evidence ("I answer that . . .")
- The replies to each objection.

The Fichtean/Hegelian dialectics is based upon four concepts:

- Everything exists in the medium of time and is transient and finite
- Everything is composed of opposing forces/contradictions
- Gradual changes lead to crises as turning points where one force defeats its opposing force, which leads to quantitative changes creating qualitative change
- Change is helical not circular, meaning that there is no return to the previous point; no negation of the negation but instead periodic change without returning to the same position.

The Jain dialectic is quite sophisticated in that it ensures that any statement is expressed from seven relative and conditional points of view (known as "saptabhangi") and so form what is known as the theory of conditioned "syāt" – perhaps, perhaps, in some way, maybe, from a certain perspective – predication.

1   *syād-asti*: "in some ways it is"
2   *syād-nāsti*: "in some ways it is not"
3   *syād-asti-nāsti*: "in some ways it is and it is not"
4   *syād-asti-avaktavyaḥ*: "in some ways it is and it is indescribable"
5   *syād-nāsti-avaktavyaḥ*: "in some ways it is not and it is indescribable"
6   *syād-asti-nāsti-avaktavyaḥ*: "in some ways it is, it is not, and it is indescribable"
7   *syād-avaktavyaḥ*: "in some ways it is indescribable"

Modern dialectics

Dialectic thinking in Europe has flourished in modern times, borne by the ideas of existentialism and thinkers such as Jean-Paul Sartre, who states, alongside others, that the synthesis in dialectics found in a moving, dialectical actualisation, manifests in history and culture to become the world. In Western philosophy, there is a split between European thinkers and Anglo-American thinkers, with Europe having embraced and utilised dialectical thinking from ancient times to the present day. Jean-Paul Sartre's "Critique of Dialectical Reason" being a prime example of dialectical thinking, in his existentialist views, with existentialism being the search for the truth and concrete synthesis to be discovered in experience by philosophy becoming history and the world.

Dialectic thinking remains a central principle of understanding and relating to the world in continental Europe. Formalism became an additional movement towards providing a mathematical foundation to dialectical logic by authors such as Stephen Toulmin (*The Uses of Argument*, 1958), Nicholas Rescher (*Dialectics*, 1977), and Frans H. van Eemeren and Rob Grootendorst (*Advances in pragma-dialectics*, 2002), alongside other scientists and practitioners involved in informal logic and paraconsistent logic. At the same time, using theories of defeasible reasoning, a number of logics have been developed in the fields of artificial intelligence and law, to define well-formed arguments, rules for arguments based on fixed assumptions, and rules for shifting burden. In addition there is also the need to formalise dialectics in order to build decision-support and computer-supported collaborative work systems.

Meanwhile, in the Anglo-American culture dialectics play no significant part, instead being overwhelmed by positivism. Positivism applies the simple principal of clarity to divide the world into two categories: that about which things can be said clearly and that about which we better keep silent. Evidently this position raises the question of whether everything that is clear in the world and can be expressed (tautologies and trivial truisms) comes anywhere near all that cannot be expressed clearly, due to the extreme complexity that the world represents, and which, in fact, represents the larger part of existence but will nonetheless, be left outside our enquiry.

This obvious weakness has been questioned by German sociologists such as Max Weber and Georg Simmel, who rejected the doctrine at the turn of the twentieth century to found the antipositivist tradition in sociology. Later, positivism was also criticised for becoming an ideology (scientism) and caused respected scientists, such as German Nobel Laureate (for quantum physics) Werner Heisenberg, to distance themselves from positivism. Not surprising given how many phenomena in quantum physics prove a non-binary reality in the states of small particles of matter.

A contemporary use of dialectics is to be found in understanding how we perceive or should perceive the world and acquire knowledge (epistemology), or in the way we understand the origin of things as being a result of interconnectivity, contradictions and a dynamic nature of the natural world (ontology) or simply a method of presenting ideas or conclusions.

Scientific thinking: complexity theory

The theory of complex systems and evolving systems has been developed mainly within sciences such as computing, chemistry, biology, mathematics and physics. The theory is in fact a unified point of view, based on research cumulated and merged, coming from both the US (Santa Fe Institute and work by Stuart Kauffman, John Holland, Chris Langton and Murray Gell-Mann between 1992–2000) and Europe (Peter Allen, Brian Goodwin, Axelrod and Cohen, Casti, Bonabeau, Epstein and Axtel, Ferber, Prigogine and Stengers,

Nicolis and Prigogine, Isabelle Stengers, Gregoire Nicolis, Humberto Maturana, Francisco Varela, Niklaus Luhman, Mingers, Gleick and Brian Arthur 1985–2002).

A complex evolving system (Mitleton-Kelly, 1998) could be defined as a system where at least the four principles operating in what are known as complex systems are present and interact with another set of six principles, defined by further research, natural sciences (dissipative structures in chemistry/physics, complex adaptive systems in evolutionary biology, autopoiesis in biology, and cognition and chaos theory) as well as social sciences (increasing return in economics). Together, they create the ten principles operating in what is known as complex evolving systems.

In complexity thinking, the systems rank from complex, to complex adaptive, to complex evolving, each level being superior and also integrating the previous level. Whilst natural sciences have proved to stimulate a lot of work in the complex theory field, the same has been considered for social systems since the 1990s.

Complexity principles

The initial four principles used in systems theory are: connectivity, feedback, interdependence and emergence. The complexity theory adds new dimensions to these principles, meant to further explore and define a deeper level of inter-relationships, not only between these four, but also between them and the other six principles of: far from equilibrium; space of possibilities; co-evolution; historicity and time; path-dependence; and creation of new order (Mitleton-Kelly & Papaefthimiou, 2001).

Connectivity, feedback and interdependence

The principles of connectivity and interdependence qualify the fact that within a system or complex structure the components are very deeply interrelated and intertwined. So much so that if an external force impacts the system, or an internal component functions in a different way from usual, this will cause a reaction throughout the system. In terms of human systems, at work or in everyday life, the interaction of a small group of people, for instance, will be changed by the topics brought in by its members, and also by who joins or leaves the group, and so on. It is also a mechanism that operates in relationship management, where the behaviour of individuals interacting is directed and regulated by the information going back and forth between individuals.

In a human system, connectivity and interdependence mean that a decision or action by an entity (group, organisation or individual) may affect related entities in different ways, depending on the state each entity finds itself in. For one entity an action may be the catalyser for new and better ways; for another it may just be the last drop into a glass already too full.

Far from equilibrium, and space of possibilities

Given that complex systems are live and dynamic environments, the occurrence of an external force or a variance in internal forces will push a system outside its equilibrium, which otherwise is maintained as long as the variance of force is within certain limits. Beyond that the systems will be caused to adjust to this change and as a result move to another state of balance, which will provide equilibrium as long as all the parameters of that system remain unchanged.

The advent of a new baby in a family, for example, will cause the dynamic and the routine that the family has established in order to maintain its functioning equilibrium to be pushed away from equilibrium and the family will have to seek another way of operating to establish equilibrium again, albeit of a modified kind. The quest for a new way of operating, to regain equilibrium, may lead to exploring a number of possibilities, which would, once embedded, provide a new context for equilibrium of a different kind than before.

For an entity, individual or organisation to survive and thrive there is a need to explore its pace of possibilities and generate variety in its interconnection and interdependence to adapt and co-evolve. A variety of strategies may be available at any given time; however, not all are best and one may be better than the others at different times and under specific circumstances. A complex system will therefore be able to explore the whole space of possibilities, perhaps follow different strategies to test them, and then settle for a single strategy to which all resources will be committed.

The important thing in moments when systems are pushed far from equilibrium is to allow the systems to find their own path out of the possibilities in a creative way, and not design the new order, ignoring what the system will naturally do pushed by historicity and its own ability to self-repair. In this way the new order is creating an enabling infrastructure for the new patterns and order to emerge and become established.

Historicity and time, and path-dependence principles

Out of the exploration of possibilities, only one critical choice will be made, to become, in the future, the history created, by this single path taken out of several possible options. For an individual it means that future solutions, chosen out of a space of possibilities and alternatives, will not be due to random occurrences, but will be dependent on that person's history, style and specific identity, making it very personal and coherent. Whilst one single path is chosen, the alternatives explored prior to that decision remain as sources of innovation and diversification, to keep other possibilities open. The same principle allies to groups and nations or organisations, for example where the past plays a role in the future and the evolutionary options of that group are informed by what has gone before. So history plays a very important role in complex systems and their evolutionary future.

Co-evolution, creation of new order and emergence principles

One of the key defining features of complex evolving systems is their capability to adapt and evolve and create a new order and a new coherence and equilibrium. This is achieved by the creation of new structures and organisations, new hierarchies, relationships and ways of working. In this sense, systems are self-maintaining and self-repairing and can act at a local level, independent of what the larger system is doing. When connectivity relates to different systems or subsystems within an ecosystem, the changes that are triggered in one also influence another, leading to co-evolution, as a result of adaptation in neighbouring systems to the changes occurring in the other. Adaptation in one system will cause a change of landscape in the other.

This co-evolution relates to interactions and reciprocity, and the way the relationships between them evolve. To have co-evolution it is necessary to have an ecosystem that is more than one isolated system, so that interaction can take place between systems (not within a system). Systems as such will adapt to a change in the environment (a distinct and separate environment or element) but co-evolve with other neighbouring systems, as a part of their ecosystem. In social ecosystems, all subsystems, such as business, global, cultural, technology, legislation, etc. are all related. Changes in consumer perception have created a change in the way organisations work and the organisations also respond to changes in legislation as a result of changes in public opinion, for example. The subsystems have adapted (for example, the organisational practice in response to change of labour legislation), but by co-evolution, the overall global picture today is very different from ten to fifteen years ago.

Practice Co-evolution also suggests that no one entity is powerless and ripples of that one impact will sooner or later show through the wider system (the example of the velvet revolution or that of Ghandi's passive resistance, which led to Indian independence and later to the collapse of the Empire). Co-evolution is therefore also subject to boundaries of responsibility and ethics. As co-evolution reverberates well beyond an action-reaction response, going much deeper into the intricate fabric of the ecosystem, serious consideration for consequences is of paramount importance. For instance, one could take the view that the enormous problems experienced by the transport system in the UK today are linked to blanket privatisation in the 1980s. Pursued at the time to boost the economy and create growth, it also caused, as a by-product, a possibly unhealthy reverence for shareholder satisfaction, which in turn reduced the possibility of investment with long-term returns, thus leading to a short-sighted management of assets, such as transport assets, that became twenty years later, a dreadful casualty within an economy otherwise prosperous.

Equally, the trend of moving call centres and service centres outside specific countries to regions where costs are lower has resulted, perhaps, in savings for the organisations but increased stress and discontentment among users and consumers, who eventually put enough pressure to cause a reverse of the trend. Co-evolution implies a change that happens at the same time; however, in reality, systems seem to adapt in the short term and co-evolve in the longer term with a new coherence and new order as its outcome. Co-evolution also happens within an entity's subsystems as well as outside, between systems of an ecosystem. Ecosystems are defined as within and without the system, the two aspects of co-evolution also being interdependent. The learning within one team will also impact the learning transfer between teams working together, leading to the establishment of an organisation as a "learning" organisation, which when culturally embedded will become a new order.

By the same token, the organisation may also foster and encourage learning outside, in the wider community, as its wellbeing and equilibrium will also depend on the social community at large, which will be able to supply the organisation with individuals who are learning individuals and better prepared to work effectively within it. The term endogenous co-evolution will therefore be applicable when referring to co-evolution within the organisation, and exogenous co-evolution when referring to learning co-evolution outside the organisation, but within its ecosystem. Co-evolution of a complex co-evolving system comprises multiple, intricate, multidirectional links and influences, direct or many times removed, which are propagated and established by the levels of connectivity and interdependence, in various degrees and variable amounts.

Self-organisation, emergence and the creation of a new order are three of the key characteristics of complex systems. Natural selection is not the sole source of order in organisms and self-organisation is necessary for evolution. Emergence is a process to be considered as a whole, and creates a new order together with self-organisation. Emergent properties rise above and beyond the sum of parts that they arise from and represent an interactive whole different from an assembly of parts. For example, the relationship between the brain as the supporting neuronal system that enables sensory perception as well as, at the most complex level, consciousness, represents very well the concept of emergence, as a transition from local rules applicable to components, to global principles applicable to the whole, through coherence and resonance, which provide the links between local and global.

The process that enables the transition is equally important; phenomena such as consciousness or representation, for instance, remain, in this respect, still areas for scientific research and are also up for debate between scientists and philosophers. One other key co-evolutionary process is that of the interplay between microscopic events, which can cause macroscopic structures to emerge. Also expressed as quantitative accumulations causing qualitative jumps, and sending the system into a different level altogether, this is in turn, through the feedback mechanism having an influence on the microscopic event and so on, results in a continuous co-evolutionary process. Conservative self-origination is reversible, and dissipative self-organisation is irreversible. Both combined with the presence of constraints pushing a system far from equilibrium will result in the phenomenon of self-organisation in a system.

The important notion about human systems is that they tend to create structures and ideas, an emergence that becomes part of individual and collective history and as such is irreversible. With this new knowledge, the building of the new continues by connectivity, interdependence, self-organisation and emergence. These, however, also have a negative side, in that connectivity is not infinite, because viable sustained connections are limited in number. This may provide some food for thought about the latest belief in the power of the "silver bullet" called networking, with "networking gurus" proudly claiming ownership of thousands of names in their databases, inspiring others to follow their example! The cautionary information about systems shows that emergence resulting from connectivity without enabling environments and other contributing factors is not always efficient and positive.

Complexity and chaos

Applied to human systems, the chaos and complexity theory are specific in that they describe the reiteration (repetition) of certain patterns through the system, which can range from simple to complex, and give rise to very intricate outcomes, in spite of the original pattern being simple. Emergent order and disorder coexist in complex systems, at the edge of chaos, but complex systems are capable of adaptation and evolution, and of changing the rules of interaction, breaking the pattern. This is due to human behaviour being able to suddenly break repetition that natural systems may sustain. One peculiarity of complex systems is that similarity and similar characteristics can apply to both levels and scales of one system as well as between the system and another adjacent one (rules applicable in one organisation, across several functions of that organisation, in one business sector, also apply to another organisation in the same or another sector).

One pattern that can be repeated across different levels and scales is known as a fractal. It denotes the multiple levels of a system whereas hierarchy denotes the levels of an emergent property. The interesting thing about fractals is that although the initial pattern can be relatively simple, by repeating itself it gives rise to unbelievable, complex structures that do not much resemble their humble beginnings.

Theory of individual development

Individual development refers to a number of aspects such as:

- Development of thinking
- Development of morality
- Social model of development
- Individual development and leadership

And there are scientists who have made these domains the object of their life's work and put forward theories that have an important value and place in our understanding of these complex human capabilities.

Development of thinking

Jean Piaget represents one of the most established models related to the individual development of thinking in humans. The development of thinking has been the realm of philosophy but more specifically psychology, and the Swiss developmental psychologist Jean Piaget is considered to have made the most significant contribution to the understanding of the development of thinking in the 1980s – not least because of his rather novel way of conducting research, by closely observing his own three children as they grew up, to collect first hand, day and night, invaluable information that provided the foundation to his research and developmental stages theory.

A psychologist, Piaget was also a philosopher and epistemologist; three disciplines very closely interconnected. His object of study was the source or knowledge (epistemology; branch of philosophy) and how our cognitive processes develop. In addition he was also interested in the impact of genetics in epistemology (how genes may influence the way we develop our cognition and acquisition and developmental processing of knowledge).

A polymath thinker, he had been interested in biology and natural sciences since childhood, and had produced scientific papers at age fifteen, having focused his interest on the albino sparrow at the age of eleven. Later on, he explored psychoanalytical theories and worked with Alfred Binet to develop intelligence tests. Piaget worked both in France and Switzerland, holding academic roles but also advisory and consulting roles related to education and research.

Unlike other psychologists, who thought that infants saw the world as a source of unstructured, confusing and blooming stimuli, Jean Piaget proposed instead that from the earliest dates infants learn how to structure information about the world and make sense of it. He developed a model of development for thought, judgement and knowledge (Piaget, 1950). He suggested that knowledge is constructed (constructivist school) and organised into different sets of mental representations or schemas of the environment. New information about the world will be organised by assimilation into an existing schema (if a match could be found) or will be accommodated by changing the schema (if there was no match). And so the process of cognition is driven by a continuous activity of assimilation and accommodation of information coming from the world. As a result of this developmental dynamic he formalised four stages of development as follows:

> *Sensorimotor (birth to 18/24 months)*: The stage during which infants are aware only of what is in front of them. They have no concept of the permanence of the objects and the idea of causality, so they keep experimenting by direct physical interaction (throwing, shaking, tasting, etc.) with objects in an ongoing trial and error activity, which is not goal-oriented. From 7 to 9 months they progressively sit, crawl, stand and move and their exploration of the world increases their knowledge. Once they start language they add a symbolic ability.

Preoperational (18/24 months to age 7): A stage where toddlers increase their symbolic ability through language combined with memory and imagination. This enables them to understand past and present and also engage in make-believe. But their thinking is intuitive and not necessarily logical, lacking the grasp of cause-effect relationships or comparison or full appreciation of time.

Concrete operational (ages 7 to 12): The stage when children become less self-centred and increasingly aware of external events. They realise that their own feelings and thoughts are not necessarily known or shared by others and may not be part of reality as such. They demonstrate logical concrete reasoning but most still cannot think abstractly or hypothetically.

Formal operational (from age 12 to adulthood): During this stage adolescents become able to logically use symbols related to abstract concepts (algebra and science), think of multiple variables in systematic fashion, put forward hypotheses, and work with possibilities. They can weigh up abstract connections and relationships and concepts such as justice.

Piaget's view was that the actual age when children demonstrate various stages may vary around the average age points that he set (slower or faster development) and that some children may demonstrate signs of being at more than one stage at a point in time (individual variability). But he believed that the sequence of stages cannot be skipped and that each stage brings about new intellectual abilities and greater complexity in the understanding of the world. However, he insisted that the formal operational stage is the final stage of development and what follows is a lifelong accumulation of knowledge.

Summarising, the key elements of Piaget's proposition are that individual thinking is constructed and evolves by structuring external stimuli against mental schemas, which increase in number (assimilation and accommodation) in an evolutionary manner, from simpler to more complex stages of mental processes, with each stage having its base in the previous one, and that these stages cannot be skipped. And he based his model on the direct observation of his own three children from birth to their teens.

Development of moral judgement

The introduction of the social impact on cognitive development also brought about the significance of cultural values and beliefs that adults and culture transfer to the young. And so thinking and cognition cannot be separated (except artificially and for research only) from one specific aspect of human intelligence, namely moral development. Lawrence Kohlberg (1927–1987) significantly developed the field of moral psychology and moral education in his pioneering work. A polymath, Kohlberg's intellectual interests in philosophy, sociology and psychology enabled him to look back at moral reasoning and judgement from Socrates to Kant and Piaget, alongside American thinkers such as James Mark Baldwin, John Dewey and George Herbert Mead.

Lawrence Kohlberg (1958) took a specific interest in the theory of moral development and pushed the pre-existing ideas further. He studied groups of children at different ages and collected answers to questions that he put across related to stories that involved a fictitious character called "Heinz", who lived somewhere in Europe. One such experiment involved seventy-two boys aged ten to sixteen, from Chicago. Fifty-eight were also followed over twenty years. His objective was not about getting right or wrong answers; instead, he was interested to know what the reasons were behind the answers, when the children were presented with ten dilemmas. In the process he noticed that the reasons given were different depending on age. Kohlberg's empirical research resulted in his proposed model of moral judgement, which had three distinct levels, each with two sub-stages, which became influential and further stimulated the field of research (Kohlberg, Levine, & Hewer, 1983). The stages evolved from:

> *Level one*: pre-conventional morality; moral code is in culture, authority is external
>
>> (stage 1) blind obedience to rules and authority and fear of punishment, then seeking to pursue one's interests, understanding that others do the same, and using a calculating instrumental approach to decision-making,
>> to (stage 2) trying to live up to others' expectations of good behaviour, fostering close relationships and having good motives.

> *Level two*: conventional morality; moral code and authority are internalised
>
>> to (stage 3) concern for maintaining the social system, order and welfare,
>> to (stage 4) judging the moral values and trying to live up to the expectations of others for good behaviour, by having good motives and by fostering close relationships.

> *Level three*: post-conventional morality; moral reasoning and judgements are self-made principles
>
>> to (stage 5) maintaining social system to promote welfare and social order,
>> to (stage 6) judging the value of social rules by fundamental values such as liberty, utility, human rights and contractual obligations under universal principles of justice and human autonomy.

Kohlberg also thought that the higher stages were not necessarily better stages and that one had to make a philosophical argument in this regard. In addition, just like Piaget, he considered that these stages are being constructed and reconstructed by individuals, through interaction with society, rather than giving priority to either the environment or the individual. He also posited that the stages of moral development are universal and appear in a fixed sequence (no skipping or reversals) and they represent holistic structures or patterns of moral reasoning.

Regarding moral education, he was of the view that civic and moral education are the same, and to avoid the use of an arbitrary personal or religious belief in teaching virtue, he chose the US constitution and its fundamental principle of justice as a reference for this research and developmental model. He also promoted the idea that schools should have a role in moral education and that they should provide an interactive environment for this type of learning and development, to stimulate discussion and debate and use the Socratic questioning for students to examine their own arguments in the exploration of moral discussions as a way to develop higher levels of moral reasoning. To him role modelling or the value classification approach were limiting and did not address social issues such as racism and social inequality. Kohlberg believed that moral education should transcend culture and subcultures towards universal principles of justice.

Kohlberg's most important contribution in the last thirteen years of his life was his work on the just community approach, working with students and teachers in three schools. The key elements of this approach were to ensure a direct participatory democracy and to build a community based on a strong sense of unity (drawing from Emile Durkheim's collectivist theory of moral education). His commitment to developing just communities was based on his belief in shared values of caring, justice, trust and responsibility (from both students and teachers), and was also a reaction to what he believed to be too strong a focus on private interests prevailing in the American culture. He promoted the idea of revitalising the sense of democratic and civic engagement in and against the prevailing American culture.

Social model of development

But an individual's development – be it moral development, such as studied by Kohlberg, or cognitive development, such as described by Piaget – takes place in human society in a context of carers, family, friends and the wider social context. Children develop almost literally in the hands of adults. The importance of this aspect of development needed a focus of its own and Lev Vygotsky (1896–1934) was a Russian psychologist who positioned a cultural-historical theory of cognitive development (1978), where culture was instrumental in the development of speech, reasoning and higher mental functions. For the learners (children) the social and cultural context is a key ingredient of the cognitive development. Vygotsky's theory proposes a variety of significant influences to the development of cognition, namely:

- Social interaction
- The more knowledgeable other
- The zone of proximal development for learning.

The social interaction precedes development (unlike for Piaget, where development precedes learning), and for him the child is first exposed to social interactions of learning (inter-psychological) and then to individual development (intra-psychological). The more knowledgeable other can be any person or device that may have a higher understanding, ability or performance level than that of the learner. Therefore it can be someone that is a teacher, coach, older adult, but also a peer, a younger person or even technology (computers, robots and AI).

The zone of proximal development refers to the distance between a learner's ability to perform a task under adult guidance, through shared experiences – mediated by cultural tools such as language, writing and technology – and what they could achieve in the absence of such additional external influences and resources. Whilst initially such tools are developed to communicate needs, eventually they internalise to become higher thinking skills. Vygotsky's theory impacted the way learning was organised, from a one-way transmission of information (teacher to student) to setting up an interactive environment where the teacher becomes a collaborator who facilitates discussions and feedback. He also argues that culture is the key factor in the construction of knowledge, because it provides a lens through which we learn rules, skills and abilities, by interacting with others, and so being shaped by our culture.

There are six main assumptions in Vygotsky's theory:

- That adults convey knowledge to children in the way their culture interprets the world. The meaning they attach to objects, experience and events is informed by the culture of the parents and adults in general
- That thought and language become increasingly independent in the first few years of life
- That complex mental processes begin as social activities. Gradually they become internalised, independent and personalised
- That children can increase their capability for complex tasks when assisted by a more competent adult. This pushes the children's ability from the actual development level (by themselves) to a potential development level (when assisted by more competent individuals)
- That challenging tasks facilitate and promote a maximum cognitive growth (known as zone of proximal growth – ZPD); that which a child can attend to with help from competent others but not by themselves
- That play stretches a child's cognitive field because it allows them to take on roles otherwise not possible for them to take. The make-believe offers

them the possibility to stretch their cognitive capability for a greater number of scenarios than the ones offered by their reality as it is.

Vygotsky also places great importance on the activity of play because of its critical developmental outcomes:

- Enables children to make sense of their worlds, learn thinking skills and acquire and develop language
- Holds not only entertainment value but also a complex process that affects all their lives and a crucial component of child development
- Enables language development, because children need to create a story, characters, a dialogue with themselves, imitate others and use a vocabulary to navigate the world around them. Language internalises the world, uses symbols to convey cultural and historical accounts and meaning-making through inner speech (talking to themselves loudly) and also serves for regulation and self-control over thought and memory (cognitive processes), enabling transition from being other-regulated to self-regulated
- Helps with the development of cognition, because children first observe the social interactions around them and imitate adults in speech and behaviour, but in play they can take different roles and imitate different situations and in doing so eventually internalise that experience and also become self-regulated in thought and action
- Enables problem solving during play, and children may be assisted by others, which provides for them a "scaffolding" on which they can stretch their problem-solving capabilities to the next level, when mediated by a more knowledgeable other
- The make-believe and different scenarios of the imaginative play provide the opportunity to increase cognitive capability.

Summarising Vygotsky's contribution, he positioned development within a social context and highlighted the importance of surrounding culture and the impact of adults on the development of cognitions in children. He also believed that children can increase their achievements in relation to their untapped potential, if enabled and helped by adults or others, who have a superior skill or knowledge base. He believed that children's ability to perform and develop their practical, problem-solving, intelligence and symbolic capabilities (through language) can be improved and develop as a result.

Individual development and leadership

There is a long line of scientists who have contributed to the idea that from childhood into adulthood and beyond, throughout life, individuals evolve and develop as a result of increasing abilities to expand an understanding of and relationships with the world.

It is also widely accepted that in adult life, individuals experience a number of overlapping but distinct stages of development that evolve people's ability to solve problems and interact meaningfully with their world. This view is supported by a strong belief in the potential for continued learning and growth of people, if properly motivated and supported, to develop new ways of seeing and engaging with life. This development is also instrumental in the working lives of people where increasingly the need to be capable leaders has been highlighted by the fact that the world of work and the individual working life have changed beyond recognition. In such new socio-economic environments leadership as a capability is necessary not only in organisations but also at an individual level, for people to make sound and sustainable decisions over their own working lives and the way they position themselves in a society that is increasingly divided by wealth, unstable geopolitical structures, potential lack of individual agency, uneven ownership of skills and assets, all on the backdrop of an unpredictable future.

As with most ideas, the question of how individuals develop in their given environment has been long standing and the roots of such modern considerations go back to ancient Greek, Hebrew, Hindu and Buddhist cultures. In modern times, Darwin's work triggered renewed interest in the understanding of how it impacts our knowledge about humans. Freud, Adler, Jung and others (psychologists, philosophers, psychiatrists and polymath scientists) explored our understanding of how the human ego develops in adults.

On the strength of the work done by Piaget, Loevinger, Cook-Greuter, Graves, Kegan, Kohlberg and Wilber, in 2005 Rooke and Torbert created a model of development based on researching leaders in organisations.

Widely known as Torbert's theory of development; this model proposes that the stages of development in adults are not a direct mapping onto personality traits and they specifically reflect the ability of meaning-making, which results in the way individuals act. These stages of development are known as "action logics" and are regarded as independent of personality traits, although some may consider "action learning" as an overarching trait.

The model postulates successive stages of development involving greater levels of empathy, responsibility, complexity, understanding of the world and appreciation of the potential of each moment.

This is known as the seven stages of development, an overview of which follows, starting from the first level.

| **Opportunist** | Self-oriented; manipulative; goes for wins by all means possible | Views luck as central; has a "happy-go-lucky" attitude in life, and is focused on the concrete; presents a fragile ego and is generally distrustful; does not accept feedback; deceptive; rejects rules as loss of freedom; works with the "eye for an eye" ethic; legitimises getting away with things; seeks opportunities and personal gain; externalises blame; fragile self-control; short-term outlook. |

Diplomat	Wants and needs to belong; does not rock the boat; sticks to group norms; conflict averse	Conflict averse; sticks to protocol, clichés, platitudes; conforms; avoids hurting others; feels shame if they disregard rules; seeks membership; loyal to close groups; is the social glue and participates in social requirements.
Expert	Searches for improvement; uses strong expertise and logic; searches for efficiency	Own logic and belief systems; problem solver; critical; perfectionist; values efficiency; values feedback only from experts; dogmatic; values facts; wants to be an expert; internal moral order and external sense of obligation; strong individual contributor and pursues improvement.
Achiever	Meets strategic goals; delivery of results by most effective means; success-focused	Inspiring; visionary; welcomes behavioural feedback; values long-term goals, results and effectiveness; initiator; seeks mutuality; compelled to meet own standards; sometimes unorthodox; not aware of own subjectivity; resourceful and adopts goals.
Individualist	A few fixed points but relativistic position; interacts with the system as self and in relationships; new process innovation	Special interest in and understanding of systems and complexity; focuses on self rather than actions; operates through relationships; deepens personal connections and relationships; changes roles and adapts to the situation; less self-absorbed; questions assumptions; likes change and individuality; less focus on goals; increasingly questions assumptions of self and others.
Strategist	Makes links between judgement, theories, contracts and principles; creates transformations for self and others	Creative; both process- and goal-oriented; appreciates importance of judgement, contracts, principles, theories and creativity in conflict resolution; aware of contradictions and paradox; aware of own world views and opinions; values individuality and uniqueness; has a sense of humour and enjoys playing different roles; aware of dark side; post-conventional morality.
Alchemist	Transforms self and others; operates on a social scale to generate transformations that involve thinking, awareness, action and outcomes	Involved in society-wide preoccupations and awareness; pursues spiritual transformations; creates situations to reframe events; continuously focused and attentive; seeks the opposite in situations and a positive outcome; creative integration of opposites; works with order and chaos; seeks interplays of logic, actions, ethics and effects; works with symbolic, analogical and metaphorical time and events; involved in a spiritual quest; helps others with their life questions and challenges.

In early 2000, Torbert and his associates increased their interest in exploring what Torbert calls action inquiry, as a way of increasing individual presence in the moment; a place from where the future emerges and where one can be alert to current opportunities and threats, and act effectively in a transformational and sustainable way. Enquiry in the moment helps us attune to the development of self and the wider world. Action inquiry (Torbert, 2004) can be practiced and developed by acquiring the capacity to make incremental (single-loop) changes to increase timely, effective action. Next comes the capacity to make transformational (double-loop) changes; further still comes the ongoing (triple-loop) listening into the dark, into the present, and into the range of possibilities from which emerges the future.

Action inquiry is a process that cannot be practiced by learning a few rules and then following them in a mechanistic way or learning it by simply imitating others. Instead it is a dynamic process of being alive and learning anew, by moving from moment to moment with openness to transformation, to vulnerability, and to possibilities of how best to act in the now. This is not an easy process, but it results in a profound sense of growth in personal integrity, in interpersonal mutuality, and participation in wider world sustainability.

Torbert also has a world view about the development of humanity as a whole, now entering what he calls the third age, which follows the first pre-1500 age of dependence and the second age of independence, enabled by science, democracy and market forces. The third age is the age of interdependence, where mutual enquiry, power and love all merge and create full responsibility for us to live with others, on our common home, Earth.

Philosophy and science applied in self-development and career coaching

As humans we are biologically prepared for social interaction and most of our learning comes from all around us, through imitation, social immersion, memes, communication, teaching, exchanging ideas, role models, common emotions and value systems. Therefore there is absolutely no doubt that any person-to-person interaction based on trust, through language, and a close, personal, caring rapport will work! In this respect what our friends and family and colleagues tell us is certainly useful and we practice this type of growth, learning and problem solving as a matter of everyday life. So why and how is coaching different?

Coaching is different from the advice and wisdom we receive from friends and family, because although coaches use similar and common methods such as language, conversations, enquiry, etc. they have an independent position; they are outside the history of the client's evolution and apply methods and knowledge that have been researched, can be repeated, relate to common standards of practice for all practitioners and refer to a body of knowledge that is universally recognised. This is why the models and formal thinking presented in this section (and the book) may indeed be useful to us, in our work and life choices, in the present and for the future.

Career is just one window that opens into the wide landscape of a person's entire life and includes the personal journey, individual circumstances, good and bad luck, preference for certainty or not, appetite for risk or stability, repetitive habitual patterns, chaos and chance – the entire complexity of our personal and social world within which our professional and personal journey unfolds.

Career happens in context and the context is everything outside the person, but it also includes the inner world of the person, which in turn opens into wide inner spaces, also complex and impactful on the world outside the person, and the path one builds through reality, determined by design, or by chance, or by something in between.

And there is complexity involved; starting with personality, leading to attitudes, beliefs or emotions which define each other, in a circular way, as inner co-dependent sub-systems. But values and beliefs are also evolving with age, society and surrounding culture. In turn, this evolution causes changes of behaviour and different work and career choices. And science backs such findings with, for example, constructivist theories of cognitive and moral development. Developmental steps involve both design and chance. And we can meet chance halfway, by an attitude of openness and belief that a solution will be forthcoming. Obliquity, chaos and complexity theory provide scientific underpinning to this reality we all experience in our life and work. Often such changes of direction involve a transition to a new state or location, all enabled by the legacy of experience and skills that have been gathered as a result of the decision of the past. And so all specific aspects of our identity manifest as an integrated expression of ourselves, at all times. Everything is connected, interdependent and in motion, in the inner and outer systems of our individual and social existence. And the science of complex thinking theory offers operating principles that map the dynamics of the way we manifest in our personal and working life.

Our history also reveals the strategies we have developed to negotiate the intricacy and complexity of events that provide contents to our individual history, beginning with what we have received from family and friends through to those we have encountered in work, significant others and the socially structured educational and employment systems, our national culture and our global ecosystem of people and nature, with whom we are connected.

We develop and continue learning throughout our lives, and the constructivist approach in the science of cognitive and moral development offers models and stages of early and adult development. There is a wealth of knowledge that we can use in self-development or coaching, including the skilled, personal, respectful, hopeful, confidential conversations that we may choose to have with another complex, competent and professional person.

Career coaching with complexity in mind: chaos and chance

Work is part of life and life is subject to complexity, change and the unexpected events that can randomly bring good or bad luck. We deal with this by pretending that it is not there and prefer to control our anxiety and exercise our preference for certainty and the familiar by thinking that things remain forever as they are. But they do not and we are today, more than ever, subject to seismic changes in economy, politics, value systems, governance and stability. Technology has changed everything and the ripples and tectonic movements have only started.

In this context it would be amiss not to acknowledge that work and careers are also subject to hazards and change and respond by acknowledging this and embracing complexity, chaos, chance and transformation as part of our career and future of work conversations with all age groups from children to retirees. Everyone needs to review and reframe their expectations and build the readiness required to navigate those changes successfully and adaptively. This perspective has been formalised by academics in what is named the Chaos Theory of Careers (Pryor & Bright, 2011), which posits, based on research and practice that careers need to be reframed from being a lifelong plan and a predictable stable course of activity into a more flexible adaptive ability to live well and remain resilient and steady when faced with unexpected change. It also questions the ability to predict future behaviour based on the past and takes into account that small changes can lead to significant outcomes (sliding doors). It requires career counselling to accept that the only predictable element of the future in a complex world is that this world is unpredictable and to replace current methodology and focus from fixed and linear to a paradigm that acknowledges our world as driven by complex concurrent multicausality and interconnectedness. It also predicates the replacement of career management as a lifelong skill by another skill – that of living well with uncertainty and complexity.

Pryor and Bright introduce the Luck Readiness Index (LRI) as the ability to recognise, adapt, utilise and create opportunities that can be brought about by chance. Significantly, this is an index of attitudes to describe a person's ability to deal with chaos and uncertainty, as follows:

- Flexibility: adaptable, not threatened by the unfamiliar, ready to respond to change, comfortable to alter thinking and action
- Optimism: hopeful, open to new experiences, seeing possibilities as opportunities not problems
- Risk: fearless and not put off by the possibility of failure, able to make a decision when faced with change, confident
- Curiosity: disciplined learner, learns from others and from experience, explores and seeks possibilities
- Persistence: staying power, endurance, tolerates some failure and repetition, not discouraged by obstacles, tenacious and determined in pursuit of goals

- Strategy: plays and plans to win, no matter what the chances and risks; seeks opportunities to improve and achieve goals, believes that chance can be influenced and helped
- Efficacy: self-control and self-direction, believes that own destiny need not be determined by external influences, focuses on what they can control and uses or creates opportunities
- Luckiness: expects or believes to be lucky.

John Krumboltz's theory of career also challenges the established belief and method that focuses on planning as a long-term approach to career advice (Mitchell, Levin, & Krumboltz, 1999) based on the belief that things are predictable and can be controlled. In this tradition "indecision" is wrong because it delays decisions and prevents taking control of the future and planning a set of goals and actions. But complexity is precisely a state where predictability is low and uncertainty is high. In this reality, usefulness of careful planning is greatly reduced and such a traditional approach to career is no longer fit for purpose. He suggests that instead we need to introduce the ideas of chance events and impact of external unexpected factors into our considerations and build potential around luck and happenstance. We have to learn to be prepared for the unexpected and abandon the wish to plan and control everything, welcoming luck instead (Krumboltz & Levin, 2004) as a career-influencing factor that needs to be considered, appreciated and leveraged.

Krumboltz also offers four main attitudes as key for uncertainty preparedness, namely:

- Curiosity
- Persistence
- Flexibility
- Optimism

These attitudes reframe career development from a linear, planned and controlled approach to a flexible and positive state of readiness for what comes, instead.

Reflecting on group findings

The often limited time and focused scope of career conversations with my clients, did not allow me for specific explorations of their philosophical or scientific perspectives. However they were expressed and evidenced in their behaviours, choices and the narratives they presented about themselves. Unsurprisingly this resulted in an endless individual variety alongside common trends and patterns shared by them all, as a client group, which have been explored in some detail in Chapter 1.

My case study

As I was covering the research part for this section, I found that a lot of the information I was reviewing refreshed what I had learned a long time ago in high school and university (Vygotsky). The foundations I had then came in very handy to structure the research information I was now gathering. And this process helped me understand the origin of my own thinking (Piaget, Torbert), of my values system, and of how significant others, society and my own preferences – together in a dynamic and dialectic fashion – embedded the fundamentals of my thinking and moral fabric (Kohlberg) that have informed me throughout life.

I discovered that the labels I could use linked me to materialist dialectics, which formed the world view, so closely related to the cosmogony proposed by quantum physics and science generally, based on my childhood enjoyment not of fairy tales, but of science fiction, illustrated short stories and later the novels of the great science fiction writers. The idea of an infinite universe, perpetually moving and transforming, is comfortable for me, even if at times a bit daunting (complexity, dialectics). I also value and believe in the interaction between different factors, such as nature and nurture, in a dynamic equally important measure.

I have also increasingly embraced the understanding that chance has a role to play due to the passing of time that enables all sorts of events to occur, with a significant and often unforeseen impact either way (Prior and Bright's Chaos Theory of Careers CTC and Krumboltz's Happenstance), and which we cannot predict or control (obliquity, chaos, complexity). And the best way to adapt is to respond the best we can (Prior and Bright's Luck Readiness Index). On the other hand I know that a lot of decisions and choices we make are under our control and there are many possibilities for exercising free will and for opting for one alternative or another (Krumboltz's four attitudes in complexity), which made me always take full responsibility for my own actions and decisions. I also identified the significant others and what great advantage I gained from their influence (next proximal space). The patience and encouragement from my father, who spent a lot of time with me in activities related to school and homework but also arts and science to expand my knowledge, imagination and creativity (Vygotsky). The pragmatism and sense of duty from my mother (Torbert, Vygotsky, Kohlberg), who was such as strong role model for how to get things done effectively and for never thinking that obstacles could stop one's will and commitment to a goal. This attitude – I later discovered – was a great advantage when engaging with the task of living, working and just getting things done in the world. This approach also provided me with an increased time to enjoy the less pragmatic pursuits of reflection, imagination and creativity. This in turn, led me back to new exciting projects that I wished to implement. And so creating a dynamic state of being and doing, an ongoing motion of enrichment, increasing the breadth and depth of my existence, in mind and action, in time and space (Torbert).

The admiration I had for the superior understanding of psychology of my dear school friend, Maria, who at the age of fourteen fired my imagination and led me to my first books on the subject; a small step that led me to a career and a lifelong passion (Prior and Bright's Chaos Theory of Careers CTC).

The examples of my aunt, father and mother, who took great pride in the way they looked and had a sense of style that resonated with me, which later influenced my own style and appearance (Prior and Bright's Chaos Theory of Careers CTC). The values of fairness, generosity and honesty that most members of my extended family and friends embraced and embodied, are just a few examples of the legacy I received in my formative years (Kohlberg, Vygotsky).

This stretching influence of others, created a strong foundation for one part of my identity, upon which my adult life built the rest, informed by my own experience and appetite for learning. (Piaget, Vygotsky) I could see clearly how and what aspects of my knowledge, beliefs and behaviour have remained the same or have been transformed by the passing of time as I was creating my own life's story as opposed to representing the life history of others (Torbert, Kohlberg). This change did not happen without rebellions, confrontations, disagreements and reconciliations (dialectics); without me asserting new beliefs and ways of being that did not resonate with all the people around me all the time (Kohlberg). But such contradictions have also been a part of the new me that was emerging from what I learned from others, from what I left behind, and from what I learned by myself and what I embraced anew as a new dimension of my emergent adult identity at different points in time (Prior and Bright's Luck Readiness Index).

Writing this book has also enabled me to map the thinking style that I use today to the roots of my continental European education, and it has also highlighted why in an Anglo-American intellectual context I was at times puzzled by the lack of some theoretical concepts that I had been accustomed to. Now I understand that it is due to regional differences and the way they have been filtered in or out, in education and professional practice, and do or do not play a part in mainstream thinking. Unlike the Anglo-American thinking, European thinking has long embraced dialectics, and today its usefulness is being confirmed in science; for example, by the superimposition principle in quantum physics and also in the complex evolving systems theory.

All these aspects of myself, as a unique individual but also an interconnected and interdependent part of the wider social structures – themselves evolving and changing – have been forming as I advance in time and cross geographic spaces, moved by design or by chance. Meeting significant and more knowledgeable others (Vygotsky) and progressively changing the ratio of action, reflection, ethics and meaning (Torbert) have all played a part in my developmental journey and my way of being in the world. And this has been a complex, evolving and dialectic process, where each transformation of my Self has progressed to another level (dialectics, Tolbert), leading me to becoming increasingly independent and increasingly connected to others through my better understanding of their uniqueness and also our common connection with the world.

My own career panned out organically and without a plan, and my first significant career decision was to not practice after graduation what I had learned at university; instead disrupting the predictable and taking a completely new direction, in an age when such things were really not done! This was ominous, although I did not know it at the time; indicating boldness in my resolve to have a strong independent grip on my professional destiny alongside the decision that my path was not to be that of a specialist. Decades later I was giving an overview of my somewhat meandering career history to a senior career coach colleague. After listening, she commented with a smile: "you took control of and exercised your own career management, well before the concept was coined". I realised that it was true. And now I also realise how nicely my career history so far, maps to what Krumboltz (2004) currently views as a way to navigate the uncertainty of the future world of work and careers.

Indeed my focus has always been on something else than the specifics of an actual work content. Instead I simply pursued opportunities where I could:

- Successfully use exiting skills whilst learning something new
- Be in working environments that reflected my own personal interests in science, technology, creativity and innovation
- Enjoy opportunities for change and variety
- Ensure my financial independence
- Stretch my capabilities and be pushed to new levels of performance.

But there is one factor that, upon reflection, is also worth mentioning: in my case I caused some uncertainty, myself. I pushed myself to the edge of chaos, at regular intervals: I disrupted the exiting order and hypothesised on what the next may be like, taking a chance without really knowing. I hoped for the best, and I was confident in the ability to deploy the personal resources I knew I had. In doing so I may have partly prevented time from showing its hand and bringing unexpected circumstances to me. Given that I have frequently exercised change on some aspects of my life – with some memorable exceptions when I changed all! – I effectively distributed the odds of events occurring across multiple fields and played my hand first, at relatively close intervals. With my eyes set on the horizon, I have outpaced time with at least fifty-fifty odds to win, as it is the case in games of chance. And looking back, indeed there is a balance of wins and losses, good disruptions and not so good disruptions, distributed across different aspects of my life, with mainly material losses in exchange for self-actualisation wins.

To successfully exercise this ambition I certainly embodied Krumboltz's recommended attitudes: curiosity, persistence, flexibility, optimism.

And these are without a doubt a direct undiluted legacy from my parents and the way I saw them live their lives. In action, my mother was a persistent optimist whilst my father was driven by curiosity and flexibility.

Alongside nurture I also used nature and preferences with additional values and attitudes that map to Pryor and Bright's Luck Readiness Index (2011), including strategy as a reflection of my appetite for endless possibilities, and an opening to take and mitigate risks; effectively initiating regular planned changes as opposed to unplanned changes. Both deplete resources and cause disruption, but in one case I could somewhat prepare, in the other, I could not. And the implications in the respective costs and benefits are significant.

I recently met Charles Handy (the founder of modern management theory) at a professional event where he was sharing his latest idea that the way of future adaptation for organisations and people in an uncertain world is to prepare and think about a next phase, whilst at the height of the current one, instead of waiting for decline to signal that it is time for a change. I was happy to agree and reflected that indeed this seems to have been a strategy I embraced, directly translated in the way I managed my own career.

A useful exercise

There are many useful questions you could ask yourself to increase awareness of influences from the past on your developmental and career paths, explore how and what other experiences of your own you have accumulated and how you would position yourself for the future. Such questions may relate to:

1   Your overarching beliefs and thoughts that represent your world view, from philosophical, spiritual, scientific, secular or religious perspectives, and how you embody this frame and how it guides the way you live your everyday life as well as your career choices. For example:

- Have you found philosophical and scientific models that resonate with you?
- Did you already know about them?
- Is there anything that you would like to explore more in depth, in life or work?
- Are your actions connected to your beliefs?
- Are you aware of how and when they came about in your history?
- Can you use some of the ideas from philosophy or science to help you with your life and work?

2   Your individual development and the various stages of development you relate to – be it in thinking, moral or personal development – and your own views on the levels of development that you have experienced so far. For example:

- What models have captured your imagination and how can you use them in practice?
- Are there significant others in your life, and what have you specifically learned from them, or what specific influence have they exerted on you?
- What are the significant shifts in your life and how did they happen?
- What do you identify as your current top three to five beliefs, behaviours and capabilities. How valid, adaptive and useful are they? Would they help you in the future, and if not what can you do about that to become better prepared?

3   Your connection to the world and your perception of how it works; whether in a linear, straightforward clear fashion with events linked by clear cause and effect connections, or in non-linear ways as complex, sometimes unexpected and incomprehensible, with its fabric of explained and unexplained events. For example:

- Use a combination of directed and focused reflection and open-mindedness to listen to what the surrounding environment may whisper to you
- Trust your intuition and instinct and also cross-check it with your thoughts and your new knowledge
- Plan actions around your findings and place yourself on a continuous review path where you reflect on your current life and project it in the light of a mapped future to see if there are any gaps and to see how you are tracking your course to achieve your purpose
- Select a few developmental areas and just allow your mind to absorb and integrate the new ideas in connection with those themes
- Define and review your purpose! In relation to yourself, but also to your close and loved ones and the wider society.

Summary

The way one may look at the relationship between philosophy, science, self-development and career coaching is similar to the way nested universes may fit together, one within another within the next.

Philosophy has been "the science of all sciences" with a quest to rationally explore and consider truths and principles about all big questions on life, identity, conduct, meaning, our place in the universe and the existence and future of the universe itself. Later on, specific domains of enquiry broke away from philosophy to become stand-alone sciences and use evidence, research and falsifiability as frameworks for legitimacy and specialist progress. Humankind represents the reflective aspect of our universe and within it individuals also develop, by asking big questions about their own existence to map a specific path for their lives that includes work, professions and careers. And so all these facets of reality and related thinking nearly fit together, one within the other, from the overarching dialectics of philosophy, to complexity theory in science, to development and the meaning-making of individuals, to specific choices that one has or makes about work and career; again considered within the much wider context of the world of the future, itself subject to dialectic transformations under the prevailing forces of our time. From the big philosophical picture to a narrow personal decision, all are connected and fit neatly as systems, within systems, within other systems.

Philosophy has offered a multitude of thoughts and systems that have helped us make sense of our existence and answer major questions about life, the universe and everything, over the thousands of years of human civilization.

And of significant importance may be some schools of thought that hold their value to this day when applied and tested in the reality we experience now.

Such an example is the dialectic thinking represented uninterrupted from antiquity to these days by Mahavira's Jainism, Babylonian philosophical lore, Socrates, Plato, Aristotle, Heraclitus, Hegel and Marx, all representing schools of thought as evidence of an evolutionary process. Dialectic thinking embraces the view of dynamic opposing forces, evolution in stages and helical development, an evolutionary interplay between quantitative and qualitative changes, a world in constant motion with a lot of relativity and predications around truth and perceptions of a world that is complex and manifold.

The complexity thinking in science mirrors dialectic principles and offers a view of a world as being interconnected, interdependent, changing and subject to complex dynamic principles that are at work and result in expected and unexpected consequences. It also considers that chance, chaos, time and history are all at play in mapping future events.

The theories of individual development related to psychology also embrace a dynamic constructivist perspective, with a belief in continued lifelong learning and development. This development covers aspects such as thinking, judgement, ethics, emotions and social interactions. There are psychologists who support the idea that this development is continuous, ongoing throughout life, with development in one stage providing skills and abilities that enable the next stage. Other psychologists believe that development occurs in a discontinuous way, with specific skills and abilities that have a clearly set start and finish. However the specific feeling, thinking and abilities do not occur spontaneously but develop gradually for some time, prior to becoming visible.

Constructivism embraces the idea of development in stages (stage theory: Piaget, Freud, Kohlberg, Maslow, Kegan, Loevinger, etc.) and posits that the stages evolve from simple to more sophisticated; that not all individuals develop at the same rate and in the same way and that this development happens under influences that come from society, starting with the initial small group of family and friends and further expanding to all other people that can act as guides and catalysts, to stimulate the learning process in others. This learning is also open as far as the potential of an individual will allow and is not necessarily directly correlated to personality, although personality informs development.

This rich tapestry of thought can be brought to bear in self-development and coaching, a journey that itself is dynamic, evolving, between complex individuals that bring to the table an identity defined by personality, emotions, values and beliefs, life and work experience and aspirations to drive them forward to new paths of self-realisation and adaptation.

The degrees of separation between the mundane and the philosophical are few.

Starting with everyday questions such as what makes us happy, what type of work do we want to do, what do we wish to accomplish in life, what do we want to be remembered for or what is the meaning of our life and activity, we quickly move from the mundane to individual psychology. Because we explore personality and identity, likes and dislikes, our motivation and values and how all this causes us to communicate, behave and be in the world. And so we are back to philosophy, as we ask and answer questions that are in the domain of ethics, logic, ontology and epistemology.

Chapter 3

The future of the world in the age of learning machines

Life and work on the cusp of the fourth industrial revolution led by AI

The post analogue world of the new millennium

Technology and the state of the world

With increased frequency and from multiple sources we are being exposed to "sound bites" of information about how the world around us is changing and what we might expect in the years to come.

Visions for 2020 and beyond are increasingly projected across conventional and new media. And there is a sense of increased urgency to these messages and an awareness that this change may be significant and different, alongside the notion that a lot of the future has now become difficult to predict due to a lack of historic data. But for the general public, the messages projected by mainstream media are like dots of information scattered across an ill-defined canvas. Except for futurists and think tanks, there is little cohesion about the full view, particularly at the level of the ordinary people, busy as they should be with the daily chores, challenges and routines of life, in a world that is in fact unstable across the large geopolitical zones.

Whilst uncertainty is unsettling, people fail to join the dots and make sense of this information, not necessarily due to lack of interest but rather lack of time and practice. Instead, most get on with their lives, understandably focused on the immediacy of the mundane. On the one hand, they continue to pick up scattered fragments of news, whilst on the other hand, they reassure themselves, thinking that this is not going to impact them and if so, not just yet, and tomorrow is another day to ponder if need be.

This is why this chapter is an attempt to create a useful, practical and integrated picture of the future world by bringing together various sections of the puzzle, from the future of work, business, professions and technology to the future of society, politics and governance. The future will impact our working lives sooner or later, and in business the future is already here for some groups and in some countries, with Airbnb and Uber as early, and now already embedded, examples of serious disruptions to previous business models.

There is no doubt that humankind's progress has been strongly determined by technological changes and advancement. And technology has in turn caused ripple effects and changes in all the related systems, whether social, political or economic. Such impactful changes are known as the industrial revolutions. Broadly speaking, an industrial revolution is defined as a set of complex changes brought about by a method that enables a significant increase of productivity efficiency, on a wide or massive scale, and which in turn causes major shifts in socio-economic and political systems.

The first industrial revolution happened in 1784, with the advancement of mechanical equipment powered by harnessing water and steam. In 1870 the second industrial revolution was defined by electricity, new capabilities to mass produce, and the division of labour and new jobs. The year 1969 ushered in the third industrial revolution when a new form of nuclear energy was being explored, transistors and microprocessors gave rise to electronics, new materials were being created, and space exploration and biotechnology were supported by telecommunications and computers. And productivity and automation were increased due the combined power of IT and electronics whilst paving the way for robotics. Again a new range of products, ways of working and jobs were opened up by a new source of power – energy and information processing.

The following decade (1980–1990) brought about an exceptional cluster of technological advancements which irreversibly transformed our life and work.

To name the most significant two, the fax machine (replacing the telex machine and often the post) and the PC (complementing and eventually replacing manual and mainframe information processing, storing and transmission) brought about unprecedented speed and flexibility in information and data management. Not only accuracy but speed of processing – in both business and personal transactions of all kinds – increased and reduced the duration of end-to-end exchanges from weeks, days or hours, to real time, instant completions.

The fax machine transmitted information as it was being sent, raising just the one concern of authenticity. The PC followed soon after, to steadily conquer most business desks in many companies, working alongside and then all but displacing the mainframes, which required complex data manipulation and tedious interventions by specialists, instead of the actual information users. Within years the PC became mass produced at ever-decreasing prices and invaded millions of homes around the globe. The internet then opened the gates of information, products and services to all who could access a PC. At the same time, the Baby Boomer generation was challenging monopolies, and budget airlines opened the gates to affordable travel worldwide. Now, not only knowledge but people, too, could move around the world in greater numbers and faster than ever before.

The same went for goods, which could now be transported everywhere much faster since the related paperwork could be done in minutes, allowing pallets to come and go as soon as products were picked and packed, whilst related documentation was being sent to banks and logistics suppliers electronically.

E-commerce, placed consumption – literally – at the fingertips of the customers, who have become more and more aware of their power (actual or perceived) to expect or even demand a bigger choice of products and services (needed or not), pushing competition to another level, where diversification and sophistication of choices have become an endless race of – one may argue – futile sophistication, when considered against what most people habitually use or consume.

All these fast, unstoppable and significant changes led to rapid growth in connectivity and a greater complexity of exchanges. The new technologies created and integrated software to run manufacturing, financial transactions, ordering of materials and services in the supply chain, sales and servicing after sale, and they ultimately placed "everything online".

In addition, the new software generation that was modular, scalable, integrated and housed in increasingly portable and miniaturized devices literally linked everything to everything and everyone to everyone else, bringing together the head and tail of the most complex of business processes, and so align all aspects of the value and supply chain, from customer demand to raw materials, to logistics and distribution to after sales support and customer satisfaction surveys, to consumer behaviour and back to research and development, to restart the business cycle anew.

The analogue star performers – information technology (IT) and telecommunications (Telcos) – themselves evolved and advanced to the next level due to the increased processing power of integrated circuits (also known as microchips) and they formed – combined – the formidable Information and Communications Technology (ICT), a hybrid of IT and Telcos that continues to evolve now in its integrated and digital guise, supporting the future of Artificial Intelligence (AI) and Robotics.

E-commerce was also rolled out, supported by somewhat less glamorous but critically instrumental Call Centres, also known under the more user-friendly names of "Contact Centre", "Customer Care Centre" or "Client Support" centre. A twenty-first-century version of Taylorist performance, they break the barriers of geography, biology and time, as they operate 24/7 around the world, following the sun, and are never asleep.

They are still with us today and are run by call centre agents who work against stringent performance metrics such as: Average Speed of Answer (ASA) indicator or 'wait time' of 20 seconds for 80% of the calls – currently the most common service level for voice calls – or for emails, 80% of emails answered within four hours, and for chat, 80% of chat answered within 90 seconds.

Every individual agent's response time is strictly monitored, and deviation from expected metrics is not well viewed. This environment is not for the faint-hearted, and the turnover of employees in this industry is, understandably, amongst the highest.

But this technology-related human activity has itself been impacted by technology. Increasingly, call centre agents are replaced or aided by interactive voice devices that so far have not been too popular with consumers. For all the advantages enjoyed by the DIY customers of today – who can order products, pay bills, print statements and install and fix products themselves – they also represent the people who get quite frustrated for being left to wait at the end of a telephone, hoping to eventually get attention from a talking machine, which only offers a narrow range of options when it answers, unlike the human mind which is open to all options and can do much better in such dialogues with ease and speed.

All things considered, it is technology again that is positioned to deal with this current limitation, and the more sophisticated range of options, algorithms and Robots of the future integrated AI, may help us overcome it in the fullness of time.

A new definition of work and the new globalised workforce

The world of work today has little resemblance to the world of work of the 1980s, and it impacts all aspect of our lives. It is also a world that is fragmented and full of contradictions between division of high versus low skills, low and very highly paid jobs, a multitude of ways to deliver work and new challenges to regulation and legislation. This redefinition of what people do in their work and how work has changed is not new. There have always been vintage skills and skills in high demand related to new technologies. And the 1980s were a time of formidable technological advancement that simultaneously brought together personal computers, the internet and the mobile and later smartphones.

This is an unbeatable triad that today enables a person to leave home with nothing other than a phone in their hand yet still have access to any and all needed services, such that they can function with absolute effectiveness across all activities that people undertake in a normal working and personal life, at home or away.

The mobile phone has become an alter ego of the human, ubiquitous from the deserts of Africa to the high rises of the USA and Japan, to the quaint villages of France and the UK, to the icy poles of the north and south, all around the globe.

What this means is that people can work from home, on weekends, at night, across time zones, all the time or just some of the time.

This also has an impact on real estate and office space, on the challenge of engaging and managing a scattered remote and diverse workforce, of developing new skills whilst other skills may well become under utilised, on the way work is regulated and legislated, on the division between those technically skilled and those who are not.

In the face of significant change, the new structures of global companies also had to integrate – alongside process and technology – one other key element of their operations; namely, the workforce. Organisations have been facing the challenge of integrating workers from around the globe, often managed remotely by bosses sitting at the other end of the planet, trying to motivate and roll out workers into cultures, models and work practices generated at the other cultural pole. This phenomenon was only reflecting something that was organically happening across the world, with large numbers of people crossing borders, of their own volition, spurred on by perceived differences in affluence, increased communication and ease of travel.

Today more people travel from any point to any other point on the planet faster and cheaper than ever before. Such movement of peoples across the planet and at such speed has never been seen before, and with the air travel monopolies broken and air travel being so affordable, there is no stopping this phenomenon of travel and migration for both tourism and economic reasons.

The planet has become increasingly integrated, culturally cosmopolitan and economically globalised, with companies worldwide becoming micro-representations of society at large. To keep pace with this new, slimmed-down operating model, a new way of organising a company was needed to render it more flexible and nimble and able to respond to market and client require-ments faster and more efficiently; hence, the matrix organisation was born. This involves the utilisation of skills and resources on a project basis, deploy-ing and re-deploying a company's pool of people, quickly and in accordance with the latest business demand.

The implications of this in terms of job nomenclature and skill sets are as obvious as they are deep. Many of the jobs we casually talk about these days simply did not exist even five years ago, and many that existed ten years ago or still exist today will no longer be here tomorrow. Skills are commodities; as such they change and fluctuate in price and availability. This lack of skills stability is something that will increasingly try and test employers, recruiters, businesses and economies at large.

E-commerce and the new savvy and empowered consumer

The whole effort and transformation that organisations have experienced through technology and globalisation was focused on a return to sharehold-ers and also satisfying the consumers in order to increase sales and business wealth. In this process a lot of importance was placed on empowering the client, through increased market awareness and changes in legislation that pro-tected the consumers.

The concepts of "market" and indeed "customer" greatly evolved in the last few decades. The client of today is a powerful figure – educated, sophisti-cated, informed, demanding and discerning – someone who can make or break organisational profitability and who demands of organisations not only a good product, but much more; corporate responsibility and global citizenship terms and demands, which were nonexistent in the '80s but which today can change the position of an organisation on the stock exchange. Behind the visible paying client (the consumer), shareholders and other stakeholders have also gained status through various interests related to products and services. This new complexity has highlighted the importance of connections, influence and relationships in the value and wealth chain.

In this context the quality management function has embraced the more holistic approach to business – through total quality management, continuous and continued improvement, sustainable and green businesses and so on – to create standards and hold the balance of forces coming from innovation in products/services, the providing organisation and the market (with multiple clients) with people, leadership, culture, processes and technology between supply and demand. It is a complex, dynamic landscape and therefore not so easy to control and manage.

E-commerce has redesigned business processes to enable people to buy online everything from groceries to furniture with a promise of delivery the same or next day.

Companies advertise two clicks or one click or three clicks as measures of effectiveness and speed. And with every click on the front end of an attractive website page full of pictures, reduced prices and deals of the day, a vast and complex supply and distribution chain is being triggered.

The logistics and supply chain industry is one that has been growing steadily and significantly, unaffected by the economic downturn and, quite the contrary, stimulated by globalised trade, the concentration of manufacturing hubs in just a few global locations and the need for moving goods from one side of the planet to another, or from a warehouse in the south of the country to a location in the north of it, as fast as possible.

Every click on a website galvanises huge warehouses – the size of many football pitches, filled with thousands of tonnes of goods – into action, and orders get passed down to pickers and packers, humans or machines, followed by trucks large and small that arrive and load pallets and containers, to take them to local and global destinations.

The workforce is set in motion by websites and technology. But the workforce is rather divided between the software specialists who programme the supply chain and website functionality at one high skilled end, and the lorry and van drivers and the pickers and packers that turn the magic of the click into a delivery of goods to our doorstep, at the low-skilled or unskilled end.

In many countries the low-skilled workers are a migrant workforce labouring for low, unregulated and often exploitative pay under unsecured, seasonal, zero hours contracts.

In between the click and the delivery, there is also fuel consumption, pollution, traffic jams and the brute muscle force of individuals of any age, who lift and carry packages, or push heavy stacked delivery trolleys. In the case of large international logistics companies, there is a significant level of automation; there are no unskilled workers, and the skilled people are there just to make sure that machines do their work properly.

And this is how by just a few degrees of separation, we cross the line between the front end and the back end of e-commerce, to contemplate the depth and complexities of the space between the click and the dynamic shadowy world of globalisation, geo-economics and geo-politics, potentially also staring at the face of human exploitation, economic migration and modern slavery. Not something that immediately comes to mind when consumers conveniently purchase more or less needed, wanted or necessary goods at low or very high prices. Because there is an absolute principle that typically informs business and quality management thinking – namely, that there is always an actual price for everything (even a bargain) and someone somewhere does pay it. The question is: Who? Which rightly and thankfully also triggers the related concern for "ethical sourcing" that goes hand in hand with technology and globalization.

Manufacturing, supply chain, logistics and distribution are industries that have vigorously pushed the boundaries of software development, automation and robotics and have been implementing related applications for many decades now. The first wood stacking robot was built and developed in 1937, followed in 1956 by robots that moved objects, and then the articulated arm robot for use in assembly in 1969. Almost two million robots are estimated to be working today in applications such as welding, assembly, manufacturing of printed circuit boards, packaging and labelling, palletising, picking, product testing and inspection, performing with high precision, speed and endurance.

Today the sight of advanced distribution platforms (represented by Ocado, Google, Amazon) is quite extraordinary with thousands of robots working in tight and precisely configured spaces to satisfy end game solutions for volume and speed. Today robots bring goods to human packers, but the research is ongoing to develop a robotic hand capable of the same dexterity as the human hand, itself a miracle of adaptation and key contributor to human civilisation. This robotic hand will be able to identify and handle properly any object, from small and fragile ones such as an egg, to larger, heavier and shape changing ones, such as a bag of potatoes, to geometric regular shapes where the weight has no direct correlation to the size, such as a bar of chocolate or a bar of metal. Once this is achieved, picking and packing in warehouses will be fully automated whilst the technical support will be provided by robot technicians who will proactively keep the automation in good shape.

And this will put an end to low-skilled repetitive work, exploitation or inequality allowing people to aspire, upskill and do something that makes better use of their human potential. Because it is hundreds of software engineers and human supervisors that still retain the edge on more complex and value adding activities, such as developing new technology applications and controlling the complex flight paths of thousands of robots. Whether this will also become autonomous in the future is an open question. As things stand, higher skills combined with human judgement and decision making provide the better option for now!

New generational values and expectations

The changes in demographics and the need for people to work longer – and, as things stand in most countries, until they are close to 70 years of age – require the businesses of today to accommodate within their workforce several generations known under different names, from Baby Boomers (1946–1960); The Generation Jones – also known as the lost generation (1954–1965); Generation X (1965–1980); Generation Y or "Millennials" (1980–1994); to Generation Z (1990–2001), who may be applying for internships and work experience at this very moment as many of their future colleagues will be contemplating retirement soon.

But generational classification such as this is not universally applicable across all geographies.

In countries under different socio-economic regimes (communist vs. capitalism or private vs. state economies) that may have changed in one direction or another (China, Eastern Europe, etc.) the generations are pre or post or in transition, and are also active together in the workforce today. One generation has spent most of its life under the regime of a state-owned economy, another one has been in transition, and finally the third has grown up under the exposure of a free-market economy and industrialised countries, aspirations and values, creating a very interesting melting pot. In addition, there is also the group of people who, around the globe, may have left their country of origin for political, personal or economic reasons, spent a good number of years elsewhere and then may be invited to or wish to return. One example is that of the "brain drain" of people born between 1946 and 1960 in Europe – in the totalitarian regimes established behind the "iron curtain" after the second world war, and who during the '60s through to the '80s left their countries as political refugees; they are typically a highly educated intelligentsia who gathered their life and professional experience in the free-market economies of the world. Today they are encouraged to go back to their countries of origin and share their expertise, but it is debatable how well they would re-integrate in an environment that is just managing to catch up on market economy practices and embrace a new open culture, given that they are likely to bring with them values, aspirations and a life experience that has little in common with their former compatriots.

What remains true regardless of generational or other labels we may use to identify groups of people, is that process and technology alone cannot align and harness such diversity in any one country or indeed a given organisation – quite the contrary; process and technology may well become jeopardised by lack of buy-in from the various groups, unless beliefs, vision, motivation and inspiration come into play in their critical role. Different generations and groups are driven and motivated by different and sometimes opposite goals and expectations, plus all the other external and internal environmental factors which together create a very complex and potentially uncontrollable dynamic mix.

It is a changed and new culture that could become the unifying factor to generational differences, and achieving a common shared set of values and cultural practices, meaning and collective purpose is the way to bring together a great diversity of generations and groups that are now increasingly compelled to collaborate as a globalised and diverse workforce, today and – even more so – tomorrow.

And this is one important and challenging task that the leadership needs to take on, a task where failure is simply not an option.

The advancement of Robotics and Artificial Intelligence (AI) in the digital world of work

Alan Turing is arguably the founding father of modern computing, and in his famous 1950 paper, "Computing Machinery and Intelligence", he asks the fundamental question: "Can machines think?" and proposes the idea that machines can learn. The objective of a learning machine has been the dream of AI experts, and the actual term was coined in 1956, whilst the field itself has existed since the 1940s, at least in modern history. Over time the field of AI was challenged mainly by inadequate supporting technology (speed of processing) and research problems, until the 1990s, when a narrowing of the research field to real sub-problems occurred (such as medical diagnosis and image recognition). In 1997 a seminal moment was marked by the chess game won by Deep Blue (IBM super computer) against a reigning world champion. Learning and speed of processing seemed to come together in a winning formula. Machine and human, bar the visual inputs, became indistinguishable in the game.

The modern "Turing test" indeed challenges a human judge to guess if the conversation counterpart they engage with is a human or a machine, in the absence of visual inputs (blind experiment), and if the machine can trick the human into believing the dialogue is with another human, the machine is called "intelligent". Examples of such wins include the success of self-driving cars in the DARPA Grand Challenge competitions in the 2000s, Apple Inc.'s Siri (based on DARPA's Cognitive Agent that Learns and Organizes [CALO]) or IBM's Watson and his victory on the TV gameshow *Jeopardy!*.

The AI revival of the 2010s was powered by the availability of information known as Big Data (aggregated from business, social media, e-commerce, science and government – all excellent aggregated backgrounds to enable learning), improved algorithms and processing capability combined. In addition, investment in AI has also stepped up.

The definition of AI varies, and broadly speaking it is about a computerised system that exhibits behaviour that needs intelligence or a system that is able to solve problems rationally, or act appropriately to achieve its goals in a given circumstance. There is also a taxonomy of AI as follows:

1 Systems that think like humans (e.g., cognitive architectures and neural networks)
2 Systems that act like humans (e.g., pass the Turing test via natural language processing; knowledge representation, automated reasoning and learning)

3   Systems that think rationally (e.g., logic solvers, inference and optimisation)
4   Systems that act rationally (e.g., intelligent software agents and embodied robots that achieve goals via perception, planning, reasoning, learning, communicating, decision-making and acting).

Venture capitalist Frank Chen's taxonomy of AI involves five general categories: logical reasoning, knowledge representation, planning and navigation, natural language processing and perception. AI researcher Pedro Domingos' description of AI is more organic and symbolic against human tribal models, with the five AI "tribes" described as: "symbolists", who use symbols for logical reasoning; "connectionists", who use the human brain to build structures; "evolutionaries", who use the Darwinian evolution method; "Bayesians", who use probabilistic inference; and finally "analogisers", who extrapolate to new settings the cases seen previously.

But the distinction in AI between the problem-solution aspect, on the one hand, and the performance and accuracy of the algorithm used in Big Data analysis, on the other hand, which has been developed by humans, who then became AI algorithms themselves, is not well defined. The boundaries between the respective human and machine operating principles and contributions are indeed somewhat blurred. The soft permeable boundary line between humans and machine in the evolution of AI is in itself telling of the fact that the "merging" of human and artificial is already happening and that both sides co-evolve and feed each other in a helical motion that establishes what may become in time a "natural" hybrid outcome, and in so doing normalises the "human machine" concept as it translates in actual reality.

But AI has been making great progress by chunking down bigger problems into more specific ones, known as narrow AI, which is specifically applied, for example, in image recognition, self-driving vehicles, playing strategic games and language translation, trip planning, medical diagnosis, education, shopper recommendation, ad targeting, and scientific research.

There has also been the development of "deep learning", which expands somewhat the narrow AI field at the moment. In a way, machine learning is a general approach to finding solutions for a wide range of problems rather than finding an algorithm for a specific problem. Machine learning needs an initial input of a lot of historical data used first for triage and then for testing sets. To recognise extremely complex patterns in data, deep learning uses many layers – more than a hundred – with each layer itself a number of units. Constructing and training such very complex networks is at the heart of larger and faster computers that have emerged, enabling much larger deep learning networks. The success of such machines has caused surprise and enthusiasm for AI amongst researchers and practitioners.

Machine learning aims to create trained models that can generalise and extrapolate from specific examples to new cases they have not seen before. Modern machine learning – learning from data – is different from the previous "expert system" approach to AI, where programmers work with human experts about the rules and criteria used to make decisions and solve problems. This new approach relies on statistical methods to find a path to a decision, which can then be used in practice. Their approach works even when it is not feasible to write down the actual rules for a problem. An example can be that of detecting user log-in attempts that are fraudulent, where the starting point can be data of attempts labelled as fraudulent and work a solution from there.

Machines today can achieve better than humans results on narrow tasks; they can also fail in unpredictable ways by, for example, labelling images that are in fact noise – and should be eliminated – as a specific object of interest, thus cluttering the process instead of optimising the steps to a valid conclusion. It is a case of misinterpreting along the same principles but with a false outcome. Another challenge is that it is not possible to have a clear explanation as to why a particular trained model is effective, because trained models have a very large number of variables – hundreds of millions. They could be models that work well but are not necessarily the simplest models that work.

Humans on the other hand can work with a situation where not enough data is presented, yet humans can make a decision because something just "felt right", which a machine cannot do. But just like with the progress from the third to the fourth industrial revolution, where the key differentiation is the overall integration of systems all talking to each other, and accessible from all/ any point of entry into the entire network of subsystems, the vision for future AI is the whole system – that is, general AI (GAI), also called AGI (Artificial General Intelligence). Achieving GAI/AGI has proven challenging, since the development of narrow AI-specific solutions makes it impossible to roll out an overall applicability across all problems and all cognitive and practical takes that people are capable of having, and because human intelligence and related activity can be deployed anytime anywhere, in all terrains, and has this exceptional flexibility of application, transfer, recognition of differences, and an adapted response to complex changes that is swift and appropriate, with great flexibility to be able to move from one objective and problem to the next.

Somewhat like the quest for a "theory of everything" where different aspects of physics – quantum mechanics and Newtonian mechanics, for example – could be unified under the same set of rules and principles, AI specialists envision a day when they will unify all the AI styles and methods under one large tent; a single elegant method suitable for a large number of applications. Achieving that is not about broadening the scope or unifying the many models, but it is about opening up new paradigms for the solution going forward.

The progress is relatively slow. It took forty years for a machine to defeat a human at chess. And the ability to translate across all languages rather than just between specific languages is yet to come, whilst even one-way translations have only become available recently and not with perfect results, because it is not a linear option to extrapolate from the ability to solve a specific task to a broad and deep range of capabilities that imitate or replace the general intelligence that humans possess. This is why the prediction of making significant inroads into GAI is not foreseen before a decade from now, with a potential for a real GAI arrival, unlikely before 2030. But accurate predictions are themselves difficult. Reviews of technology forecasts over the last fifty years have found that forecasts with time horizons beyond ten years are rarely better than coin-flips (Mullins, 2012).

AI technology is not only about "thinking" but also about action; this is why AI is closely linked with autonomy and automation. Automation refers to work – mental, cognitive or physical – previously done by people that is now done by machines but still requires human supervision and corrections if needed (for instance, in manufacturing, logistics or mining industries where machines do a lot of the heavy and hard work and people supervise their activity).

Autonomy, on the other hand, refers to the ability of a system to adaptively operate with no – or significantly reduced – human control; for instance, the self-driving car. And autonomy operates all around us, even if in less visible activities, such as financial trading or content curation, or self-repairing faults in systems, or in the detection and resolution of security vulnerabilities, which all take place without us noticing or intervening.

The human need to provide the brief and initiate the activity that thereafter happens without human intervention has been present since at least the industrial revolution. Such consequences rightly raise the issues of human–machine teaming or inter-changeability. AI and Robotics are particularly sensitive subjects since they are perceived as a direct threat to human employment and role in the world of work and in the economy. There is no doubt that AI will automate some jobs, but the difference now is whether the impact will be similar to that which we have seen before during the previous industrial revolutions, or much greater.

Machines are not only created to replace human work, but, better still, to complement it and give rise to machine–human teaming, also known as intelligence augmentation. Together, they become more effective due to complementarities of strengths and weaknesses. Humans and machines need not compete but rather partner, in order to enable people to realize their full potential.

The benefits of humans and AI working together are enormous. Smart vehicles can save thousands of lives every year, and provide mobility for those less mobile; buildings can save energy and reduce carbon emission; precision medicine can extend life and improve quality of life; smart governments may serve the citizens better and at a lower cost; and AI can enhance education. These are just a few of the benefits that can change human life for the better. But the magnitude of the potential and the task also needs to be managed and supported at central and governmental level, in tandem with business and civil societies, from research and development to deployment, governance and regulation, to delivery and efficiency, in order to thoughtfully and safely reap the exceptional benefits that the fourth industrial revolution promises to deliver, like no other before.

And there are a good number of sources to inform us about what the future of work may look like in the rising digital age, for example, the "Global Challenge Insight Report"; "The Future of Jobs Employment"; "Skills and Workforce Strategy for the Fourth Industrial Revolution", produced by the World Economic Forum in January 2016; "Preparing for the Future of Artificial Intelligence", prepared by the Executive Office of the President of the United States and the National Science and Technology Council Committee on Technology, released in October 2016; or "UK Taylor Review of Modern Working Practices", which informs on the global challenges facing government as a result of the changing world of work. What follows is an overview of such information alongside an invitation to personal research, to explore themes or professional aspects of specific interest.

On the cusp of the fourth digital revolution: impact of AI and Robotics on the wider systems

> We must develop as quickly as possible technologies that make possible a direct connection between brain and computer, so that artificial brains contribute to human intelligence rather than opposing it.
>
> Stephen Hawking

Today we are on the cusp of the fourth industrial revolution, which will be defined by cyber-physical systems. Increasingly, the work is now driven by the mind and not by the body. Some industries have all but disappeared and others are already fully automated. Many industries are now almost fully automated, particularly in regards to jobs that are hard, dangerous or repetitive. This fourth revolution is set to be the most impactful and transformational of them all because of its all-encompassing span and the way it will fundamentally alter the way we work, live and interrelate.

And the impact goes all the way down to actual skill sets that are increasingly required and those that are becoming obsolete. With technology at the helm of modern life, technical skills remain and are likely to increase in demand because it is technology that finds itself at the heart of our human existence today and we all need to know how to harness it. The skills in demand today in the market are vastly different from those required say ten or even five years ago. All those of us who have been employed for at least fifteen years – including the Millennials, who are today the main generation involved in the workforce and with the potential to become a significant influencing force in 2020 and beyond – have enough past work experience to see how things have changed around us. And the pace of change remains a critical risk factor, as it challenges our ability to adapt and increases the urgency of our ability to predict future trends. Nonetheless, we have to somehow plan and strategise for the future.

Individuals and governments alike need to respond to this demand quickly in order to grasp the opportunities and avoid or mitigate potential negative impacts and challenges. At national levels there is some activity by government to increase the importance and spread of STEM (science, technology, engineering and mathematics) capability amongst graduates and the young workforce, to have it more prepared for the future. But this category of skills and workers does not represent the entire workforce. With people likely to work into their seventies, and the work market featuring all generations from Baby Boomers to Generation Y, each more or less technology savvy, the need for reskilling and upskilling a significant amount of workers in "hard knowledge" is huge.

With changes in skills required and not required, the availability of new skills is increasingly scarce and reflected in the famous "war for talent" that gives the HR function and recruiters a problem without an effective long-term answer. This skills instability or shortage is looming on the horizon and has created a related new indicator: "skills stability". There is effort to try and close that gap but a concerted and systemic solution is not yet in place and time is ticking. Modelling for future needs is possible, but the actual definition of skills and categories of skills is something that needs to be done first. Easier said than done, since the definition of skills is volatile and moving at the same accelerated pace as the change itself. We are dealing here with a moving target that is moving too fast for us to catch up in our upskilling and training plans. By the time one such initiative is in place, things have already moved on again. Big Data could potentially be useful here, but again it is a matter of understanding what data and what models are correct and useful to begin with. Such rapid and impactful change is quite understandably causing anxiety around finding a solution that will rally all stakeholders involved.

But again, not all regions or industries or jobs are being impacted at the same time at the same rate. Some regions and industries or job families experience a stronger sense of urgency around this challenge than others. Overall consensus and adequate solution-modelling is being outpaced by this momentous transition. AI has become an increasingly normalised presence in our lives, alongside hybridisation of bio and artificial materials, from the discovery of new drugs to materials engineering, where symbiotic combinations between our bodies, the products we consume, microorganisms and synthetic biology are mixed by computational design used by engineers, architects and designers everywhere, from our bodies to the buildings we inhabit.

Industrial revolutions have always been and remain all-impactful, across demographic, social-economic and geopolitical systems and will cause significant changes everywhere, from production to employment and consumption. This latest revolution will force adaptation and change on everyone from individuals to business and governments and will create a significant ripple in all directions, across all systems, some predictable and some not, some destructive and some constructive. The drivers of change, spearheaded by technology, will interact in all directions and amplify each other across all demographic, geopolitical and socio-economic systems.

Technology and AI can be a major beneficial driver of change and progress if government, civil society and industry work together to manage and harness the impact of change and mitigate threats and differences.

Those in the growth industries, connected to the driving technology and close to the factors that cause the change, have the advantage of perspective and preparation for what is to come, whereas those that find themselves, personally and organisationally, in industries that are being overtaken and replaced have a harder task at hand.

Industry and HR leaders, who are in charge and close observers to this landscape, are the first to be called on to map a trajectory and a strategy for jobs, skills and recruitment across geographies and industries. A new measure called skills stability has been introduced to ascertain the disruption to skills within occupations, job families and industries. Their measure enables our understanding of how opportunities and losses will be distributed across the job markets. It can also map potential job dynamics across workforce diversity (age, gender, neurodiversity). Clearly, there will be a skills shortage in the market alongside skills that the market will stop procuring. Two examples come to mind in this regard; one is historic, related to the introduction of mainframe computers in the 1960s, when highly skilled humans, talented in mathematical

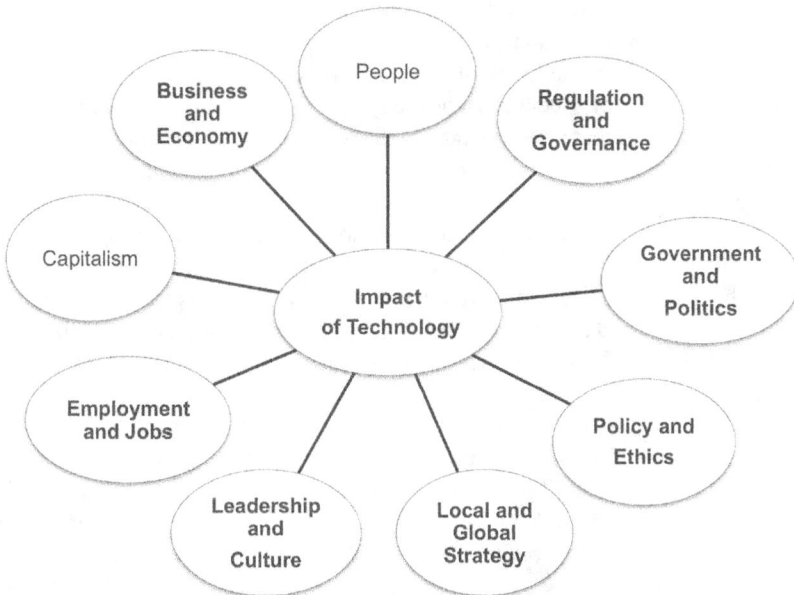

Figure 3.1 Impact of the fourth industrial revolution and AI

calculations, were used in very large numbers to calculate everything that represented the mathematical side of NASA engineering, including spacecraft launch and landing trajectories. Such persons were actually called "computers" in the 1960s, because they did highly complex computations. The introduction of mainframes to do such calculations at a speed impossible to even understand let alone match by humans displaced large numbers of workers in the field, who lost their well-paid and well-respected jobs, except for those who used their pre-existing skills, in a lateral move, and swiftly learned how to run the "electronic computers" by learning to programme them. Human intervention was not eliminated but simply displaced to another step in the process of executing accurately and quickly complex calculations. One set of skills was indeed made obsolete but enabled the development and use of a new set of skills, related but not identical, which caused the "human computers" to be relabelled as computer programmers and actual controllers of the "electronic machines", which in turn were now called "computers".

The second example is from my own career in the 2000s, when a corporation I was working for released a new software application into the global market, which had a strong take by clients. The skills challenge at that time was that there were only about ten people globally that were fully competent in installing and testing this software. And so the initial challenge at this time of change and introduction of a new method was quiet significant. The ten specialists literally spent their time on a plane, flying from client site to client site around the world to supervise software deployment projects. Those of us in resource deployment management could not find similar talent in the market to hire and needed to set up a parallel plan of training to upskill new specialists and in so doing increase the pool of capability. Of course, a few years later a much larger cadre of specialists was ready to fulfil the market demand and the needs of expertise that new products in that category were generating.

Both examples illustrate the impact of significant change and the way such an impact can be managed by adaptation and co-evolution, with overall long-term positive effects, whilst some of the short-term results may be negative for those who do not manage the transition effectively. This may involve an imperative change of attitude and a proactive mindset in the workforce of today, to remain dynamic and alert to changes, skills and upskills, and open to a lifelong learning culture. In turn, governments need to enable this activity to take place by all related channel, old and new.

Collaborations between government, industry, education and individuals are key to a successful implementation of these needs and adaptation to massive changes ahead. Multiskilling and the flexibility to be productive across a multitude of work opportunities may well become a strong asset in the future; an effective form of high specialisation branching into multiple work capabilities.

The polymath of today may finally come into their own tomorrow! AI education and related skills are needed to provide for the future and for the current rapid transition. A gap of skills and income is quite likely to be created, with some jobs and skills becoming obsolete, or "low paid/low skill", at the same time as opportunities for exciting new jobs are emerging in the market that are "high skill/high pay", giving many a chance for an exciting and rewarding work life and good income. It is also likely that owners or providers of intellectual or physical capital – shareholders, innovators, investors – will gain a greater power and impact in the economy, and so create or increase a gap between them and providers of labour, who in turn are divided between a high- and low-skilled workforce. This inequality is creating anxiety and disillusion amongst workers who have previously seen their input to economy valued but now no longer benefit from the same advantage.

Social media now provides a democratised platform to global users at a significant rate and enables all voices to be heard. And great access to information and learning brings along a great opportunity for cross-cultural communication and understanding of diversity and exchange. By the same token, it also provides for propagation of extreme ideas and unrealistic expectations. Privacy and security are also of concern, and there is a dystopian view of a world that is dominated by super-intelligent machines, a "singularity" created by an "intelligence explosion" that will gain control over critical systems and play havoc with society. On the other hand the optimistic view is that such systems will become helpers, teachers, trainers, assistants, who will team up with humans and so create a much higher performing outcome for society at large and the benefit of individual users and humanity at large.

Governments have to face head-on the cyber risks to state and individuals and properly assess what fears are founded and which not, and create policies and regulatory frames for managing such future developments. In addition, researchers and practitioners of AI should demonstrate leadership and responsibility in the way they approach and disseminate technology, considering upfront the longer term implications.

The same security risks are seen at global level, with international relations and security across countries. International AI considerations must be on the agenda of multiple agencies across the globe from defence to research and development, across multilateral institutions. Design and operations of security systems is currently in the hands of experts. But automating such systems could increase security across systems and lower costs. Using AI may well improve the ability for fast response and maintaining systems security.

Once again this positive outcome depends on the agenda of the humans that produce such systems in the first instance.

Impact on people

This revolution, just like the previous ones, has the potential to improve the quality of life for the global population, and so far those who have benefited have been the consumers around the world by digitally accessing services and goods. Ordering cabs, meals, booking tickets and flights or downloading entertainment and information have become regular activities for millions of individuals around the globe.

In addition, technology has now become part of our identities and our passport, everywhere from banking to purchasing, to planning our lives, to interconnecting to those we know and many more we do not personally know. Today people can leave their house and engage in any activity at all, from travel to work, carrying just a mobile device in their pockets. No need for keys, bank cards, IDs, tickets, entertainment materials or the packed lunch. All can be obtained and arranged via the mobile phone. So this reality will affect our sense of ownership, identity, privacy, consumption, time management, work and life balance, leisure, careers, skills, health and relationships: an endless list limited only by our imagination.

Alongside the advantages, this adoption of technology raises questions about privacy and security, about human capacity for compassion, cooperation and empathy; also about our social and communication skills and the time to reflect and pause and find purpose and meaning in what we do and how we live our lives. We are also targets and assets of cyber tracking, food for the Big Data needed by technology, and targets for personalised sales and advertising. In all cases, privacy is an omnipresent component, with related concerns about loss of control and use of our personal data. This in itself is triggering the need for an urgent and comprehensive review of moral, ethical and regulatory boundaries that span across all aspects of our lives, from longevity to health, cognition and capability. And as a result there is another trigger for a new contract that individuals have with governments and governance.

The matter of trust based on a sense that individuals were once protected by governments is now eroded and populations at large are increasingly suspicious and vocal about their feeling of having been let down. Lack of timely regulation to provide some necessary restraints to what seems to be a moving target of technology travelling at great speed is leaving individuals and national, political and governmental structures in an uneasy rapport disrupted by suspicion and a degree of confusion. From an individual perspective, this situation is unsettling and requires a resolution that needs to take into account not so much the present as the fast approaching future, which remains somewhat unclear. In addition, the AI technology requires a new type of data-literate citizen, who can use, read, understand and communicate data-related information and in so doing actively participate in the decentralised policymaking debates on matters related to AI.

New platforms and technologies enable citizens to engage directly with governments and confront them, voice their discontent, organise political activism and circumvent the plans of the establishment by any means, from complaint to political and revolutionary uprising. As a result, governments will be forced to review and change policymaking for public engagement as their centralised position is undermined and shifted towards a more distributed and consultative ownership of power.

Impact on government

In this unprecedented rapidly changing environment, governments can only survive if they become more flexible and nimble at fast adaptation and behave a little more like industry.

Transparency and efficiency are new indicators that public authority are increasingly asked to demonstrate. They need to be competitive to survive, continuously adapt and reinvent themselves to truly understand what it is they are regulating, and crucially to collaborate with business and civil society. Unlike in the second industrial revolution when they had the time to study and reflect upon an issue before making policy and a related regulatory framework, in a linear and mechanistic fashion, with a top-down rule, the fourth revolution is fast and furiously disruptive, across entire systems concurrently and this has placed policymakers on the back foot. They struggle to keep up. Whilst the new technology has increased their power to control the populations by pervasive surveillance, and control the digital infrastructure, they must also protect the interests of the public at large.

The fourth industrial revolution will also impact national and international security, and redefine the notion of conflict. Historically, international warfare, security and technological innovation have been intertwined and now there is no exception. Modern conflicts are becoming "hybrid", combining traditional warfare with new "non-state" aggressors and players. The boundaries between war and peace, aggression and non-aggression (cyber threats) or combatant and non-combatant enemy are blurred and uncomfortable. Autonomous and biological weapons are easier to procure and use, with potential for mass harm. On the other hand, technology increases the precision in targeting and in so doing the potential to reduce the scale of destruction.

The new AI technology is also hungry for skills and another challenge for governments is the adaptation and transformation of the related workforce and skills. Education in science, technology, engineering and mathematics (STEM) is a priority for governments, to address objectives such as economic sustainability and growth through technological advancement and change, and to research, so that they develop and embed AI-related disciplines and comprehensive curricula for the future workforce. The catalogue of related skills is comprehensive: computer scientists, statisticians, database and software programmers, primary education to knowledge partners. Government, industry and educators all agree that computer science (CS) is a "new basic" skill, the alphabet of the data-literate future generation of workers, who will need it to enjoy economic and social opportunities.

The workforce diversity, already challenged, is even more set back by lower diversity in the AI fields, where it is important to include people of all racial backgrounds, and gender diversity is already underrepresented. For example, I attended a one-day conference of the Robotics and AI week (24–30 June 2017) hosted by the EPSRC UK Robotics and Autonomous Systems Network

(UK-RAS Network) in London, and out of some 300 attendees only 50 were women. Such lack of diversity in AI research and design has given rise to questions about AI being developed only for a certain type of population group instead of a diverse AI produced for a diverse population.

Cross-disciplinary teams are more than ever before needed to research the impact of AI across social care, healthcare, economics, science and other fields, through basic and long-term research. At the strategic level, governments need to set the agenda for public debate; monitor fairness, inclusion and safety; adapt regulation; encourage innovation; and protect the public. As a result, public policy from education to economic safety, from defence to criminal justice and environmental issues, will all be challenged and in need of an adaptive upgrade. Government itself needs to maintain capacity and competence, transparency and effectiveness, to exercise its function and stay consistent with human values and aspirations.

One positive thing that the development of AI has caused is to increase our knowledge about ourselves as humans and better appreciate the exquisite capabilities that our human intelligence has to offer. Augmenting it by AI, under a controlled, wise and clear path ahead, can only be an exceptional advantage that we need to explore with optimism and wisdom.

Impact on business and the economy

Whilst even the best informed are being outpaced by the speed and complexity of change, there is the consensus that the fourth revolution and AI will have a systemic impact on business, alongside demographic and socio-economic shifts, which will have an equally strong impact on business. Automation has already changed the way people work and how they deliver the work; flexibly, remotely, on demand. The immediate short-term effect of AI manifests itself in automation, which has also been a part of the previous industrial revolutions and has created cost benefits whilst also raising concerns about jobs.

AI is likely to apply the same pressures, including pressure on salaries and income inequality, particularly for low- and medium-skilled jobs. By the same token there is a shortage of skills in the market, and the combination of talent shortages, growing inequality and unemployment will pose a challenge. Reform in education and waiting for the next generation to hit the market is not a viable option. In the meantime, upskilling is an urgent measure that needs to be taken by government policy, educational institutions and businesses alike.

Skills instability has already hit most businesses today and the trend will get worse in the next five years. Technology has also impacted how and when skills are delivered. In addition, it is changing the organisational structures and cultures – the employee-employer psychological and legal contracts – with wider socio-economic implications. The emerging markets have seen a rise in the middle class, whilst in the industrialised countries the gap between polarities has grown deeper, diminishing the middle ground space. The end-to-end value chain is disrupted at both ends, including the power and position that consumers and the market have on the service and product delivery systems.

Longevity and population age and growth have also reshaped the generational presence in the workforce and the need for new products and services for a population that is likely to live into their hundreds and work into their seventies, with all the related impact on talent pool diversity and social care and pensions, whilst at the same time increasing the impatience and desire for quick access to forever new and innovative products and services in the middle – this, alongside the "sharing" economy and mobile banking that are also disrupting the more established or conventional supply chain. At the same time the demand for transparency and social responsibility across the chain has also become stronger and more vocal, expressed by large numbers of individuals who now have a voice enabled by democratised technology and permanent accessibility.

In this light, individuals, government and businesses will have to undertake a collaborative and concerted effort to overcome the threat of the worst case scenario of such shortages. Using technology to better analyse and plan by using comprehensive data will assist the decision makers in their strategy. The implication of current disruptions to business models are far reaching and concerning, but they can potentially be overcome by collaboration and multi-agency planning and implementation of strategies that aim to swiftly respond to what data we have now and what trends we can plot for the next five to ten years. The fourth industrial revolution is impacting customer expectation, product development, collaborative innovation, and organisational structures, cultures and values.

All this activity, if measured by Big Data, can be understood and harnessed to envision the way forward and to adapt regulation and policy as well as business and economy design.

The move from single digitisation (third revolution) to interconnected integrated digitisation (the fourth revolution) is forcing businesses to rethink, redesign and reinvent their place in the economic and social world of the near and distant future. In such volatile times, business leaders and mangers are more than ever before required to understand the new world around them and provide adaptive leadership and a sense of purpose for their organisations and their workforce.

By evaluating the needs of future business, we can improve our knowledge of anticipated skills and recruitment needs and incentivise and support the partnerships between government, educators, businesses, trainers, workers and employees, to better manage the impact of the fourth revolution on business and the labour market. It seems that just as the technology itself is becoming interconnected and integrated, so is the response to this impact becoming collaborative, multidisciplinary and interconnected. All agencies, impacted entities and regulatory players that are directly or indirectly involved must come together and produce a coherent reaction plan that spans the breadth of our entire human activity from governments to individuals.

Impact on employment and jobs

Whether perceived as such or not, the impact of technological evolution has always caused a degree of anxiety mixed with a degree of hope. This reflects both our human curiosity, innovation and restlessness, and our relative aversion for change. In this light, a realistic balanced view may be the most helpful option to embrace.

The fourth industrial revolution need not be a competition or create adversity between humans and machines but rather an opportunity for individual work and achievement to be enhanced by the performance of the machines. Co-existence and co-evolution without competition needs to be the aim of this hybridisation. The real challenge is leadership and how to navigate these transformative times with minimum casualties and a maximum of benefits. And for now at least, leadership remains the domain of humans.

The development of artificial intelligence, 3D printing, nanotechnology, genetics, robotics and biotechnology, alongside smart systems for home use, farms, factories or entire cities, will help existing problems, from climate change to supply chain. And the shared economy will increase the power and use of crowdsourcing, and increase monetisation across all the range of possible resources, from empty properties to underused vehicle or excessive consumption. All these changes and possibilities are interconnected and amplify each other but also shine a bright light on what is possible, and the sky is the limit.

The AI industry itself is needing researchers, practitioners, educators, training, data interpretation and the workforce and skills that come with it; a significant change and demand for adaptation and resourcing, and not only in AI but across all industries.

The landscape up to 2020 for the workforce is quite unsettled, but beyond that there is opportunity for skills and employment growth, whilst the threat may gravitate to security and global politics. The projection for employment growth seems to be in industries like architecture, engineering, computing and mathematics, with related job families being likely to benefit from Big Data analytics, mobile internet, the Internet of Things, and robotics. On the other hand, job families related to manufacturing, production, office and administrative, education and training, legal and business and financial operations will be in decline, whilst jobs in business and financial operations, sales, construction and extraction are likely to flatline; all as a result of innovation, smart working, and automation.

The professional services industry will be automated and globalised, via online global platforms, which will enable off-shoring of project-based contracts and globalised crowdsourcing of skills, for delivery against tight deadlines, of highly skilled but repetitive jobs. Some of the major influences will be automation or globalised crowdsourcing via online platforms of high-skilled but repetitive work processes, leading to increased off-shoring of back office roles and a rise in time-limited, project-based contracts.

Healthcare will automate and use telemedicine but retain use of healthcare jobs needed for an increasingly larger aged population. In addition, the impact on the work landscape is also more complex, with consequences for family, industry and social patterns of interaction. For example, the middle class in the emerging markets will impact consumer, financial services and mobility industries; technology and innovation will impact energy, basic infrastructure and mobility industries; processing power and Big Data will have an especially strong impact on information and communication technology, financial services and professional services, whilst consumer ethics, security and privacy issues will impact the e-consumer, financial services and the information and communication technology sector. In terms of geographies, different regions will be impacted in different ways by different factors; for example, new energy supplies and technologies will impact the countries of the Gulf Cooperation Council, while climate change adaptation will be a major driver in Germany.

The change will not only affect industries as such, but job families within industries; for example, the computer and mathematical job family will be growing in the information and communication technology, financial services and investors, media, entertainment and information, mobility and professional services, because large computers and data analytics are the growth drivers in these industries. The media, entertainment and information industry is expected to flatten out, but not so for the computer and mathematical roles, which will prevail in the digitisation of the arts, design, entertainment, sports and media job family.

The same two-sided implications can be predicted for the information and communication technology sector itself, where the jobs may flatten out but the related skills will be in increased demand in the computer and mathematical field. Traditional engineering skills will see a decreased demand, whilst digitisation and innovative engineering and architecture will see a growth, particularly when used in the consumer, information and communication technology and mobility industries.

The well-established mobility industry, in its digitised and automated form, will significantly grow due to increased globalisation and movement of people and goods.

Significant growth is anticipated in transportation and logistics roles, as it plays its traditional role of connecting countries and industries in the wake of increasing globalisation.

The pattern emerging here is that skill sets will change in terms of demand but will also transfer from one profession to another, from one industry to another and in new unseen before combinations, all under the aegis of modern technology and AI paradigms. The impact is more complex and multifaceted, signalling that we must react and act to prepare for such changes and variations.

The new emerging categories of skills in high demand are new types of human resources and organisational development specialists; engineering specialties such as materials, bio-chemicals, nanotech and robotics; regulatory and government relations specialists; geospatial information systems experts; and commercial and industrial designers. Positioned for major redundancies are jobs in basic infrastructure, energy, financial services and investors, information and communication technology, as well as professional services, office and administrative functions.

There are related consequences to the changing job landscape; for example, in diversity across all new roles there is a major issue, since women are in a significant minority in IT, technology and engineering, aggravating hiring processes for companies due to a more restricted talent pool. Another change is in the business models themselves, due to flexible work and remote work, with virtual teams, freelancing, online talent transfers, telecommuting, co-working spaces all on the rise, and all redefining the boundaries between office and private spaces, between jobs and private lives, raising issues of labour regulation and shared work benefits for all; employers, employees and governments, alike. Talent resourcing is also impacted, with predicted difficulty in recruiting the necessary talent expected to increase. This difficulty is also determined by the country, geography and local demographics in terms of age and gender.

In addition provision of needed skills by upgrading and upskilling will be impacting by the changes. The current skills are likely to become outdated in a few years. In addition, the readiness of skills – not only hard and formal skills, but also competencies that current employees can use to do their jobs – will be an issue. Practical skills will also become outdated, due to the introduction of new ways of doing the same or a similar job via the ability to work with data, and general information generation, storage and utilisation.

Big Data will drive inventory management, customer segmentation and product personalisation and, in turn, consumer awareness and impact on how businesses engage with carbon footprints, food safety, labour standards and privacy. Such new consumer values need to be known and anticipated in the actual design of future delivery to them, to meet a new kind of demand.

The range of changes mentioned previously create the need for a new combination of skills by 2020 to resolve complex problems, as opposed to just having strong cognitive skills (such as creativity and mathematical reasoning) or process skills (such as active listening and critical thinking). And this catalogue of required attributes is likely to change again over time.

Strategies for the future of work and business

The impact and disruption of technology across society, economies, business, politics, skills and the world of work is significant and all-encompassing. But technology is not "an act of God"; it is made by us and it will be our mistake if we push back on unavoidable change and do not, collectively, take responsibility and acknowledge the need to embrace this process and make the best of it. As we continue to ponder over new questions and answers, choosing a positive view of the inevitable and using our energy constructively to identify opportunities and ways in which we can and will adapt to this tremendous future development, may be the most constructive option to pursue.

And there are possible strategies that could be developed around a few key aspects of concern that technology will cause.

Skills are going to be significantly impacted either by shortage or obsolescence or need of upgrade and reassignment. A transformative process that will eventually map the landscape of a new workforce capability to support and deliver the wide transformative impact of the fourth industrial revolution. We have an advantage in some visibility of the trends and forthcoming requirements and we have been through this process before, as part of the previous industrial revolutions. We have some history of successful adaptation and we can do it again; only if we accept the inevitability of this force and rally to action with clarity of purpose and aligned effort. We know about the need for certain abilities with related skills, and the need to engage cross-functionally, in cognition and action. In 2015 skills were clustering around: complex problem solving, coordinating with others, people management, critical thinking, negotiation, quality control, service orientation, judgement and decision-making, active listening and creativity. In 2020 they are likely to be: complex problem solving, critical thinking, creativity, people management, coordinating with others, emotional intelligence, judgement and decision-making, service orientation, negotiation and cognitive flexibility.

The expectation is that white collar jobs will be significantly transformed and reduced to jobs mainly in the mathematical, computer, engineering and architecture fields. Manufacturing and production may experience a decline but stabilise with a good potential for unskilled redeployment and technological enhancements. The greatest growth is likely to come from small but highly skilled job families, which are unlikely to absorb job losses and perhaps accommodate a small percentage of upskilled opportunities. In addition, there are job sectors like care and service jobs where the impact is not known, since they tend to be exercised under the typical research radars. On the other hand, it is likely that highly skilled people who may be time poor but rich in disposable income will increasingly hire service providers of low skill or unskilled services that respond to socio-economic changes, including the changes in longevity and demographics.

The year 2020 is on our doorstep, and not addressing and anticipating issues that we are aware about today will come at a higher cost to individuals, businesses, governments and society alike tomorrow. Just managing the "status quo" instead of managing the change – that for many is a hard thing to contemplate and accept – is not smart or effective in the long run.

Instead, individuals and companies have the option to use what we know and translate that information into plans of action that involve changes in early and later education, and swiftly put in place upskilling and training programs. Governments should be faster in "turning around the tanker" to support private and public enterprise to get into effective action as soon as possible. Unless the impending changes and disruptions are recognised and treated with the urgency they deserve, the way ahead will be more challenging than positive.

We need to move our gaze from short-term gains and give way to a more long-term concern for outcomes and implications, at all levels. We need to shake off the "startle" and counterproductive effects of disjointed policies, short-term lack of resources, misalignment of innovation and workforce strategy and the focus on immediate profit for investors, which together prevent us from planning a realistic, controlled and future oriented strategy.

We need to use our understanding that the strategy on skills is about restructuring, renewal, re-evaluation and redeployment of skills in a new, unprecedented way. This opens opportunities and requires interdisciplinary and interindustry collaborations to enable transfer and restructuring of new skill categories and sets that will enable talent acquisition and utilisation in a new way. Recovering skills from declining industries and packaging them with new skills will serve the emerging industry sectors and the businesses of the future. We can also use the Big Data and data analytics in a centralised and coherent manner to map the skills landscape across industries, countries, geographies and individual companies, large and small, to project the future and plan for the talent pipeline, for existing and new skills.

At the industry level we also know that the ICT industries remain as they have often been in the past, both agents of change and early adopters, ready for change, unlike other industries such as media and entertainment which – in spite of being highly impacted – remain resistant, due to the pressure of shareholders and the need to deliver short-term financial gains.

The future workforce needs all hands on deck and an increased inclusion and diversity in career path designs and opportunities to all in order to attract and welcome talent regardless of people's gender, race, religion or sexual orientation. This opens the gates to capabilities that come from all sources, including people who are different in the way they see and interact with the world, such as those with autism, or dyslexia, or colour blindness or dyspraxia. They can put forward ways of doing things and talents that the rest of the population do not offer so that work and outcomes of work, such as products and services, are created for all, not for just a segment of the market. Currently white males dominate the technology and STEM industries, for example, whilst women represent an already low and decreasing percentage in the upcoming STEM jobs whilst accounting for a higher number in currently declining jobs in sales, office administration, business and financial operations. The outcome may be that the advantage gained at great cost and effort by women's struggle to access work and equal pay and status with men will be undermined and potentially set back. In addition, diversity of age is also on the horizon, with the pension age constantly increased. People are likely to work into their seventies, whilst on the other hand the presence of Millennials will become quite significant in the global workforce in 2020. With no appetite for a "cradle to grave job for life", the Millennials are the "hippies" of the digital age, using Facebook as their weapon of choice and opting for clean, purposeful and healthy living as a lifestyle choice. Like the Baby Boomers before them, the Millennials have made their specific mark by rejecting a traditional career bent to hierarchy and authority and instead taking their employers to task on their record in social responsibility, work–life balance and flexible working.

New working arrangements have progressively been implemented but need to be leveraged to utilise an increased range of ways to create wealth by many in many different ways, from freelancing to independent professional practice, to short-term contracts and full employee status, all enabled by digital platforms where the location of workers does not matter any longer, but the talent and skill sets do. In addition, wearable technologies will transform workplace behaviours and culture, and encourage systemic change.

For government and policymakers this great diversity of scenarios mandates innovation along the lines of labour laws and regulation (which requires in itself a revolution of skills in order to safeguard the way the law treats work fairness and benefits), which will need to be applied by different employers or employment mechanisms. All industries and governance activities will have to change and transform according to new models that may be daunting and will require concerted effort to be adopt by all stakeholders.

For education, the strategy for the future means rethinking the current obsolete dichotomy between humanities and science training and skills, since the new jobs are cross-disciplinary and require a repackaging of skills to enable cross-functional capability combining technical, analytical and social skills. The training sector is facing huge opportunities brought in by a significant need for upskilling, training and reskilling – not only once but likely many times in a life – requiring lifelong learning for all who are employed or delivering some kind of work in different settings. Career transitions are likely to become a common place reality and a good, adaptive thing to do by most and not by few. Even the barriers between public, private and industry will blur with the need for a collaborative integrated activity to deliver a concerted approach to resources and skills management.

In essence, the impact on jobs and businesses is going to be significant, which is customary for industrial revolutions, but it may be the depth and breadth of this one that require a more significant and focused attention.

Beyond anxiety and considerations of individual readiness, subjective reaction and relevant experience to the current and forthcoming changes – particularly in light of the world of work, careers and employment – it is imperative that we shift our gaze from local and personal to the wider world of society, geo-politics and macro-economics, and how the ongoing changes play out and may pan out in the future, on a global scale.

It is from this wide world that companies are and will be recruiting their resources and talent, and it is to this demanding brave new world that working people will need to pledge their skills, motivation, experience, personality and creativity through the value they will add to the economic, social and political process, and the related outputs.

The role of Human Resources

It is about this world that the Human Resources (HR) function must know if not everything at least a lot, and it is this context, economic and international, that should be present in the minds of human resources specialists, business psychologist and coaches, at all times. The personnel function of the 1960's has been renamed the HR function, and since 2000 it has found itself under pressure to raise its game and be involved to various levels of impact and responsibility in: organisational culture, functional subcultures, management capability in supervision and first line management, leadership and the executive suite, corporate governance, corporate citizenship, environmental matters, work/life balance, ethics and code of conduct, overall moral transparency, the behaviours, values, beliefs, symbols, rituals and artefacts that all define the organisational culture, what the company's strategy is, who the competitors are and their weaknesses and strengths, the availability of talent and the state of the job market, the alignment between HR strategy, business strategy, and corporate policies and procedures. A very long list of involvement and responsibilities indeed!

A range that requires both specialists and strategists, a combination of the two complementary HR capabilities – tactical/operational and strategic/visionary – as a part of the HR contribution to business even when weight and sophistication of the two aspects vary, depending on the size of the company, the industry it operates in, its international span and its public visibility and liability.

More than ever before this important organisational function needs to be fast on its feet, to catch up and anticipate, ideally, what do to with the tremendous changes in skills availability and skills definition, alongside new jobs, new recruitment and assessment centres, and a new way of delivering work by a workforce that is remote, diverse, global, casual and potentially including AI workers alongside human workers.

In this context the makeup of the HR capability should also reflect the business reality and should enjoy a status that matches the contribution it makes to business, through its specialist and strategic input. Academics have dedicated and continue to dedicate time to research and map what the HR role is, or should be, or could be, whilst the function itself continues to define and redefine its identity and competencies, to build a new level of confidence and impact that can maintain credibility in the eyes of their immediate "client" – namely, the business – and deliver what matters to them – namely, the bottom line.

Now is the time when the HR function needs to reinvent itself again, under the pressures of the current complex, uncertain and shifting world.

Culture, leadership and HR

The beginning of the twenty-first century has significantly been marked by a string of events all pointing to the concerning issue of business scandals and questionable corporate governance, which have led to general loss of trust and confidence by the general public. The consequences have impacted pretty much every person on the planet, no matter how far removed from the toxic centres of corporations and financial institutions that have failed in their obligation to uphold honest business practices and a duty of care for their employees and the wider stakeholder groups. Financial institutions and regulators are still regarded with great suspicion, not to say animosity, by ordinary people for the severe consequences that greed and reckless casino-gambling behaviour have inflicted on millions, and from which almost ten years later the world has still not recovered.

A number of official bodies and professional associations have explored the circumstances and context of such derailed corporate behaviour, to highlight the importance of organisational culture. Unsurprisingly, the key ingredient for organisational functioning is its culture, values and beliefs as well as its definition of purpose and vision for the future, alongside communication, HR strategy and input towards building and maintaining engagement, providing an employee voice and promoting technology and diversity. These factors relate to internal aspects of business such as leadership, culture, strategy and employee participation, but also to the outer context and the bigger picture that involves the global economy, technology and diversity of the workforce.

In all cases of corporate failings – including financial instability and ecological disasters – the corporate culture has been found to be a significant and negative contributing factor. But it is still the corporate culture – albeit a reformed one – that can be a positive contributor to a solution.

Culture is indeed the cohesive force that holds an organisation together, integrating its people, structure and functions. But it is defined and embodied from the top down, by an organisation's senior leadership and the board who set values, define aspirations, articulate purpose and model the desired behaviours for the rest. The "tone" in culture always comes from the top, and it is also the top that monitors, enable or modifies behaviours that are in or out of line with what is desirable.

This is why the role of leaders, the board and HR – as facilitators of human resource availability and adequacy – need to actively take an interest and model a duty of care for people and values, both internally and in the wider society. Regulators have been called to address the problems of corporate governance and corporate culture issues, in relation to what should be the role of the boards, to support the CEO, whose responsibility is clearly defined, but who needs the inner circle and HR function, on the side, to expand the impact of vision and values across the entire organisation. The complex, dispersed and pervasive nature of culture makes it illusive unless actively measured and managed.

The board therefore must understand culture at board and business level and make effective decisions for the purpose of creating value for all, alongside the CEO, who is in clear view and held responsible for the organisation. In order to effectively create and monitor a culture, organisations should have mechanisms in place to listen, communicate, anticipate and react to issues in a dynamic fashion and in real time. Greater transparency, a focus on improvement rather than blame, cultural indictors that can be monitored, access and an open door policy up and down the levels of structure are all measures that will place the topic of culture on the table and keep it as a permanent item on the corporate agenda. The leaders and the board must be involved, must live and breathe the culture and align values – both present and aspirational – across the board and the organisation at large.

Employees and other stakeholders must have access to a mechanism of reporting wrongdoings without fear or consequence and be encouraged to do so as an expected action to prevent, correct or improve the workings of the organisation, as a result of a value that represents and respects the voice of an empowered employee. The HR function is ideally placed to take a key role as a co-creator and custodian of the desired culture and facilitate the relationships between CEO, board and employees. HR could lead the actions of this agenda by creating networks across the organisation that link all structural and governance levels and stakeholders.

A healthy culture is the only way to exercise sound governance and do so with free participation from all and for the benefit of all who are equally motivated to maintain a fair, thriving and sustainable business.

Policy, regulation, governance and ethics

AI alongside research and development (R&D) have already delivered benefits in healthcare, environment, transportation, economic inclusion and criminal justice. But AI also brings potential risks of competition in terms of unfair economic impact on human activity and threat to some occupations.

In this sense, private and public investment in AI has to monitor regulation and ensure that the existing regulatory frameworks accommodate the safety of the public and avoid the risk of harm that new activities and technologies may bring with them; or else review them, and overall position technology as complementary and not competitive, to human labour and capability.

AI-driven or enabled products and services already exist, with many advantages and attention needs to be focused on current policies and regulations to cover existing as well as the new or emerging applications used in the wider socio-economic context. For example in emerging and developing products such as self-driving vehicles, drones and helper robots, which are set for increased utilisation, whilst the regulation has not yet caught up with their deployment.

Such policies have to be developed not only nationally but also internationally given that applied technology is deployed beyond national boundaries and communities. The same attention needs to be given to public policy in regards to training and development and technology-related literacy, so that the public at large becomes competent in reading, using and interpreting AI-related information and in so doing directly contribute to consultation and policy making. This is a subset of the training in the wider context of the world of work with its own regulatory framework, in light of changing job families and ways of delivering skilled work, and the potential socio-economic division that this may also bring. Policy must address rising social and economic issues as well as ensure fair sharing of the benefits of AI, to all.

There is also the matter of decisions made by machines and ethical implications, as well as the unintended consequences that widespread and rapid adoption of technology may bring about. This means establishing transparency about data and algorithms involved and an explanation for the AI determination. Perhaps easier said than done, since some aspects of advanced AI are not understood, with the behaviour of AI not being predictable because of the complexity of the systems they operate within. The main challenge with AI is the transition from a controlled experimental setting to an open the real world, where unexpected things can happen. This raises the issue of building, verifying and validating a safe operating system for technology, which is challenging and lags behind the actual release of such technology to open markets.

Ethical training for students, practitioners and users becomes paramount in the light of potential unexpected consequences. Stakeholders need to have confidence that unintended failures are unlikely and therefore risks can be discussed openly and managed transparently, in line with human values, aspirations and ethics, that can be built into AI. This is how AI can enhance human intelligence rather than challenge or override it. Such an approach needs to be local and global and across all stakeholders involved, from AI students to practitioners and across business, government, educators and civil societies.

Cyber defence is also on the table, with related challenges that need in most cases to be addressed at a global level, across political lines, governments and global agreements. AI can indeed increase security across global and national boundaries but may also be a threat of equal magnitude unless governed by codes of ethics and practice that are agreed and implemented worldwide.

With security and weapons moving away from direct human control to automation and autonomy, again the issues of ethics and decision-making are raised by the possibility of machines making decision in ways that are not transparent or totally predictable, with undesired consequences. Such a matter of life and death is important on a global scale and it needs to be a matter for consultation and public debate, with strong leadership and governance at the head of the activity. For this to take place, new and reviewed regulatory frameworks have to be developed to ensure that the entire value and supply chain of AI utilisation in security remains overseen by ethics and human values and aspirations, shared globally.

The future of capitalism: how to make it fit for purpose

> Our population and our use of the finite resources of planet Earth are grow-ing exponentially, along with our technical ability to change the environ-ment for good or ill.
>
> Stephen Hawking

The fourth industrial revolution and AI will have a local and global impact – even if in different ways and at different rates – across the entire system, including: business, work, economy, ecology, governance, strategy, leadership, ethics and last but not least, capitalism as we know it. The pace of change has been rapid at both micro and macro levels. This is why it is now time to use an integrative model that considers the interconnectivity and interdependence of as many aspects of our reality as possible and is the new appropriate and nec-essary paradigm that reflects this reality, defined by globalisation, complexity and change.

As far as the history of human socio-economic systems goes, capital-ism has been a system envisioned to bring prosperity and opportunity to all and considered by some to have brought with it progress and possibly a higher degree of success than other system. And just like other socio-economic systems, it has experienced an evolution. The nineteenth and twentieth centuries saw entrepreneurial capitalism, which was focused on building business and was driven by entrepreneurial and visionary found-ers (such as John Jacob Astor). But this model did not create opportunities beyond the founders. The 1920–1980 decades hosted managerial capitalism, which was focused on process and technology, with management playing a central role, and as a result it became a burden, with too many managers and management fatigue and complacency. Since 1975, we have had finan-cial capitalism, driven by investors, short-term bottom lines, valueless or questionable value bonds, hedge funds and self-centred financial specula-tors, who only look after themselves, by way of speculating and playing the financial market casinos.

The relationship between business and society has also evolved in that the early entrepreneurial capitalism was philanthropic, meaning it was happy to make donations to worthy social causes and provide volunteer help to causes that were considered (through a moral lens) worthy of such offer. The mana-gerial capitalism and more significantly the financial capitalism brought about corporate social responsibility (CSR), which required an alignment of business with community standards, to demonstrate good corporate citizenship and con-sider sustainability; this was mainly driven by Millennials' values and beliefs.

This was supposed to mitigate risk and harm and improve trust and reputation. But as we all know, and have personally felt, since the most recent financial crash of 2008–2010, current financial capitalism is failing and is under question. It is clear that trust and patience have been running out, and society is crying out for a change. A review is needed of this capitalism that is failing the many that it is supposed to be serving as a proposed and practiced social-economic model considered better than all others. The reason being that while most people have been ruined or negatively impacted by the financial crises, another section of people – investors and financial speculators – have actually increased their fortunes. The result – in the developed economies – is an increasing gap in wealth and an impoverished middle class, with the division of society into very rich and increasingly poor, whilst the same phenomenon has given rise to an increasingly affluent middle class in the developing economies.

These paradoxes insult our deeply held beliefs about how a fair and well-functioning society should work. And we also have to keep in mind that prosperity and solutions to human problems brought about by capitalism have also come at a very high cost in terms of depleting natural resources and damaging our natural ecosystem. In addition, with economy becoming more and more complex, dynamic and, to a degree, unpredictable and globalised, the mechanistic thinking (supply and demand) that may have worked in the capitalist models so far is now obsolete and needs to be replaced by a new way of thinking, because the new players in the economy (such as banks, regulators and businesses) have introduced new non-linear inputs and outputs with outcomes that often cannot be predicted, and as a result render the old economic capitalist paradigm out of date.

Another challenge to capitalism is its fixation on money, as the absolute and single significant measure of success or progress, expressed in terms of return on investment or profit. In reality, having more money is not per se an achievement of success but, for instance, solving problems for humans at large – such as better health or better literacy for the many – and the positive solutions and change that this brings to the lives of millions certainly is. It is also true that money can be an enabler of such solutions, but only if it is indeed directed to this very purpose. The perspective and values related to prosperity should not be attached to the amount of money that someone amasses, but instead be placed on the solutions that many of us can celebrate and benefit from.

This was not the case in the 2008 US scandal of Mr. Madoff and his family business, an elaborate Ponzi scheme, where the financial value of the deceit was estimated by prosecutors to be an astronomical $64.8 billion, of which half of the investors lost their money.

In the UK, Philip Green and his wife, Tina, are billionaires who, between them, have amassed an estimated £760 million, not to mention ownership of two jets and three yachts. Whilst "hard graft" is a significant part of Philip Green's success, his business practices have also left many others worse off. Indeed his involvement in the demise of the BHS retail stores, in 2016, jeopardised the interests of its 11,000 employees, who saw the previous sur-plus of their pension fund – based on their significantly more modest savings for old age – put at risk and turned into an uncovered and unexplained £571 million pension deficit.

In both cases there are two questions that come to mind. One is: how can individuals develop such cold detachment from for the wellbeing of other fel-low humans, lose empathy and exploit or neglect the interests of – often – much less well-off people, who trust them with their livelihood or future? Another is: what would an individual, part of a family where the other members are equally rich, do with so much money? And yes, we have seen massive – some may say obscene – amounts of money spent on, say, expensive cars (each worth around one million) or people collecting multiple yachts and jets, and indulging in similarly exorbitant hobbies. But the questions of how much sense this makes and what is the point of such greed, remain open.

The success of CEOs, typically measured in the size of payouts and bonuses, is understandably seen by the rest of the population – often their employees, who struggle with mundane issues such as affording education, or decent housing, healthcare, or pensions, or avoiding poverty in spite of being employed on very low wages (they may have uncertain zero hours con-tracts, be employed in increasingly numerous low-skilled jobs or contemplat-ing poor job prospects) – as a downright insult; indeed offensive to the sense of fairness and an expectation of dignity and a normal, decent life, for the broader community.

If we measure the success of capitalism by looking at the prosperity for many and an accumulation of solutions to human problems, then this is differ-ent from, for example, whether the GDP in a country has grown or not. GDP looks at monetary values, even if the population in the country may well lead a poor and precarious life. An interesting example is that of Romania, where the public perception and opinion is that of it being a less wealthy European country, while at the same time it has much better economic indicators than many of richer European nations, including healthy finances and no significant debt to the IMF.

Capitalism at the beginning of a new millennium

Since 2008, the twenty-first century capitalism has been veering out of con-trol and it is in bad need of reform. So far, companies have improved profit-ability often at a cost to society (for example pollution), but then society has reacted – some may say retaliated – by imposing penalties; or society has regu-lated equal opportunity employment (for example, for people with disabili-ties), which businesses may regard as an additional cost to them when forced to comply. And so society, regulators, government and businesses have been set against each other, even if corporate responsibility has gained ground, not necessarily for the right reasons – that is, social benefit – but for reputational reasons and, yes, safeguarding the price of their shares, by being seen to do the right thing, even if, again, mainly for monetary gains.

These types of opposing but compulsory relationships between several parties as part of the current corporate responsibilities are known as externalities and indeed are a cost to companies, as it is money spent by companies to mainly "buy" a good reputation and indeed does not generate direct profit. At the same time, social harm – such as pollution and toxic spills, health and safety at work, employment inequality, child exploitation – do create internal costs in compensation, fines, disruption of supply and value chains and remedial costs, for big business.

To focus on just two major incidents as examples: BP has spent up to $61.6 billion as a consequence of the Deep Water Horizon oil spill in the Gulf of Mexico in 2010. The accident was due to cost-cutting-driven mismanagement of risks and a lack of interest in acknowledging and fixing leaks, but also a lack of systemic reform in working practices, which would have meant a delay in swift profitability. In 2012 BP pleaded guilty to eleven counts of manslaughter and the felony of lying to Congress. This accident is considered the largest oil spill in history; an estimated 8% to 31% larger than previous toxic oil spills, with a discharge of 4.9 million barrels (210 million gallons; 780,000 m^3). The interesting thing is that although in September 2010 the well was considered sealed, reports in 2012 still indicated that the well was still leaking.

The other example is that of the December 1984 major accident at the Union Carbide India Limited (UCIL) pesticide plant near Bhopal, India, following repeated spills and smaller incidents in 1976, 1981, 1983 and early 1984. This major manmade disaster caused 558,125 injuries (including 38,478 partial injuries and 3,900 severely and permanently disabling injuries) or, according to other estimates, 8,000 deaths within two weeks, and another 8,000 or more deaths since, due to gas-related diseases. The cause was stated as slack management, a delay in proper maintenance, a lack of responsibility for and response to repeated reports of incidents, the need for maintenance that preceded the major disaster of 1984, a systemic failure in operational and risk management, and, some might argue, utter disrespect for the value of human lives on an ongoing basis, leading to the shocking casualties of 1984.

These examples clearly position the government, business and society at large at odds with each other to say the least. There is blame, animosity, suffering and violation, resulting from the profit-seeking, corner-cutting companies, with the community affected by their unethical practices (including actual loss of lives). The government, caught in the middle, is at times also blamed for slack regulation and protecting the interests of big business rather than that of the community; at other times, it struggles to remain impartial (with questionable success) in its role of trying to regulate and balance the tensions between opposing business and societal interests.

This is an unhealthy state of affairs that is far from collaborative and that is clearly not serving the narrow objective of profitability, since shareholder gains are jeopardised by the huge cost of fines and legal fees and compensation settlements. This capitalist operating model has demonstrated that it delivers short-term gains, but also fosters risks that lead to massive losses of profit, not to mention damages to wider society and actual loss of many lives; certainly not a desirable and effective path to sustainable profitability and growth.

The new shared value capitalism: is it fit for the twenty-first century?

A new operating model, which has been positioned as "Shared Value Capitalism" (SVC), is proposed as the next better model of economic practice. In many ways similar to the framework of its business predecessor, Total Quality Management (TQM), developed since 1985 – SVC aims to create value for all stakeholders, from investors to owners, employees, clients and customers and be driven by millennial values of responsibility, mission and purpose – for a better world – to a global market.

The principle here is to embrace the idea that what is good for society is good for business, as opposed to the prevailing mechanistic thinking that what is good for business is good for society. Clearly the post-2010 capitalism based on this principle and a simplistic driver of market forces did not prove to work correctly and be the most successful economic model that it was intended to be since the 1800s. The issue that still remains open is, in a simplified way – as positioned by Marx – how profit generated by business is used and distributed. Is it used for the greater good or for the advantage of the few who own capital, which is the modern case of stock market investors and speculators and which is characteristic of the financial capitalism and means of production? So we are witnessing the end of financial capitalism as we have known it, and ideas have been put forward on what the next evolutionary stage of capitalism might look like.

The proposed new paradigm aims to refocus business interests towards the significant opportunities that are waiting to be identified and captured by innovative solutions, for the most unlikely opportunities for new markets at both ends of the social scale. For example, the mini financial transactions on mobile phones in countries like India and other developing countries with a huge poor population who nonetheless need to financially transact – even if with very small amounts of money – have created a huge socially driven market and therefore a business opportunity. With millions of people transacting amounts as small as one pound, the financial transactions that completely circumvent the conventional banks have been captured by other business entrepreneurs, via, for example, the provision of pre-paid phone cards, and run into millions in cash flow.

In this light, the shared values paradigm recognises that not only typical economic needs define markets. Companies such as GE, Google, IBM, Intel, Johnson & Johnson, Nestlé, Unilever and Wal-Mart have already embarked on the journey of defining and implementing what shared value capitalism may look like. This development is implicitly forcing the development of new skills and knowledge that leaders and managers will need to define and develop to embrace and embody the idea that companies need to collaborate and integrate social needs in their agenda of business productivity and work across profit/non-profit boundaries.

So the redefined capitalism, deploying a new model whereby a business opportunity is identified by tapping into social needs and problems that need solutions, also becomes an enabler and engine of innovation, where new ideas and the use of technology and automation translate into commercially viable outcomes and benefits for all involved and as a result at least financial savings if not outright gains.

But in fact, new technologies, swift processes and new management approaches are quite likely to increase productivity and expand markets as they deploy solutions to the social needs of the very markets they serve. The essence of the shift from corporate social responsibility (CSR) to creating corporate shared value (CSV) is that companies will leverage their resources to create economic value by creating social values and by answering questions such as: Could our design create better social benefits? Can we redesign our supply chain and value chain by using local community resources? Are our products serving all the communities and markets that would benefit from these products? Could we better use resources such as energy and water? Could our manufacturing location be of more benefit to the community? New design, supply chains, value chains and markets can be reached and achieved by new technology, processes and management styles and by overall innovation.

In addition, such achievements are likely to be realised by collaborations rather than competition and by harnessing both private and public resources in collaboration across lines and for greater social and community benefits. Such collaborations will be driven by setting clear objectives and using data to inform the decisions and implementation. And of course, effectiveness, competition and profit maximisation remain a part of the paradigm, except that now they bring advantages to all collaborating stakeholders and the wider societal and local communities.

Society will be improved and helped by business that in turn will benefit from new market opportunities offered by wider sections of the market, previously untapped. A win-win for everyone, and not just tokenism but tangible and sustainable advantages for all. The dawn of technology automation, AI, Big Data and new skills clusters are significant enablers that will make the vision achievable, if values, aspirations, objectives and related leadership and culture can be set into place to lead this transformation of the failing capitalism of today to another incarnation of capitalism that will deserve or possibly truly gain the attribute of being the most successful economic model of all time.

This new incarnation of capitalism will require significant fine-tuning, as AI and technology will this time significantly change the balance between the amount of input and actual value of human labour and the value provided by automation and AI. The relative percentages have been changing since the industrial revolution, where the ratio of importance was a relatively equal 50/50 to a current 40/60, with human labour having decreased in importance and projected to decrease even more down to an estimated ratio of 12/88 in the future AI-driven capitalist economy. As a result, the power and wealth will gravitate towards those who will own the 88% of the AI assets, rendering the 88% of humans that potentially provided labour unnecessary.

The obsolescence of human labour will place a large adult population in the precarious position of not being able to generate an income and it will effectively be dependent on a welfare system that will provide a universal basic income, paid for through a tax system by those who run the AI-enabled economy.

This division immediately raises questions of power balance, equality of access, maintaining a voice in society, fair decisions and governance, and all the aspects and challenges that AI itself is already raising as it develops and becomes increasingly deployed.

Introducing ethics in the design of products and services for the digital capitalism

The technology driven digital capitalism has generated a lot of profit and riches since the 1980s, with the sunrise and sunset of internet bubbles and the ubiquitous technology platforms for commerce, social media and financial transactions that have created complex and interconnected worlds where platform owners, advertisers, consumers, politicians, friends and foes of the state, and many more have come together in a vast and distributed net of opportunities for all to fulfil needs, wants, dreams and delusions.

Facebook alone has some 2.2 billion users, creating one point of call to a global market of the same magnitude. But after a decade of expansion and reputational growth, Facebook has run into difficulties caused by the lax way the company has considered and designed its functionalities in relation to data privacy and the safeguards around the use of such subscriber-created data/ content by other parties.

As things stand, the search engines – and we know who they are – are watching us; they know who we are, they know where we live and they know what we think. But who is responsible for the way information travels and is exchanged in this complex setting?

Is it the platform providers, the investors and shareholders, the company that has developed search engines, the advertisers who use technological platforms to position their products and services or the individual consumers who place information about themselves on those platforms?

Simplistic answers aside, the direct or indirect stakes, ownerships and interests appear distributed; so who is responsible when things go wrong? What can we do then, and how will we solve problems as they arise? And is there any doubt that things *will* go wrong even if only from time to time?

In today's world, the magnitude of negative impact when things go wrong is such that it is now imperative for questions of an ethical and regulatory nature to be considered and answered at point of design instead of being left open until accidents or misuse occur. We must now think of the very wide implications of interconnectivity and interdependencies, before we execute and deploy an idea, even when it looks innovative, exciting or profitable at first glance.

Higher needs for justice and morality are part of our human aspirations, but human actions equally extend from unintentional carelessness to appalling acts of cruelty and destruction, leaving us to ponder over big questions about variance and contradictions. This mixed potential of the human nature – for good and not so good – is something that we need to stay aware of and mitigate as early as possible and, ideally, before it manifests its dark side.

Making sense of what we know and do not know about the future

The world of the future will be mainly driven by technology and will surprise us with aspects that we have not seen before and are not able to predict. The impact of technology will be comprehensive across all aspects of human civilisation, from work to politics, economics, civil society, governance, regulation, ethics and overall culture. The changes will manifest differently in different economies and social geographic zones, but will nevertheless create a degree of change everywhere, with a level of unpredictable consequence that will challenge leadership, regulation, value systems and politics across and beyond national state and borders. For individuals, the impact is a matter of when and how, not if. It is about when we may be personally impacted and also how many years of working life we have ahead of us. Clearly the longer we need to work into the future the more likely it is that the changes will eventually impact us directly; and we better be prepared for it.

A useful exercise

With so much information, some already acquired in passing and some new, a first useful step may be to allow all this to connect, integrate and create a mental picture that is clear and provides a good foundation for further reflection on specific circumstances. This will be helpful when reviewing current work and skill sets to determine in which industries and professional activities you can use them. Ask the questions:

- Is this professional category at risk?
- Are my skills going to be useful or obsolete in five, ten or twenty years' time?

- What other talents, interests and hobbies have I got that I could upskill and prepare to deploy, should the need arise for an alternative job?
- What kind of a working environment is best for me? Am I equally productive working by myself? Can I tolerate uncertainty, in terms of my income and job security?

Depending on the answers:

- What business and work should I identify to ensure I land in a place that best suits my capabilities and preferences?
- What are the values that drive me and how able and open am I to compromise – in the short or longer term?
- Am I good with both immediate small picture and future big picture perspectives? If not, what can I do to improve my ability and tolerance to plan and hold both a short-term and a long-term vision for my working self?
- How flexible am I with change and derailments? How resilient am I?
- Can I manage uncertainty and stay positive, thinking that time and chance may well bring about solutions and resolutions that at this moment in time I am not aware of?

This process will provide the opportunity to reflect on future career prospects, what to do to improve them and be prepared for the future. Also, the way you have thought about your professional path in the past and how you may need to think about this in the future. Finally it will project such considerations on the background of your history and your professional, cognitive and ethical development to date.

This is a good moment to pause, reflect, increase awareness and chart a personal profile that will remain the one bedrock of your identity, whilst all else in your environment may be unravelling and changing.

The new life skill mandated for the future is that of being able to live well with uncertainty and turning chance and possibilities into solutions and goals for tactical actions. Enabled by developing higher strategic thinking and meaning-making, it supports curiosity, flexibility, hope and positivity in the face of risk through greater self-direction and efficacy.

Upon this solid individual core, there are opportunities to build new adaptive learning, add new skills, open up to wider societal needs, identify opportunities and innovate solutions. Building new collaborations and alliances helps adaptive behaviour and a flexible response to what the environment brings along in this shifting and to a degree unpredictable future world of work.

Chapter 4

Capturing the Zeitgeist of 2020 and beyond

No sensible decision can be made any longer without taking into account not only the world as it is, but the world as it will be.

Isaac Asimov

All change! In life and work

Initially conceived as a celebration of experience and knowledge acquired over time in career coaching, my attention was refocused by messages about imminent and future changes to our society and economy, caused by the digital revolution. I wondered what business and leadership may look like in the future and what could individuals do when faced with changes and forces over which they have little if any control. The answer seemed to be in an adaptive response and engagement with a new evolutionary approach, likely to enable us to work with ambiguity and uncertainty, by increased mental flexibility, and the use of sound judgement in assessing disjointed and changing pieces of information, to differentiate between noise and real contents, between what was true and what was not.

With a practitioner–researcher's mindset, I also looked at scientific models, philosophical perspectives and research that could bring relevance and structure to the empirical information I had gathered in practice and the research I undertook about the world of the future, in addition to extensive direct access to primary sources of information on this topic.

All this to create a unified multi-disciplinary picture of the world of tomorrow, and fit the many pieces of a puzzle that together could create a coherent and much needed integrated perspective.

But deconstruction is also a part of learning. And because there is more than one aspect to consider – the world, the world of work, the coaching process and individual self-development – it may be useful to better understand each of them before seeing how they all fit together.

The world is changing and the speed, complexity, scale and scope of the fourth industrial revolution is unprecedented making predictability of the future rather impossible. This impact will be felt globally and across social,

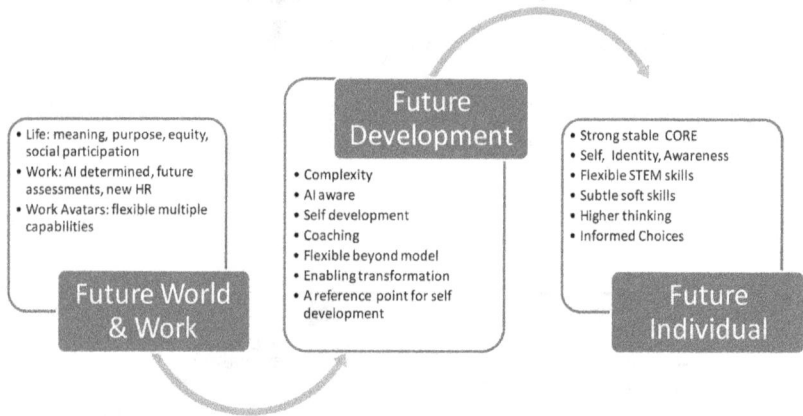

Figure 4.1 Future complexity and interdependence

economic, political and governance systems. It also heralds a new age of hybridisation and fusion between biological, physical and digital.

Our access to an infinite amount of information is constant and mobile. Billions of people are digitally connected and millions are physically displaced or on the move. Self-driving cars, 3D printing, the Internet of Things, energy storage, materials science, bio- and nanotechnology and quantum computing will increasingly bring AI and advanced technologies into our everyday lives.

New industries are being born, some are obsolete, and others are radically transforming, giving rise to skills and jobs volatility like never before. The changing nature of jobs today and tomorrow, alongside changes in technological, socio-economic, geopolitical and demographic systems, will further transform where and how people work and how they are regulated and managed.

Entire job families and sets of skills will be transformed, discarded or in high demand. Increasingly, the mind will become the driver of economies, and there is already a significant disparity between skills available and skills required – as clearly demonstrated by the ongoing "war for talent" and the new "skills stability" indicator, which continue to challenge the HR function and the recruitment industry alike.

Future evolution of the HR function

The skills required and the demands to make a significant contribution to business have seen the HR community itself change and adapt to the new reality of the world of work. For example, the "Future of Work" May 2017 annual conference of the Chartered Institute of Personnel and Development (CIPD), which is the professional organisation of the HR community in the UK, with some 60,000 members, has been focusing on the future and the role of HR in an uncertain world and put down its fundamental principles to lead those working in HR, through forthcoming times of change:

- Be a force for good for individuals, and the wider systems of organisations, society and economy
- Help everyone find purpose and meaning by contributing their talents
- Be safe and inclusive, recognising fairness and valuing human connections
- Exist for the long-term benefit of all stakeholders and balances the needs of all participants. Respectful to people, their contributions, and right to fairness, opportunity, development and having a meaningful voice
- Be led by principles, and evidence-based and outcomes-driven information
- Create value for all with responsibility for outcomes.

Having evolved for a few decades now, the HR function is again asked to step up and embrace a new set of skills and competencies for itself, such as:

- *Strategic positioning*: to contextualise the wider picture and project into the future the decisions of today
- *Paradox navigation*: to deal with interconnected, interdependent and often conflicting and tense relationships between multiple stakeholders and acting forces at play, and manage uncertainty with skill
- *Credible activism*: to articulate, persuade, direct and maintain a reputation as an influencer in complex, moving and demanding strategic and operational landscapes.

Dealing with the volatile "skills stability" factor and managing the existing shortage and the disparity between supply and demand of relevant skills accelerating at great pace is a critical task for HR. Technology itself may provide one answer, by use of Big Data analytics and mathematical modelling. There are options of modelling for the future directly and not taking into account the present state of skills, or using a gap analysis of skills between today's and tomorrow's, as long as we use correct data and have a sound definition of skills, in a context where we know that in fact we are dealing with a rapidly moving target on all counts.

Whilst the impact of "skills stability" may not be same, it is nonetheless felt everywhere. To manage organisational capability, technology can again be used to evaluate and improve performance and skills, by way of applications such as:

- *People analytics*: supporting workplace decisions in terms of predicting workforce needs and behaviours, identifying points that need intervention, and ensuring impact of interventions.
- *Turning employee experience into a consumer experience*: using technology for mobile access, immersive design, gamification and machine

learning support that is personalised to individual preferences, in real time ongoing dialogues with employees, and multimedia multidirectional feedback between central points and individuals.

- *Democratising data*: opening data to employees to access it themselves, as well as share it via internal networks (intranet, databases, etc.) in terms of availability, skills and achievements, so that a dynamic use of collective capital is enabled around matrix- and project-driven work activities, just like an internal trading platform.
- *Real time ongoing listening, interpreting and feedback*: assessing meaning and mood by analysing a large number of individual comments and summarising semantics, then enabling leaders to access this information and also engage with individuals as required, by setting objectives (Workometry analytics, Peakon) or giving real time feedback continuously (Tap my Back, Zugata) to teams and individuals, related to themes and trends; also making recommendations for developmental needs (Zugata) and updates and improvements.
- *Personalised learning by using social platforms*: access to personalised skill sets against a role and learning needs. Introduction to mentors/others and ways to apply learning (Everwise).
- *Cognitive productivity tools*: embedded applications (Microsoft Workplace Analytics, Google Goals) that capture an individual's activity levels across a number of communication systems, showing how they are getting the attention of leaders' input and how they are not; as well as drawing leaders' attention to the ratio between intense prolonged focus activity and unstructured time. This ratio can be set, as well as ranked, compared to peers.

But use of such technology needs to be approached with caution. Online open spaces come with the expectation of people to be "seen" and perform in a certain way, and not do or say the "wrong" thing. In such spaces, general group dynamics and pressures eventually manifest and – as we know from research and experience – not always for the best.

And what about those who do not wish to come out and play in full view of this "virtual village square"? If one is not seen this raises the question: why not? So how would such behaviour be "judged" by the rest? We already know that "group think" and peer pressure have often been responsible for detrimental outcomes. Big Brother from the book *1984* comes to mind because no matter the rhetoric, organisations are very political places, and political astuteness is part of one's success or failure at work, independent of actual skill or professionalism. "Thoughtcrimes" are not conducive to career progression. The power dynamic between management and staff – all thrown into this merry-go-round of public exchanges – introduces yet another dimension of complexity. And every day in organisations – private or public – around the world, mistakes or abuses are being perpetrated because people do not speak out from fear of repercussions.

We already have information on such activity and open groups interacting on social or professional platforms (LinkedIn, Facebook) where the stakes are not the same as at work, and there are no immediate penalties for "non compliance" to the group; and yet, the picture remains unsettling.

But such applications are already in use in organisations, and the questions on whether they have been carefully evaluated for impact of intended and unintended consequences, prior to roll out, or that ethics and governance considerations have been included in the design, remain open. Subtle and complex considerations aside, there is also the simple matter of workflow and time management – known to be a challenge for many people – that may be further pushed by the demand of being seen to be active in such virtual spaces, alongside the actual job at hand.

Factors such as stress, productivity, work-life balance and potential technological alienation by such a 24/7 information overload that is dynamically changing and with which people are expected to actively interact at great speed are constant sources of concern for the HR function, management and public health authorities, alike.

In many countries working hours are already too long. Employees are already asked to deal with hundreds of emails, phone calls, video conferences, meetings, routine reporting, performance reviews, profit and loss analysis, uncertainty about career progression and promotions, internal politics and maintaining the personal brand, to name just a few. It is a fact that our biology is unable to keep pace with the technology and demands that we have created and the cost in the effort to keep pace is in decreased physical and mental wellbeing. Stress, disengagement and absenteeism or indeed "presenteeism" are already costing economies billions. This alongside the huge ethical implications of such massive personal data-gathering on individuals. Issues of data ownership, rights, protection, use and distribution are a permanent feature of daily news.

Legislators, platform owners, governments and the police are often unsuccessfully trying to catch up with reality and its unintended consequences, including cybercrime, trolling and the dark web.

On the other hand, there is also evidence that such applications can be priceless facilitators for collaborations and open sources of ideas, but we need to be reminded that this is not always the case and consider all possible implications carefully, whilst monitoring the entire system for signs, one way or another.

The usefulness and hindrance of technology are mixed up in shades and shadows of unpredictable causality and consequences that have eluded the clarity of purpose and boundaries of governance from the very day they started proliferating some thirty years ago. But progress marches on and technology is also increasingly the key ingredient in the future of recruitment assessments, and this specific work-related aspect has also changed and continues to morph and adapt as a subsystem under pressure from the changing wider world.

Future of assessments and recruitment

From a pragmatic perspective, alongside the big picture about the future of work, there is merit in understanding the future evolution of recruitment assessments in the digital world, how this will impact the recruitment process and the candidates and also view this in light of the historic information presented earlier as part of the coaching trends and patterns (Chapter 1, assessment centres).

The digital world is defined as involving social connectivity, using mobile devices, benefiting from use of data analytics, and using cloud-based applications, which are already positioned in assessments. Since 2000 an increasing number of test publisher and assessment providers have offered online services. But for the early adopters – large organisations and global corporations – this service base has not been very effective, since companies have had to engage with a number of suppliers for different assessment tools. Today the market has synthesised the offerings (via mergers and acquisitions), with the rise of providers of online platforms that concentrate a significant number of assessments in one point of purchase. This type of supply chain optimisation has been driven by the procurement function of organisations, which has put pressure on the market to streamline the offering and simplify the supply chain to reduced strategic providers, with economy of price and resources to manage the relationship and reduce the operational costs.

The next challenge for both corporations and assessment providers has been to improve and modernise the candidate experience, to enable candidates to stay with the process (dropout rate may be as high as 5%, which makes the recruitment process even more costly) and see value in taking part; completing or enjoying the experience even when they do not get the job at the end of it. In other words, customers apply for a job to become employees of the companies they buy from, and the risk here is that if they get rejected and do not get the job they may also leave the company as a customer, which would evidently result in loss of sales. Therefore a lot of attention in the design of assessment centres is placed on making the assessment experience something that candidates will engage in, but also enjoy, complete and find the outcome, whatever it may be, a useful one; meaning that they get back something – reports, career advice, suggestions for alternative jobs, access to development tools, etc. – that will pacify even those who have not made it to the actual job they were pursuing (for example, Virgin).

In addition, assessments need to have mobile access, to make participation easy for candidates. This raises the challenge of multiple data display and graphics. There is also a trend whereby corporations develop their in-house expertise to create sets of tests and design assessment processes that reflect their specific context and pick and choose instruments that are relevant specifically to the job and the culture that is theirs. In this situation, again, they will connect with online assessment providers but pick, choose and exercise their assessment process and activity in-house. This customisation of the instruments is also linked to the intention that candidates are simultaneously assessed not only for skills and competence but also for cultural fit within the organisation, brand fit and social suitability. The validity here is contextual to the organisation.

Overall there is the question of whether the golden principles of psychometrics – reliable, accurate, valid, precise – are still fit for purpose. And the answer is: possibly not, because results are now sought in context. Fit for purpose "precision" assessment aims for:

- Targeted norms vs. generic norms
- Adaptive reliability vs. fixed
- Social mobility and inclusion vs. equal opportunity
- Localised validity and impact vs. generalised validity
- Individually targeted marketing vs. socio-economic group marketing
- Breadth of capability vs. narrow focus on cognitive reasoning.

So "the age of the polymath" may yet be dawning to acknowledge them as people of the future, whilst specialists have a great opportunity to upskill or broaden their skills within families of related jobs.

Technology plays a critical role in the evolution of assessments in terms of delivery and development. It is useful because it addresses immediate client issues such as logistics, feedback, tailored solutions and candidate experience; it disrupts the traditional delivery of assessment (pen and paper, supervised labour-intensive information is not properly or easily aggregated to provide an integrated picture of the candidates – it does not always provide feedback, etc.). The challenges remain around ensuring that it is acceptable from an ethical standpoint and also that indeed it predicts future job performance.

On the positive side, there is a new focus on candidates' experience and benefit to them, regardless of the job outcome. The candidate experience is really important in the new recruitment processes considering the number of touch points that candidates have, with potential examples varying between 60 to 120 in average and can be as many as 300 (considering phone calls, emails, face to face, etc.). Assessments are designed to still deliver value in terms of overall career orientation and other information that would be appreciated and, as a result, keep applicants on the side of organisations.

The new candidate experience involves enhanced convergence, personalisation, embodied technology and a consumer-grade candidate experience that ticks a number of requirements:

- Blended contents vs. different tests
- Responsive across devices vs. desktop
- Media-rich experience vs. text based
- Engaging for candidates vs. process-focused

On the other hand there are concerns about a number of aspects, for example:

- Usual IT challenges such as data collection from different sources to one point. Transfer of data from one application (recruitment) to others, such as performance on the job, or acre progression, or performance reviews, where the complexity of different systems no longer allows a direct feedback nor ERP systems, even if the collection of data is significant
- Issue of confidentiality, data protection and potential litigation related to differences in regulations and legislation; for example, between US and UK or Europe
- Automation that enables analysis of personality traits based on call centre recordings, or immersive situations, where people's reactions are being observed in virtual reality scenarios
- Use of biometrics to predict vulnerability in certain jobs and risk to health; for example, Lloyds Banking Group has been trialling immersive virtual reality (VR) for graduate recruitments, observing situation-based reaction
- Another issue is raised about validity and predictability and reliability and how to assure them; what about unconscious bias? Are relevant skills being measured? Can outcomes be predicted? Equivalence of predictability?
- The ethical implications of intended consequences vs. unintended repercussions
- The role of assessments in building a utopia vs. dystopia.

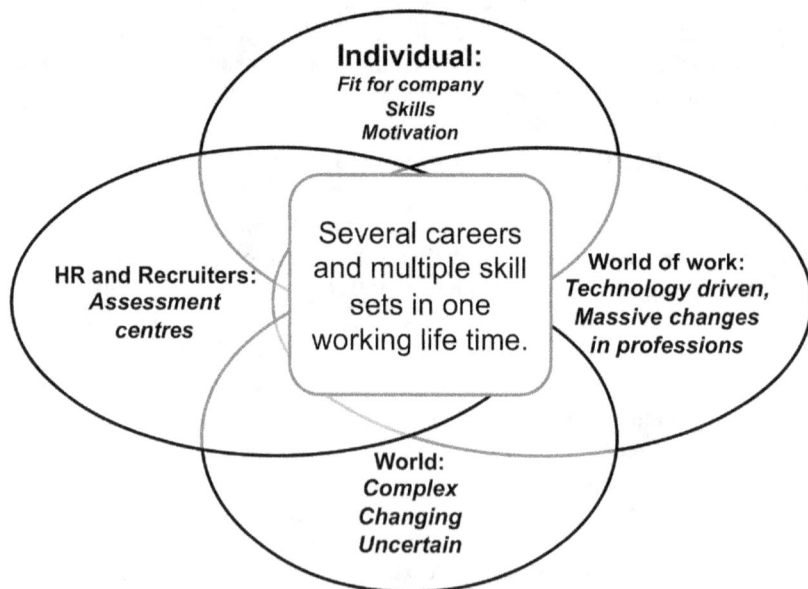

Figure 4.2 Finding a job beyond 2020

The future of assessments may be considered – depending on the point of view – at once progressive and having come a long way or, a sophisticated "weapon of mass rejection" that uses insidious and threatening ways of collecting data.

Data is already available in huge amounts on millions of individuals on the planet. The Facebook research programme that has been running for a few years now in the UK and has involved over five million volunteer users of the social platform (all details in the public domain) has yielded bewildering and, some may say, scary outcomes about the ability of the algorithms to profile people, starting with just a few "likes" as data points, and through data aggregation, to end up with information about a person, ranging from personality traits, sexual orientation, gender, race, parents' status, education, IQ, income and much more.

Our collective digital footprint is huge and in the world of AI there are no secrets and there is little legislation and regulation to monitor and control behaviour and outcomes. The brave new world of assessment, just like so many other developments in the world of work, has been spearheaded by large corporations, who have the need and the financial capability to engage with new technology to optimise their own internal operations and satisfy needs for scalability, to engage with a large number of employees and keep the recruitment and resourcing pool adequate and dynamic. But 80% or so of economies are based on the contributions of Small and Medium Enterprise (SME), which may employ any number of people from one to a few thousand. At these more modest scales of human resources, the practices of recruitment will reflect the culture and the sizes of these numerous organisations. However, far from remaining untouched by technological changes, the vision for this segment of employers is that they will gain online access to "assessment warehouses" where they can apply the DIY principle to assessment and purchase a set of fit for purpose instruments and processes that suit their need, budget and internal recruitment and selection maturity.

So the transition to technology-driven assessment may well vary in scale and complexity, depending on the organisation that needs it, but it remains nonetheless a prevailing future trend across the board.

Self-development and coaching in the digital age: challenges and calls to action!

> Humans are allergic to change. They love to say, "We've always done it this way." I try to fight that. That's why I have a clock on my wall that runs counter-clockwise.
>
> Grace Hopper

As individuals, families, small groups and nations we are all involved in what goes on in the world today, passively or actively, even when events occur at some distance. At one end, we directly feel the variations of the food prices in our weekly shopping, or the changes in cost of fuels, transport and services that we use every day. At the other end, we also get the news and learn about the activity, challenges and dilemmas that governments and legislators face at home and abroad, There is no place to hide on this planet, and all that happens on earth impacts everyone on earth; for better or for worse, sooner or later. This is something we need to acknowledge and to which we need to respond by changing the way we live our current and future globally interconnected existence.

The twenty-first century is a time when new skills and demands are being placed upon us whether we want it or not – whether we are aware of it or not. To adapt to its demands we now need to develop new skills of a higher complexity level, such as:

- Complex problem solving and creativity
- Critical thinking
- People management and negotiation
- Coordinating and collaborating with others
- Emotional intelligence and resilience
- Judgement and decision-making
- Service orientation
- Cognitive flexibility.

They enable us to manage emotions, achieve autonomy and interdependence, develop mature interpersonal relationships, establish personal identity and develop integrity and purpose.

To respond to these new demands it is time for calls to action!

Time for new thinking with dialectics and complexity in mind

> Look up at the stars and not down at your feet. Try to make sense of what you see, and wonder about what makes the universe exist. Be curious.
>
> Stephen Hawking

Clearly our world is complex and dynamic. This may appear to place us at a disadvantage. But one can equally make the argument that the more complex our world becomes the more we need to engage our potential; an inquisitive mind that can deal with complex questions and answers to reflect reality, be effective in understanding it, and best adapt to its challenges. We are chasing a moving target and make assumptions or prepare for what is to come with no foundations of equivalent historic information to use in our extrapolations and assumptions about the future. We need to accept ambiguity and become more astute thinkers, and there are already existing frameworks that can help us achieve that.

Dialectic thinking posits that the world is: constantly transforming and moving, subject to dynamic change, with only relative static stages, and full of complex processes of transformation coming into being and passing away, moving from lower to higher states by quantitative accumulations, which results in new qualitative stages, just like a knotted line where the station of a knot enables accumulation of quantity before moving onto the next level of quality.

It also offers the concept of triads, or a third option (thesis, antithesis and synthesis), as the dynamic principle of progression, where one state is challenged by another and the result is yet another state that emerges as a result of the mixing of the two; with, in the process, some of the old being developed, some cast out, and some totally new attributes being brought forward. In this way legacy as well as the present and the future are all linked in hidden connections at any point in time, even if not visible. In light of reality and the way we now look for the third option, and aim to introduce it in computing, alongside the insufficient binary dichotomy of yes/no, 0/1, certainty/uncertainty, the introduction of the third "I don't know" or "both" option, becomes imperative, as a direct reflection of our uncertain reality. And it is true that only thirty years ago, the world may have been simpler and less interconnected, the linear command and control and cause-effect paradigms worked well, and precision and repetition have been required to achieve identical outputs in large volume for the mass consumption of the society at that time. But today this is no longer the case. Embracing dialectic thinking and the yes-no-maybe options as valid could move our habitual thinking to a new level where it becomes truly fit for purpose.

Because the truth is that if asked about how safe are our savings and pensions, or how safe is the ecosystem or how stable are the political futures of countries and regions, we could answer that all will be well, or not; and that in fact . . . we don't know!

Complex vs. simple

We search for simpler answers
because we cannot deal effectively
with how complex reality is.

But reality happens all at once, all the
time and all around us.

Figure 4.3 Complex vs. simple

If there ever was any doubt, globalisation, technology, mass movements of people and changes in the geopolitical balance of power that we have experienced in the last thirty years, are all evidence of the incredible interconnectiveness and interdependence that we all experience. The financial crisis of 2008 has impacted millions and it is still felt today. Yet we also know that it has made many people very, very rich! One way or another, we are all in it, to win or lose or both, depending on circumstances. There is no doubt that embracing complex evolving systems thinking when looking at the world is not only useful but necessary.

And coaching with complexity in mind may also result in a quality of coaching that closely resembles the mental frame that individuals and coaches must have in order to fully understand, navigate and capitalise on all aspects that we face in the course of our daily but complex existence. The time of linear, causal connections is gone. Today we can no longer trace those direct lines across time and space that easily. And we can see the operating principles of complex systems at work. But complexity is not an easy option for us to embrace. It is met with resistance that prevents us from dealing with complexity, uncertainty and volatility, by beliefs, attitudes and behaviours such as:

- The reassuring nature of familiarity and repetitions
- The startled reaction to newness
- The prevailing assumption at that time
- The rigid pursuit of the "tried and tested" linear outcomes, with blindness to what does not work and external factors that make the context completely different from before
- The overriding pressure of getting a resolution and an outcome that is measurable and fast
- The power of influence of those who have the official "status" and refusal to listen to the expertise of others who are not hierarchically and formally empowered to have a voice, unless recognised as "experts" by authority and powers that be
- The "Us vs. Them" posturing
- The group thinking that overrides ideas that do not conform to majority
- Misunderstandings on the difference between linear causality and non-linear complexity dynamics.

And these are just a few of the many cognitive biases that impact our judgement in our everyday lives; for example, hindsight bias, sunk cost fallacy, herd instinct, reactance, curse of knowledge, confirmation bias, framing effect, availability heuristics, bandwagon effect, and many others. Practicing dialectic thinking is likely to enhance mental agility that in turn could combat cognitive biases, and increase open-mindedness and creativity when faced with important decisions or challenges.

Time to focus on the logic and the quality of information we use in our thinking

One of the key elements that make humans special is our ability to communicate complex ideas and emotions. And we do so by sophisticate processes which enable us to acquire information and knowledge and use it to some end, be it to inform others, or trigger emotions or encourage actions or create currents of opinion. Information and knowledge are shared and transmitted from one to many or from many to one or from few to many and so on, in various permutations. But because of its ability to cause a response, information has always been known to humans as equalling power.

Acquisition and quality of knowledge has also been the subject of study for philosophy, namely through its specific branches of logic (on form and structure of knowledge and how it is communicated across to others) and epistemology (on the veracity and quality of knowledge that we acquire through thinking and the logic forms and progression).

The critical role of knowledge and communication in manipulating behaviour have been understood by humans since the dawn of time, and this is why in early societies knowledge and communication channels were strictly guarded by those who had access to and ownership of it, typically the ruling elite, the formally educated and the clergy.

But the industrial revolutions, alongside the desire of the many to access the monopoly of the few, led to the use of the printing press and electricity to create multiple channels of direct communication to masses through books, the printed press, radio and TV. The traditional mass media did and still do have a degree of control over knowledge and information disseminated via its channels, by way of curation, censorship, industry watchdogs and legislation.

But the 1980s changed all this in one swift move. The internet, the PC and the smart phone overnight democratised, normalised and monetised the way information flows from anyone to everyone, about anything, all the time and around the planet. This has completely changed the dynamics in relation to control and distribution of the quantity and quality of information that is being exchanged globally. Today anyone from anywhere can connect any time, to anyone from anywhere else and send or receive any amount and type of information, all the time. This creates an un-imaginable volume of traffic that goes around the world and involves billions of people, at once.

The set-up of social media platforms opened the gates to "content creation" or generation of knowledge and information of all kind, and there is nothing left that is private, sacred, off limits, inaccessible or not just thrown in for fun in the mix of this global basket, where curation and quality are mainly left unchecked. Social media and other channels are constantly fed data and information that digitally track our behaviour, our thoughts, our opinions and our emotions. This data once again becomes power in the hands of those who can access and use it. As a result, decades later – some may say too late – more serious conversations are being held about responsibility, who it resides with, and how can we get a grip on the quality and behavioural impact of the knowledge and information that is distributed through democratised technological platforms.

The question of accuracy of knowledge has been raised at the highest level by politicians, public figures and states because of the significant impact that manipulating content may have on opinions and social and political outcomes, and the potential of information becoming a weapon that derails democratic and political processes. Studies conducted through various media channels and methods, such as surveys, quizzes, games and tests, designed to establish whether individual participants or an audience are able to differentiate between truth and false, have brought in varying and potentially concerning results.

In the digital age we have become accustomed to the notion of data with data and information used interchangeably; however, they are not the same. Data represents a factual description of the world in symbols that codify what we perceive through our senses, but such symbols in themselves mean nothing unless our brain contextualises symbols to takes content beyond our senses into structures that make sense and become information. Knowledge represents the way we individually process information and make sense of it to create our own mental map of the world, which we use in our interactions. Finally wisdom represents underlying common principles that define the meaning and purpose of acquired knowledge and information, widely shared by large groups of people.

Technology is data hungry, whilst humans cannot process data but need information; that is to say structure, context and meaning which help its subsequent transformation into knowledge and wisdom. And so today, we are in fact valuable products for advertisers, who are the real clients of technology platforms used as tools by business to make money but also by politicians and other groups who covet – for their selfish purpose – a seemingly unrestricted access to such an asset harvested from millions of people, globally. This exercise of power is questionable to say the least, and the scandals erupted in 2018 involving Facebook, Cambridge Analytica and other companies and bodies that use data – potentially under the cloud of questionable legality – have taken the perfect storm, building up for some time, to another level.

Data privacy breaches, data losses, theft and misuse have already plagued over two decades of intensive and extensive use of computers and automation. Observers and victims have spoken out before, with moderate impact on the will and decisiveness to put into place concerted measures to monitor, regulate and enforce the principles of protection of privacy and consent, on behalf of data and information originators. But when such breaches reached the extraordinary number of eighty million people whose data and information have been used unbeknown to them, this long-standing issue was finally brought to a head. The powers to deal with this situation under the law may be somewhat limited today, but this major incident and breach of trust seems to have finally catalysed a wider conversation about what is needed to curtail the technological invasion that has hijacked the lives of the many for the benefit of the few.

And so at an individual level, machines whispering in our ears what they know we want to hear, or fear, have to be prevented from perverting our thinking. We must take responsibility for the information we place in the public domain, what technological platforms we trust, how we keep them accountable and, very importantly, the way we evaluate – ourselves – the information to be sound and true, by pausing to reflect, think and make correct judgements about news that directly impacts our actions, decision and overall behaviour.

Bombarded as we are by huge amounts of communication and information through formal and informal, controlled and uncontrolled channels, we have become responsive to noise and falsehood as much as to accurate information and relevant knowledge. This is why today more than ever before there is an imperative need for us to pay attention specifically to the form and the contents of the information exchanges of which we may be a part, and to which we may be contributors, in order to be able to cut through the maze of disinformation and falsehood and be better equipped to make sound judgements and behave in consequence.

In some ways we seem to be in a new Digital Dark Age where technology platform owners and skilled users are also those who hold the key to power by having a monopoly on communication and information which they can use, often unbeknown to us and without our permission, in pursuit of a goal that may be useful to a few, but not to many others. Now it is time to pay attention to logic and embrace epistemology, to assess the validity of arguments and the truthfulness of information and knowledge that we process at every step. Now more than ever before, we need to develop and practice higher cognitive skills if we wish to stop being commodities and money making opportunities in the hands of those who collect and distribute data which encodes our very identity.

Time to evolve and embrace "the next" post conventional morality, which includes ethics in design

Technical expertise has played a strong role in the way we have developed in the last few decades. Achievement and pragmatism have been useful in pushing our cognitive capabilities, to advance science, methodologies and tools to the digital level it is today. But as our output is increasingly powerful, democratised and monetised, undesirable consequences of unethical behaviours have also made it clear that it is high time we considered what other or additional individual and collective developmental goals we have to set, in order to protect human values and integrity, in the age of AI and Robotics.

It is a fact that it takes a search engine about six seconds to identify us, in all ways including location, personal details, preferences and behaviours. Understandably this causes unease, to say the least, and immediately raises a few simple questions about how and when would the collection of such details specifically serve – or not – us and our interests; and how may they be helpful to others, and to whom and for what agenda?

Jeremy Bentham (English philosopher and social theorist) described in the late eighteenth century the Panopticon, a circular structure with one watchman – manager or staff – that could see (or gave that impression) all inmates of an institution and so kept them under constant surveillance and certainly enforced the impression that they were being watched. Bentham described the Panopticon also as a mode of obtaining power of mind over mind. In 1949 English author George Orwell published his dystopian novel *1984* about a super state where every citizen is under surveillance by "Big Brother who is watching you". Both examples are pertinent today in an age where surveillance is commonplace and AI and algorithms are used to interpret and use data in any way we can possibly imagine.

In some ways, and strange as this may be, Big Brother is a transparent oppressor; he claims ownership of his activity, and the citizens know that he is watching them. But in the case of our current complex technological setting, we do not know if we are being watched, by whom and when, and the involvement and access to information – and therefore power – is distributed, resulting in those involved being able to easily re-assign responsibility and displace the blame on to others.

And things are only going to get even more complicated as the internet of things enables the objects in our home and under our use to also become digitally interconnected and monitored by corporations and governments alike. Furthermore, our bodies too, can be monitored through biometric devices that measure and upload more data about our physical state on to platforms that collect it. Data about bodies, minds and surroundings can be and are today uploaded and stored somewhere, and we have little idea where and by whom exactly.

Faced with such developments in our daily lives, it is necessary to set, uphold and apply principles and make judgements on the go, all the time and in real time. This digital age demands of us the capability to evaluate situations and news and stand by what we believe whilst being willing to listen to multiple perspectives and adjust to individual needs of others, be humble whilst remaining focussed, test assumptions and take a positive stance whilst upholding integrity and principles and remain open and flexible about the ways of implementation.

Such personal attributes give way for others to express their own style and be at their best in diverse ways, enable us to take a lighter view of existential challenges, diffuse tensions, engage creatively with diversity and embody being and doing.

And we need to push attributes even further, to a new leadership capability that serves the development and enlightenment of self and gets out of the way of the development of others, is visionary, inspirational and spearheads a greater transformation. Charisma, vision and inner strength, developing an alternative view of the world, acknowledging the human paradox and enjoying complexity can all turnaround situations by using inner strength and personal courage. Being involved outside work, in a diverse range of roles and respon-sibilities, can take such attributes and capabilities to wider groups and provide constructive answers to socials needs.

Such developmental models blend capabilities that involve judgement, higher complex thinking, principles, purpose, relationships with others and a vision for positive impact all around, alongside the ability to work flexibly and creatively with tension, contradictions and diversity, and turn chaos into a posi-tive transformative energy.

Because they need – adaptively – to closely map to the demands of the world of today; complex, diverse, chaotic, polarised and full of paradoxes. A dynamic mixture of potential for the objectionable and the sublime which present to us a mixture of violence, destruction and conflict with incredible achievements in science, technology, culture and innovation for the greater good, represented, for example, by the technology for war and the technology for health and protection of human life.

Clearly, achievement, innovation, intelligence, pragmatism and positivism are no longer sufficient. A mandatory focus on ethics and principles that really reflect the imminent changes in accessing and using data – a specific enabler of digitisation and key source of power and wealth in the future – as a result of democratised technology, cannot be emphasised strongly enough.

Aristotle talked about logos, ethos and pathos as three pillars of persuasion, and indeed our intelligence and logic, as used in technology and AI, cannot be separated from our emotions and the ethics that surround how we use the appli-cations that our extraordinary mind can create through its cognitive function.

Every age has presented different and specific ethical and moral dilemmas, and the digital world of today is no different. In this digital world data is the "new oil", and platforms like Amazon, Google, Apple and Facebook gather data about billions of users. When such data is acquired across nations and from a global source, and can then be utilised globally by multiple interested parties, for commercial and political purposes, the landscape that results is much more complicated and therefore less easy to manage, control, regulate and govern. With a combination of no regulation, self-regulation and regulation, in various degrees that varies from country to country, but with a client base that counts billions of people, globally, these companies have acquired huge power and influence and an ability to have a say in policy and politics, directly or indi-rectly. In addition people have lost confidence in the governance systems whilst governments have lost the edge of protective and regulatory powers that they were supposed to have to safeguard liberty and protect individuals at large.

The Panopticon comes to mind in relation to CCTV surveillance but equally pertinent is the question: what about us being objects of data capture in our pri-vate space, at home as we use PCs, tablets and our mobile phones for example, to swipe between screens and check various URLs? In this case there is no "eye" watching us at home, or is there? Soon Google's Brillo and Apple's HomeKit will enable everything from washing machines to sex toys to communicate between them (the internet of things) whilst GPS footwear and biometric wearable devices collect all they can about our bodies, adding to the vast data gathering baskets – commercial and government – that are already in place.

And so the exposure is going to get even greater with our objects and our bodies also going online to be captured by "the others" beyond the technology platforms that gather all this wealth of details about us. We do not know where that body of data begins and ends, and this may give us a sense of privacy, security and anonymity. But people live a lot of their lives online, and so the exposure is significant whilst the preoccupation with consequences is not at the forefront of people's mind.

The whistle blowers have got their work cut out for them, and their revelations provide now and again a real wakeup call to the wider society. But society does not appear to be cohesively respectful and encouraging of "whistle blowing". More often than not people who take such risks – because telling the truth always comes with some risk – end up suffering serious consequences and a life that is never normal again, as a price they pay for moral rectitude. They lose jobs, are rejected by peers and may end up legally pursued themselves by various entities. No wonder the truth comes out significantly less often than the frequency with which breaches of trust and bad behaviour occur.

Between the information and surveillance that government agencies collect and the data that commercial organisations and social platforms collect, there is a lot of data that is being held about individuals, with little clarity on why, how and when exactly it is used. And this should invite us to reflect on how much interest do we really take in what goes on, beyond our immediate and safe universe that we think we control. We should be curious about and more engaged with the wider and specific aspects that this age of technology, combined with overt and covert financial and political interests and gains, present to us. As consumers we should exercise our voice and ask that products and services are designed with the users in mind and defend consumers' rights to opt out, to have a voice, or to retain privacy – for example – and make sure that businesses rank such considerations above profit.

This is a time when we should individually develop the capability to play a role and respond by asserting the need of including ethics in initial design and develop our own ability to define and apply "the next" post-conventional morality that is fit for purpose and reflects the immediacy of events unfolding in our current digital capitalism.

Time for a new "Digital Adaptive Leadership" to pro-actively enable and adaptively respond to the digital future

The current disruptive threats to the existing order are quite significant, and whilst some outcomes can be predicted others cannot. In addition, there is the matter of speed of change and of transformations and the unravelling of the existing order. In this light the importance of providing leadership and strategy are self evident. But we know from experience and research that leadership and strategic capabilities are not common and not easily developed even in those with high potential.

This is a time when a new form of leadership is imperative; because notwithstanding the urgency, leadership in organisations is a moving target, and developing such an organisational capability in itself has so far proved to be a challenge. Yet new leadership is needed to implement a series of integrated measures that can prepare us for the future. We need to increase diversity and attract women in the workforce to join the emerging opportunities in STEM jobs as well as leverage the experience of the older workforce; open up collaborations within and between industries, but also with educators and government; hire more short-term employees and international talent; encourage and empower polymaths to innovate and contribute across different fields of practice, support employees' mobility and internal job rotation with related career management options, and support a government strategy connected to business in order to redeploy talent and skills across industries at a national and international level.

All these critical aspects require a new type of leadership; a leadership that adaptively responds and pro-actively enables the new digital economy and the new digital world.

Because right now, actions lag behind both requirements and the rhetoric or intentions expressed by a leadership that has been outpaced by change and is slow to implement wider and faster applications of the strategic vision, if the vision indeed matches the actual needs.

The new "Digital Adaptive Leadership" will confidently face the relentless march of technology with related transformations and changes – which understandably right now cause anxiety, confusion and a sense of powerlessness – with flexibility, agility and resilience. Because technology is made by humans, and just as we have demonstrated innovation in creating AI, we must develop new leaders who take responsibility for the way technology will impact our lives and future.

The "Digital Adaptive Leader" will work collaboratively, to develop a shared purpose and vision that enables collaboration and cooperation well beyond the boundaries of organisations or nations, by aligning local action to a global vision intended to harness potential and creativity with technology, whilst minimising risks and harm to individuals, society and the planet.

Such a global, innovative and adaptive perspective is currently hindered by mechanistic thinking and by a narrow focus, which clearly indicates that we must look deeper and change our ethics, values and beliefs and replace them with new attitudes and behaviours. This will lead to a more sensitive and effective application of a vision that embraces the digital age, by being complex, integrative, collaborative and solution-focused, for an outcome that will benefit the many and not just the few.

The new "Digital Adaptive Leader" will embrace inclusion and harness diversity, build consensus and unity of purpose and action for all stakeholders, from government to business to individuals. Sharing responsibility and bringing in contributions is the way we can collectively, meet our challenges under a digital adaptive leadership that embraces technology. This should provide a fit for purpose visionary strategy, a flexible and enabling response, multi-stakeholder partnerships across disciplines and delivery bodies, and allow fluid boundaries. A "Digital Adaptive Leader" should embody capabilities that best reflect the reality of an emergent changing world – full of promise and challenge – unfolding in the guise of our shared digital future.

Time to pursue a capabilities framework instead of the competencies framework

The world has changed and requires us to exercise a sustained higher order of thinking and use meaning and purpose as a guiding approach to the uncertainty of events and lack of historic data to extrapolate and predict the future. Causality today is no longer linear due to increased interdependence and interconnectivity of our global setting, which has been driven by technology and has caused shifting boundaries in professions and skills, geo-economic rankings, regulation, governance and politics, to name just a few. This state of affairs calls for a range of skills that no longer rest within the competencies framework but calls for capabilities that go beyond the linear box-ticking evaluation of resources and linear prediction of outcomes. For over two decades the world has been squared and neatly arranged on a tick list of competencies applied in recruitment, assessment, accreditation and rigid performance review processes. It is a method that is based on: behaviour checklists, prediction of future performance based on the past, individually checking sets for narrow isolated activities, demanding linear alignment between explicit criteria and explicit evidence provision, and use of a "black box" model that evaluates each individual against the same simplified common denominators of a "one size fits all" set of criteria.

The alternative to this approach is that of capability assessment, which looks at: individuality and diversity of a person, having a holistic approach to tasks and relations as a source of good performance, appreciating individual knowledge, experience and meaning-making as attributes for future success, valuing and being curious about a person's richness of knowledge and developed self, holding a contextual and systemic perspective in personal and professional interactions.

The suitability of the capability approach to our times is self-evident, and this is a call to action for coaches, HR practitioners, assessment designers, recruiters, management and individuals to embrace a times-appropriate, fit-for-purpose framework, particularly when it comes to complex jobs, or complex environments, management and leadership roles, or evaluating highly experienced and highly skilled people. Being able to assess, develop and utilise resources at an appropriate level by embracing a capability evaluation model will increase our chances to successfully deal with uncertainty by having the right people for the right task at the right level, as one critical way of facing the future with hope and the confidence that "we can".

Time to pursue multiple interests and become a successful polymath

Popular wisdom has been cautious in its view of polymaths with sayings such as "Jack of all trades and master of none (UK), "Nine trades and the tenth is . . . hunger" (Estonia) and "Knives everywhere, yet none sharp" (China). It may well be because polymaths are not representatives of the majority population and we know that society normalises a common denominator and maintains social cohesion by discouraging deviations from the norm. But hypothesis aside, it is a fact that polymaths have existed since time immemorial, have questioned and challenged the status quo and have embodied significant change, innovation and progress.

It is the polymaths who have pushed civilisation forward and their impact remains significant to this day even if their contributions have been made centuries ago. Names such as: Newton, Galileo, Aristotle, Kepler, Abbesse Hildegard of Bingen, Doroteea Bucca, Maria Sybilla Merian, Leonardo Da Vinci, Descartes, Huygens, Maria Wnkelmann, Laplace, Faraday, Pasteur, Ptolemy remain relevant to us, as well as those that came after them, such as: Hooke, Leibniz, Euler, Darwin, Ada Lovelace, Marie Curie, Richard Feynman, Ben Franklin, Lise Maitner, Thomas Edison, Rosalind Franklin, Rear Admiral Grace Hopper, Barbara McClintoc, to name just a few. In modern times, it is the polymaths again who have been leading innovations with Bill Gates, Steve Jobs, Warren Buffett, Larry Page, and Jeff Bezos, as examples. The contributions of polymaths such as Piaget and Vygotsky – significant in the context of this book – have been explored in some detail in chapter two.

This is a long list of names we recognise, yet by no means comprehensive. And just like the academic – practitioner divide, the divide generalist – specialist has also been around for a long time, with specialists acquiring increasingly more expertise and recognition for a specific domain, whilst the generalists have been regarded with relative caution on the quality of their contributions in the several fields they embrace.

Yet it is the polymath who have driven progress and innovation and have given rise to new hybrid industries such as biotech, green tech, internet of things, mobile app development, internet contents marketing, alongside new hybrid fields of science such as quantum biology, nutrigenomics and bioinformatics which have merged different domains of thinking, into new single disciplines; very much following Leonardo Da Vinci's inspiring call to: "Study the science of art. Study the art of science. Develop your senses – especially learn how to see. Realize that everything connects to everything else."

And there is no better time than now to do just that, and indulge one's curiosity and appetite for learning. Today portable 24/7 technology enables endless access to multiple democratised and free sources of information in an unprecedented way. With unlimited access to unlimited information, today is the time where there are no restrictions to learning new subjects and skills; a perfect time to fulfil motivations, aspirations and dreams, without hindrance or delay. This opportunity exists for all, regardless of gender, class, age, creed, thinking or learning style. Any preference can be satisfied by what is available to all. Structured or unstructured, self directed or mediated, e-learning is open to all and many people indeed use this unprecedented advantage.

On a macro level, complexity and dialectic principles move the world and we – individuals and society – need to adapt to this increasingly dynamic and unpredictable wider context. Therefore, the new evaluation, restructure and redeployment of skills – necessary for our adaptive and proactive engagement with a world, itself, a hybrid between humans and technology, between biology and machines – has to transcend narrow specialism.

And the future is hungry for polymaths. With capability for complex thinking and complex problem solving and need for innovation in the digital age, polymath capabilities are needed more than ever before. With access to free information on every imaginable subject, satisfying people's appetite for learning, curiosity and multiple interests, there are no barriers today to becoming a polymath and if so inclined, follow your motivation and belief in the contributions you can make across a number of fields of interest.

Modern polymaths build an unusual combination of skills and accumulate knowledge across at least three areas of expertise, integrate them in a top set of skills that they use with new ways of thinking, then deploy them in specific and possibly successive areas of need or core area of practice/expertise, over and over again, by using flexible and adaptive mental models.

Combining psychology, neuroscience, sociology and evolution to understand, influence or improve the way they manifest in the complex histories of peoples' life and work (explored in chapter one) is just one pertinent example of such multiple disciplines, coming together, and all – and more – relevant to our very field of interest.

With the demands of the future pulling our society in all directions, becoming a polymath is likely to be the new norm as a way to future proof our handling of multiple jobs, increase our chances for global employment, be able to ride waves of skills re-evaluation and redeployment and differentiate ourselves from others. Future demands, only amplify a recipe for success that has come through from the past; namely that innovation and advancement have resulted from combined skills and a cross disciplinary capability.

The future beckons to polymaths!. This is the time to expand and augment learning and capabilities, and embrace the belief and the aspiration of becoming "A master of many existing trades and an innovator of many new other"!

Time to embrace a complex world where human coaches and clients as consumers, adaptively integrate with digital devices, AI coaches and helper robots

> Robots are programmable machines and not people, even if we make them in our own image. The ownership of commercial Robots may eventually have to been regulated to prevent their use to cause harm. Robots cannot be considered legal entities since they are programmable machines.
>
> Adina Tarry

Technological devices have filled out product lists and have become the "go to" source for individuals who are interested even superficially in their own activities and performance. We are dealing with consumers that have been attracted to what is "on trend" to have and know in the world of personal tech devices. It is not only a matter of personal curiosity and genuine interest but also "memes" and "fads" initiated by peer groups and others in a community of users that gets excited by supporting one brand or another. This is a consumerist society and brand loyalty for prestige is one social phenomenon that goes with it.

There are those who side with Apple and those who go with Microsoft or the "imitations" that may come from the tiger economies; there are those who like inspirational leaders and therefore buy the product whether they need them or not; there are those who feel they have to be busy and not have a moment unscheduled in their lives; there are those who genuinely believe that running on busy city roads, and measuring their effort will change their body shape and make them more fit and desirable. There are others who embrace an entire lifestyle change for the long game and adapt what they do to what they know is sustainable for them because they take responsibility and are happy to put in a moderate but realistic effort.

It is not clear how impactful and beneficial such behaviours and fashions may be for the long game, and whether people do change for good without reverting to their usual default state. But it is clear that just as the world has embraced Facebook and other social media, come what may, intentionally or by imitating others, they may also adopt self-monitoring and self-developing devices available on the tech gadget market. Our coaching clients may well be such individuals, children of generations that are known for their appetite for independence and self-direction. And we need to work with this reality and add value to what they believe they are already getting from devices but which is not enough. In my experience many such enthusiasts buy devices and some related behavioural change occurs for a while; they then drop the device, seeking some other type of answer and knowledge that is missing and that can apparently be found elsewhere, over and over again. Without proper analysis and investigation I have no conclusion other than to note that the successive quick uptake of new devices and activities dies out sooner or later and leaves people in a constant search for the answer. The fact that at one point in time they knew how many steps they had taken that day, or how many calories they had eaten, did not make them achieve lasting fitness or embrace radical and permanent change in their lives, because those activities and behaviours were quite likely on the periphery of something else much more significant and deep, which such devices cannot surface, and so are left obscured and unexplored.

Random technology and activity changes do not bring meaning and purpose but do fuel the hope that somehow they will help in a deep and lasting way . . . yet often they do not. Results and consequences of such choices are of course variable, but sustainability over time and radical changes of behaviour and ways of thinking are much harder to achieve by quick fixes. And so the high touch of personal and personalised interaction and the related ability to make sense of things and find meaning remains and continues to remain in the domain of human interactions.

AI can do many things and tech devices can gather a lot of information, but what they cannot do is extrapolate, connect, skip intermediate steps (heuristics) or transfer experience and meaning. They cannot swiftly and flexibly respond by fine-tuning to the feedback they get, or bypass binary options and work with "hunches" and "intuition", whilst holding still the vision of what the best outcome may be in a given situation. But humans can do this instantly, naturally and effortlessly without pausing to ask for direction and more details, by exercising exceptional flexibility in the use of experience and evaluation of multiple available options. They are able to make a judgement in real time and immediately put forward a solution or a path to follow.

But online options for self-coaching and therapy already exist and many clients prefer this alternative that gives them privacy and control, and they find this useful. People can choose to do that by themselves when they have the time and draw whatever benefits they can. There is no doubt that just as with anything else, some people will benefit and some not; some people will prefer this method and some not. It seems that in the immediate future, coaching may become a hybrid between humans, technology devices and machines.

The engagement with hi-tech or high-touch or both is a matter of personal preference, and as we know this is driven by individual uniqueness. No two people are the same. And there is a lot to choose from, with more to come: there are monitoring devices for fitness, for health, for movement, or for security. We can now measure in real time bio data such as: glucose levels, cortisol levels, blood pressure, brain activity, eye movements, skin conductivity, heart rate, sweat and temperature. Such information is interpreted and related to stress reaction – via tone of voice – physiological resilience, and behavioural flexibility. There are tens to fifteen gadgets to monitor and improve sleep alone. The sales of such devices are running into the hundreds of millions and generate sales into the billions but cost around £150 per piece, which is affordable for the population that may be attracted to such purchases. The latest wearable health gadgets offer new capabilities and sleekness.

From headsets that measure brainwaves, to clothes that incorporate sensing devices; personal health monitoring is the wave of the future. There is tremendous growth in wearable wireless health devices, as well as sports and fitness devices, and devices worn on or close to the body are expected to produce the most groundbreaking innovations. Technology such as Preventice's BodyGuardian Remote Monitoring System or Avery Dennison's Metria Wearable Technology are able to seamlessly deliver patient data to doctors. Textiles included in AiQ Smart Clothing bypass the need for add-on sensors by incorporating them in clothes to collect data. Emotiv is a device that provides neurological feedback, and measures six states of the user's brain, including arousal and focus. It helps users to monitor and manage their state by using, for example, meditation. Products in the neuro feedback range use a mix of audio and visual guided meditation to readjust brainwaves and bring someone back to a state of calm energy and improved mental performance. Thync, for example, induces calm by neurosignalling to bring specific brainwaves to a positive state and with practice makes this possible for users to bring it on, on demand.

The same can be said about the organisational environment. In the world of work, there are a range of gadgets and applications that our potential coaching clients may already use for their own goal-setting and goal-tracking such as: Stoick, GoalsOnTrack, Habitica and Strides, all with evocative names as to their utility and related to turning goals into tasks, timelines and feedback, with swift check-ins and dashboards of goal and intermediate achievements. The power of the group has long been known and devices such as Slack and I Done This help involve others who are partners in the process and provide support and challenges, give feedback and share progress. Staying on track with activities and plans can be supported by a number of tools such as: Productive, Momentum, Tiny Habits programme, and HabitBull.

Another set of applications already available on mobile phones, such as Clear, Wunderlist and Todoist, prompt for specific activities that support goal achievements by reflections and reminders. There are also devices that help with deeper explorations of mood, feelings and values and attempt connections between such pieces of information, with suggested strategies for self-regulation, such as: Mood Meter, Mitra and Lifetick. The simplest search on the internet will provide hundreds of results and inform us all about what is available and what we may not even have imagined yet but may suddenly find useful. And no doubt they are useful in some cases at some points in time for some people. And there is just one small step from personal tech gadgets to digital little helpers; steps have already been taken with the creation of Siri, Cortana, Alexa, Echo and Google Home, which can handle a range of questions and tasks for us, should we choose to use their services. This is due to AI and what it can do today in its current stage of not being integrated. The next generation of AI called general AI or artificial general intelligence (GAI/AGI) is much more ambitious because it aims to replicate what the human mind can do; AI cannot, but GAI/AGI may well be able to, at least in a primitive form.

Research into robotics and AI is a driver of innovation in a number of sectors, including healthcare, manufacturing, transport, aerospace, oil and gas. The robotics and autonomous systems agenda is gaining momentum and support from investment and governments. Its aim is to answer at least a few key challenges to improve our lives in the future, such as: robotics for social care and independent living; robotics for surgery and global health; robotics for emergency response and disaster relief and resilience; robotics for resilient infrastructure; and robotics for self-driving vehicles, etc. Such challenges create a common agenda for collaborations between research, industry, innovation, government and investors, with the purpose of producing solutions to problems that face populations today. And there is no doubt that achieving such vision will help humankind.

In a nutshell the only barrier to the march of progress is our imagination, and science fiction has already turned into science facts. The natural fate for coaching is to follow the same path. The current and – increasingly – future coach-coachee interaction may mean that individual responsibility and inputs are brought along, as a result of data gathered via high-tech personal devices, to be used in combination, made sense of and integrated into the wider picture of human context and purpose. There is no doubt that human coaches are headed for disruption just like all other practicing professionals, and it will be up to us as a community to decide whether we embrace progress and deal with reality as it is or resist it with little chance of stopping the technological progress. The digital coach, looking and sounding like a human that is able to deal with complex thinking and processes in real time and the many pieces of information that come its way, as well as generating new options and using them sensibly in a real conversation with a coaching client, is not yet here to directly threaten and take the place of human coaches. However, robotics and automation are marching on, and it would not be wise to ignore that what is not here today and what may sound like fantasy may well become reality tomorrow.

After all, the magnitude and landscape of scientific achievements that exist today would have looked like magic and sorcery to the humans of only 500 years ago. The magic of science remains because humankind continues to be curious, innovative and keen to push the boundaries of the unknown and unreachable, further and further. And digital coaching will find a market just as personal gadgets have already found one, whilst the digital assistants are already in our homes.

This progress is unavoidable and we all need to get on with reality as it presents itself. What is now needed from the coaching community is acceptance, preparedness and proactive thinking about how to define, represent and safeguard the real value that human coaches may bring to hybrid, democratised, accessible and technology-led current and future incarnations of self-development. Coaches are not going to stop the progress of technology in its tracks. But we can certainly influence attitudes, ethics, governance and codes of practice, both in the world of our clients and our own. And it may be a good place to start with our own community so that we know what we are doing before we engage in working with our clients.

Time to embrace happenstance, chaos and complexity in career management

In complex environments, cause and effect are so disconnected and so distanced in time that they become almost unrelated and unrecognisable. When the context of events is changing and volatile, using pre-set tools and reacting with set behaviours is no longer sufficient, because set answers only work when the circumstances have also been set and remain so. And in our times, they change continuously.

The future of careers is no longer predictable and careers as well as professions no longer operate within known and agreed boundaries. Whether we like it or not, uncertainty, chaos and change will play an increasingly significant hand in our choices and our personal and work-related path, which as a result will get increasingly meandering and unexpected. We are in the eye of a global storm that keeps moving its centre, sending waves from one location to another, with unintended consequences that require us to build another kind of a response to it.

It is imperative that we become at least familiar with dialectic and complexity thinking and more importantly use it in our daily lives, by reflecting deeper on what happens to us to adjust our responses in a flexible and decisive way. We need to be more skilled at holding on to uncertainty without losing our self-belief and deeper centre.

Nurturing attitudes such as: curiosity, openness, flexibility, self-belief and self-directedness; being both tactical and strategic; sustaining a higher order of thinking; placing lower level tasks in the context of higher levels of reflection, purpose and meaning-making is necessary for the future of work. Facing the future from a strong, hopeful centre will enable us to live well with uncertainty and meet change, chaos, chance and complexity with flexibility and a self-belief that we can make luck and have luck.

Inhabiting multiple work avatars as one strong and hopeful self

The world of now is what it is, and as individuals we live and relate to our context whether this is our local neighbourhood, country or continent. And this may be the case for our individual everyday life or for a more involved participation in the activities and preoccupations – cultural, political, social, ethical, operational – of the human groups (family, friends, community, social, work groups) to which we belong. In all cases we fulfil a role and we have to answer the bigger questions about life, in simple or more sophisticated terms.

Asking questions about this path and dreaming about becoming someone or doing something meaningful are expressions of our humanity, and behind every mundane role there is a core of feelings, desires and values. There are people who will say that their life's achievement was to raise a family or get an education or be able to provide, or be able to serve the community, or just achieve happiness for themselves and those around them. Simple statements that nonetheless involve an aspiration, a belief, a value system, a cognitive engagement to implement those aspirations and an effort to adapt and relate to a complex reality to best stay on track.

Others dream to reach for the stars, become astronauts or rid the world of some terrible disease or make a fundamental change in humankind's history, and again, on another level of complexity and involvement, the same personal enablers have to engage and keep such aspirations alive, help the accumulation of knowledge, gain the experience needed to implement the dream and hold on to guiding values and beliefs; and potentially stimulate reflection on what the implications of that contribution may be for the wider world of others.

From VIPs to successive generations of farmers, or from people of humble beginnings who through social mobility and sheer determination have reached fame and fortune, all have been driven by a set of enabling factors and achieved a modest or enhanced awareness of what drove them. We all have our drivers and use them; the difference is in the degree of awareness and purpose that we place around them.

Having language, reason and will enables us to exercise a level of agency that is informed by a common source. And that source is knowledge, experience and the way we work with these as we manifest our existence in the world to become ourselves. Implicit or explicit, this process of enquiry and action is triggered by ourselves or by events and others around us. And always, our actions and reactions provide that answer, even if embedded in what we do, with no explicit articulation. We are bio-psycho-socio-philosophical creatures, and whilst our brain and society remain as they are, the way we work as human beings will also remain unchanged.

We can identify, trace and recognise every documented emotion and action that people have experienced, going back thousands of years of human civilization. What tested and challenged them then, still challenges us now and is likely to challenge us tomorrow. Regardless of what technological and socio-economic stages have prevailed in times past, what has always won the day is the fabric of the human nature. It is only the generation of babies born in the last decade or so who are literally growing up with smart phones in their hands, playing baby apps before they can talk and walk, that may give us a first set of answers about the future. By their mid-twenties they would have been a social experiment that could potentially confirm whether their early exposure to technology has modified the psychological drivers that have been our defining traits from the dawn of time and whether this will still apply again in the future. Biological evolution is slow and certainly many times outpaced by the speed of technological advancement.

If the technological environment does not cause genetic mutations soon – unlikely since natural genetic mutations due to environment take hundreds of thousands of years, or even millions of years for a mutation to become prevalent – and our biology remains in the foreseeable future as it has been in the last few thousand years, they will be asking the same questions that we ask ourselves today, including the in-between generation that is now in their teens and mid-twenties. Unless we intervene technologically to manipulate genes which may adapt us to the very technology that is challenging us in the first place!

But as things stand, whilst technology has changed at a dizzying pace, our biology has not. Humanity has survived political and geographic conflicts that have led to wars raging over decades, and has seen the rise and fall of huge powerful empires that have disappeared off the map and shrunk to nothing after hundreds of years of domination, alongside innovation, new technologies and territorial expansions that have often come with the price of death, destruction and sometimes the extinction of entire peoples across the old and new worlds. Major and troubling disruptions and setbacks have nonetheless not defeated humanity or prevented it from continuing to exist over millennia and make further progress.

And what we know from the history of large groups and societies has also been true for the individual history of my coaching clients. Across the entire group of many hundreds, I have only witnessed a few extreme examples of unthinkable challenges where all the odds appeared stacked against the person in front of me; people who may have been experiencing at the same time serious illness, financial difficulty, redundancy, a career transition and responsibility for family and others, and who were just at a loss to know where to begin

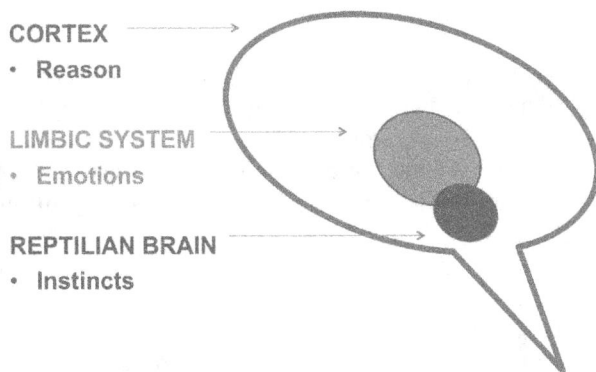

CORTEX
• Reason

LIMBIC SYSTEM
• Emotions

REPTILIAN BRAIN
• Instincts

Figure 4.4 The bio-psycho-socio-philosophical nature of humans

to manage so many difficulties, as well as the darkness brought about by defeat and serious threats to their very existence.

I was shocked by such personal stories, and my inner thoughts went to their unbelievable enduring power and the resourcefulness they needed to keep conjuring up, in order to remain as they were, seating upright in my office, holding with dignity and coherence the most difficult and painful of conversations, trying so hard to work out a way forward from despair to a solution. They had to suspend reality and ignore the fact that their entire world was crushing down, and find the strength to enable hope and believe that when one door shuts another opens, that things will turn out all right in the end, that an answer will come if only they keep asking and looking for it, that miracles are possible, that luck will gift them a winning hand just this once, after what they have suffered. And I also wondered at such times, how would I have reacted in a similar situation . . .?

But such extreme cases have – thankfully – been rare and in a way demonstrated just the opposite of defeat and hopelessness. Because throughout my work I have been witness to an incredible range of common strengths across the entire group:

- Tremendous resourcefulness and the energy to bounce back after difficult times
- Ability to identify new opportunities, move on and rebuild
- Power to recover and return to an even stronger self, after adversity
- Resilience to never give up and just pursue the belief in a good future
- Remaining empathetic and considerate of others, whilst themselves at a low end
- Transferring and repurposing professional competence, by reinvention, after setbacks
- Nurturing a life force, in times of destruction, when commercial worlds and companies around them had been turned to ashes

Witnessing this collective, inspiring and often humbling experience of others, has in turn filled me with a great sense of admiration and empathy for my clients and has nourished my own commitment to support and serve them the best I could. This in turn, gave me clarity of purpose and a sense of achievement and professional gratification, in addition to the opportunity to self-develop and evolve, by benefiting from this privileged, rich, unique, co-created environment. In this exchange I have learned from them as much as I hope they learned from me and in these co-created systems of dialogue and collaboration, we have experienced good partnerships. This book is a testimony to the indomitable human spirit and an acknowledgement of the contributions made by all the people I have worked with. They have demonstrated an exceptional and inspiring resilience, not only by surviving and overcoming adversity but by continuing a happy and fulfilled existence, often enhanced by what the unplanned challenges revealed about their unexplored potential, which enabled them to thrive beyond and in spite of setbacks.

Far from being just a part of our life – as it is for work today – our work in the future may well become the essence of our life itself. Because the type of work and our ability or even opportunity to work will define our income, our independence, our position in society, and our right to access representation and to have a voice. The way the world of work alongside technology, artificial intelligence and the fourth technological revolution are unfolding, will have a tremendous social impact on our ability to ask questions and on the equity of power and wealth distribution, at large.

The whole restructuring of professions as we know them today, as well as the importance of labour input into the general wealth, the matter of ownership of means of production, capital and artificial intelligence, and the massive growing difference between people who are extremely wealthy and people who are increasingly poor and dependent on the rich for maintenance, is likely to cause new and challenging social tensions. In fact the changes in our work are going to change our entire life, our status, our self-esteem, our value system, our social input, and gender equality, and so it will raise philosophical, social, political and mainly ethical and regulatory questions.

Unlike in the past where work was to a degree a given and was an important part of our overall life, work in the future may become an activity that will not involve everyone and not for a large amount of time or within the same range of opportunities. So our future life is directly linked to the future of work. And for this we need to be prepared and empowered by the vast amount of possibilities for gaining self-knowledge that are available today, more than ever before, freely, online and also mediated by all the beneficial talking interventions and interactions with qualified people, with coaching being one such option, along the others. Certainly, combined skill and effort between individual ownership of a developmental agenda and qualified support will ensure that the way ahead can be navigated in the same brave and successful manner as it has been for thousands of years, and, hopefully, with less effort, enhanced intelligence, enhanced methodologies, and enhanced possibilities of additional resources in the pursuit of answers and best outcomes.

The future of the fourth technological revolution is a future where ambiguity, ambivalence, many concurrent alternatives, volatility of information and permanent change are indeed calling for thinking and a connection with the world that is much more flexible and adaptive, and where we need to embrace tensions, uncertainty and contradiction. To this end we may be better served by a new way of thinking – dialectic and complexity – that allows us to make sense of ambiguity and a shifting reality whilst maintaining self-belief and the ability to evaluate situations and make useful judgements.

The new resilience is about maintaining a strong human core of aspirations and purpose that is relevant and supports the direction that we set for ourselves. It has to provide a strong and adaptive centre to enable us to manifest in the world, empower us to navigate a shifting and unravelling reality, use and realise our potential and pursue a happy and meaningful existence. The path ahead is likely to be meandering and challenging, but our humanity may be our greatest asset and with all our resources primed we can stay on course, adapt to change and new contexts and enjoy a good life.

"The Immortalists" and the quest for "deus ex machina"

> Humanity has the stars in its future, and that future is too important to be lost . . .
>
> Isaac Asimov

For better or for worse, technology is now outpacing our biology and we humans are curious and impetuous creatures. We are also defiant in our belief that we can dominate all that surrounds us and have become impatient with our poorly designed and really vulnerable biological vessel that is our body, which carries such a timeless, boundless and fearless force that is our human spirit. We have had enough of the tyranny of time! Impatience is in our genes and so science is once again expected to do its magic!

The "Immortalists" have been called upon to get working and find a solution that will project our human essence into infinity. The ambition is to unlock and capture the essence of the human spirit, extract it from its fragile container and place it into a more robust shell that can survive entropy, biological decay and time. An entity that can exist forever! The so-called Immortalists are not fiction writers! But scientists at the top of their profession; they are the leading minds in neuroscience, brain physiology, AI and robotics. Their quest is eternal life!

There are two schools of thought. One, that the mind and personality are just information and can be mapped as such, to be downloaded from the human brain and then uploaded into a machine. Which means that the entire activity of 86 billion neurons has to be mapped. With current technology this is not actually possible, but if the hypothesis is correct, it may be possible in the future. In this scenario, the brain is considered to be just a very powerful computer that operates with inputs from the environment and translates them into neuron impulses – effectively zeroes and ones (on/off) – which in turn generate behaviour. Therefore it is assumed that the entire self, or psyche or consciousness or personality of a human, including feelings, motivators, thinking, cognition, behaviour and communication plus all the attributes of what we call consciousness could be mapped as data and then transferred by download, recoded, stored and obviously uploaded or copied just like we do with any data today. And with robotics making significant progress in building machines that look so much like humans, any person could download their individual self then upload it into a machine and . . . live forever, as well as in many embodiments of the one self, cloned as multiple machines. The possibilities are endless in that with multiple selves that live forever we could be in space, just like probes and spacecraft travelling thought the universe, potentially forever, unimpeded, because machines are less affected by decay than a life form like us and could so become potentially immortal. Or we could be in different places at the same time; one version of our Self on earth, another on a newly terraformed planet, and a third travelling, indefinitely, out of our galaxy and into deep outer space. And, for many, this is a compelling vision!

The other school of thought is that the self and consciousness are not data but something that we do not quite understand yet; something more dynamic, emerging and not easily translated into data or driven by algorithms and computation rules. This school of thought does not consider the brain to be a computer, because the mystery that links the matter of the actual brain to the intangible outcome cannot exactly be mapped back to linear connections between neurons and neuronal networks, but instead emerges as an outcome of a different level altogether, quite difficult to capture and define in binary terms. The brain and the mind may be connected but are qualitatively different states of matter, just like, say, water, steam, ice and snow, for example; all the same, yet all different and with different shapes and properties of their own. So the brain is not considered a computer; and what it supports – self and consciousness – is something that we recognise indeed, but we do not fully understand. This school of thought is faced with two challenges: first, to map the human brain and then understand how it generates something so different, called consciousness.

And so we are back to the challenge of mapping 86 billion neurons and their activity, which in fact is not currently possible. But one may attempt to map a nervous system that is simpler. And to this purpose a micro-organism called the Hydra (class Hydrozoa, Cnidaria) has become an object of study for neuroscience and brain physiology.

Hydra, a freshwater invertebrate organism, looks like a translucent tube of about thirty millimetres (1.2 inches) and is capable of great contractions. The body is made of two layers linked together by connective tissue and housing its digestive system. Its mouth is at the top of the body and surrounded by four to twenty-five tentacles. It moves by creeping or looping in somersaults, by attaching on a base. But most importantly, it is equipped with a diffuse nervous system, the most primitive one, which is made of nerve cells distributed throughout the organism. It lacks a large concentration of neurons, such as a brain, but it has smaller pockets called ganglia. Most importantly, primitive as this system may be, this does not preclude it from coordinated, prolonged and integrated behaviour in reacting to the simplest stimuli. This modest creature has been the object of intense studies to great success, and all 3,000 or so neurons of its primitive nervous system, have been mapped. Furthermore, the activity of this network has been made visible with dyes and can be seen working just as we see the rivulets of light from above, at night, if looking down on a city. It is a vision to behold, full of motion and beautifully luminescent.

But quite against the given premise that neurons are activated by stimuli and then cause the organism to react (behave), what we see with Hydra, is an organism that behaves, but also does not behave, whilst remaining neuro-physiologically active outside the input-output loop. Meaning that it fires and talks across the network in the absence of stimuli, according to algorithms, principles and a dynamic only known to itself, but not yet to us. In other words, it seems this network creates activity of a different kind, not based on what it has received from the outside world, but something that originates from within, independent of external sources. A parallel inner world of self-generated stim-ulation and dynamic responses.

So what is it doing? Could it just be . . . "thinking . . . or dreaming"? Or is it processing the information that it has first received from external stimuli to transform it into another kind of self-generating information? Does it initiate or does it continue an activity in line with some necessary processes that relate to the inner life and workings of this creature, and the dynamics of the environ-ment within? We do not know. And that which we can now clearly see . . . we still do not understand!

The network is talking to us in a language that has its own meaning and rules, except that we do not know the rules or the vocabulary used. We cannot map the 86 billion human neurons, but mapping Hydra's 3,000, has not explained the internal dynamics of such a network, either. And we remain unable to code such knowledge into information and data. But scientists are not giving up and continue watching and thinking about what is going on and how to unlock the mystery of the inner principles that drive the visible and baffling activity that they can now at least observe at will.

Wherever this quest to capture the essence of humanity and make it immortal leads, one thing is sure: the imaginings of the visionary Isaac Asimov (1919–1992) are coming to pass. Professor of biochemistry and a prolific writer, including of hard science fiction (fiction based on scientific consistency), in the league of Jules Verne and Arthur C. Clarke, Asimov predicted that the next synthesis of the future inhabitants of the planet will be found in the middle, between machines becoming more like humans and humans becoming more like machines. This process appears to slowly but surely be on its way.

Such dreams have captured the public imagination and been expressed in popular art. The number of films starting with *The Matrix* (1999) and followed just in the last few years by *Robot & Frank* (2012); *Gravity, Elysium, Her, Europa Report* and *Under the Skin* (all 2013); *Automata* and *Lucy* (2014); *Ex Machina* and *The Martian* (both 2015); and *Passengers* (2016) all deal with themes of the future of humanity in the age of the machine, outer-space colo-nisation, and generally the subject of continuity or immortality for the human race on earth or elsewhere, by some means or other.

And what we already know is that when humans set their minds on something, they never, ever, give up!

Embracing the third option: a hopeful vision for the future

But the subject of this book has not been science as such; but rather people, and how they relate to science and technology and how this relationship will pan out in the future, as we contemplate it now, at the dawn of the fourth digital revolution. And every time we discuss science we talk in fact about ourselves! Artificial intelligence more than anything else is raising questions about the knowledge we have of our brain, our emotions and our need to make meaning.

To answer some of these questions I chose an integrative multi-disciplinary and cross-functional approach to combine experiential findings with theory and science, in light of current information gathered from primary sources in the last 24 months. This enabled me to sample and to some extent cover a wide range of relevant topics from psychology and philosophy, to the future of individuals, society and business, to new technologies and the impact of artificial intelligence and robotics, to ethical, deontological and epistemological aspects, and what are the ambitions of the future technology, itself.

The triad of logos, ethos and pathos is a reminder that our intelligence and logic, as used in technology and AI cannot be separated from our emotions and the ethics that surround how we use the applications that our extraordinary mind can create through its cognitive function.

We are already approaching a time when the cost of AI technology, the open source and use of natural language in AI programming and the ability of people to create AI and distribute it, will become affordable and accessible to many.

In the UK today an AI start-up business is created every few days, and the new "buzz" word is "algorithm" replacing a similar wave of enthusiasm of a decade ago when the word "app" captured everyone's imagination and hundreds of new apps were released every week; and soon the market will be crowded by over supply and then rebalanced in the way such changes have panned out for technology, industry and business in the past, towards the point of a new equilibrium.

With a level playing field for all – just like with information technology in the last three decades – competition and commercial edge will be gained not by the technology itself, but by how well technology serves human needs and the quality of human experience. Competition will intensify redefining the product category with human instinct at its centre, and a new vision to build brands around lifestyles and helping people feel alive will determine success. The future agenda of technology is to fulfil social aspirations, enable us to spend more time with other people, have more time to do things that we want to do, build relationships and live in the moment.

Tomy, the vintage robot of the 1980s, is a primitive – if cute looking – ancestor compared to the interactive robots of today and tomorrow. In 2018 we enter the era of natural language and conversational computing which will enable expression of emotional intelligence and a return to storytelling.

If we may say that in the last decades technology has encouraged isolated individual utilisation of connectivity through the Internet and login protocols, in the future human natural voice interaction will change the way technology enables communication and connectivity and will truly serve the purpose of creating communities and a better life experience.

It is now evident that we must be sensitive and respond to what works for people and not only what works for technology. The importance of communication between people is not to be underestimated and often accounts for half of the variance in overall performance and happiness. Isolation is a killer as powerful as any physical disease that is incurable today.

And this is why the pendulum of technology is swinging back towards the human centre to satisfy human needs, human emotions, human aspirations and human lifestyle choices to enable a better life experience where a higher degree of choice and freedom can be exercised naturally, whilst blending work, life and the enabling technology in a seamless and natural way.

The three pillars of persuasion coined by Aristotle and embraced in Greek antiquity come to mind as an ideal, integrated and dynamic way of exchange between technology and humans. If technology is to be trusted and embraced, it needs to speak to humans by appealing to logic, with reason and facts, by speaking to emotions through impassioned storytelling and by an ethical assurance based on domain authority, trust and credibility. We are complex beings, and we respond best when all aspects of what makes us human are acknowledged and addressed.

And this offers an overarching principle that mirrors the one found in my coaching work. Namely that when all has been said and done, whether it is about technology, or society or individuals or the future of work or coaching and self-development, it all comes down to ethics, meaning, purpose and governance. The conversations and unknowns today are no longer just about technology or where it is going but increasingly about how to ensure that it is used for the greater good and for all. It is about ethics, values and purpose. The capitalist economic order is today looking for a new path to integrate the new awareness that the needs of many have to be taken into account; that what we value must shift to another level of responsibility and exchange, for a collective greater good. The same applies to the use of the internet and data protection generally; that is, how to keep it safe from misuse by the dark side.

In this age, data is the most valuable asset of the future, and in digital capitalism, harvesting, storing and utilising data will make the critical difference in wealth generation and distribution, in favour of those who are in the game. Data is for the future what steam, electricity, gold and oil have been in the past: an immense source of opportunities, power and wealth. In the digital world data is at the centre of global economic and financial power with serious social and political implications.

Now more than before it is all about ethics, but ethical decisions are quite difficult to make and may significantly vary from individual to individual and from group to group.

For example, to further develop and deploy self-driving cars, a wide survey has been opened to the public where people are asked to volunteer their views and make choices related to a number of scenarios which involve ethical dilemmas and where they need to make a decision. This exercise is needed in order for this information to be used as input data for the operating brain of the car, to enable it to react and decide, as a human driver would.

But the range of human decisions is wide; some people may rescue a pet and sacrifice a human, other people may sacrifice individuals if they can save a group, others would rescue a young person or a baby instead of an older person and so on.

This is why debates on any topic are always interesting; they demonstrate how every side and view can put forward an argument to support it and how, typically, one view may prevail if those arguments appear to be robust enough. However this is not to say that they are always right; all so reminiscent of the Jain predications.

Scaling up the question of ethical dilemmas to include the provision of a robust ethical framework for the wider society is even more challenging, and it is the job of governance, regulators and legislators, informed by public consultation.

But people have lost confidence in leadership, and politicians are struggling because the values have shifted and the masses – enabled by technology – can be vocal about their expectations. This is also about attitudes and motivators.

Humankind's resilience on this planet, in spite of so many changes and transformations over millennia, suggests that success has been based not only on technology but more significantly on aspirations, culture, leadership, identity, inner strength, self-belief, motivation and ability to innovate and cope with adversity, the capability to reinvent ourselves, and the ability to dream, imagine and explore possibilities.

And this may also be due to the fact that we are the only species designed for cultural accumulation and creation of wisdom, which is shared by and passed on from large groups to other large groups over time, again and again.

We have shown exceptional flexibility and used both chance and planning to get to a better place to overcome a temporary adversity or difficulty for a better future existence by catching or creating opportunities to survive and thrive. And this human imperative is now recognised and making its way in technology design.

We have always had the ability to use our minds for good or ill, and if our purpose, mission and vision for the future are bright and fair, we will create and follow that constructive path with courage and readiness, and we are likely to get to our desired destination.

Spiritual and higher needs have been a core of human existence, and individually this is also about developing and using the inner core of the individual self and how it connects to the wider society. It is about emotional and social intelligence, about imagination and adaptation, about being able to use the foundations of the past and life wisdom, to better connect and co-evolve in an adaptive way within the wider ecosystem – social, economic and global – in the now and into the future, as part of a continuous process of cultural accumulation.

From such a strong centre everything is possible within the context of the time and place where we are. Just like the symbolic tree with strong roots and floating flexible branches and leaves, the roots of the self are fed by society, to grow from within and then provide the flexibility for the rest of us to move with the winds, seek the sunlight, be nourished by storms, adapt, auto repair and fight entropy, by leaving a biological, cognitive or spiritual legacy to the wider society.

Humankind is set to indulge once again its unstoppable curiosity and push the boundaries of exploration well beyond our planet and solar system whilst trying to bend time to its will and live forever in one guise or another. There is no boundary to human ambition, and all that makes it weak may yet be its greatest strength.

And a unifying thread emerges upon reflecting on so many sources of information to establish that human continuity and our footing are planted firmly in what may also be considered our humanity and our weaknesses: such as feelings, compassion, beliefs, dreams, appetite for risk, curiosity, restlessness, mood and irrationality.

Paradoxically but not illogically, in the context of complexity, dialectics and evolution, these human attributes have been and are most likely to remain – in chartered or unchartered times – the firm power behind individuals and groups, to ensure resilience, adaptation and survival, no matter the challenges and changes.

And perhaps we need to change our conversation about the future from binary to a third option, where some things will pan out well and others not, where sometimes we will succeed and other times we will fail, where there are going to be gains alongside losses and where there is going to be a price to pay for the advantages we will win.

Hope supports the expectation that things will pan out well in the end, even if they may not; resilience enables us to recover from loss and defeat and get back on track, hopefully enriched in some way; and sustainability takes care of our present and future on a wider scale using ethical and responsible principles for human and natural resources and respecting the balance of consumption in order to make this planet inhabitable for future generations.

The combination of such attitudes and capabilities can provide for us the third option, a much more adaptive, realistic and helpful projection, instead of a binary perspective of utopia or dystopia.

In the end, focusing on hope, resilience and sustainability at an individual and collective level will map the way through transition and mark the next evolutionary landing point as a desirable one.

Nothing has stopped the innovation and ambitions of the human spirit, which has prevailed over adversity time and time again over millennia. And the same is likely to continue, provided we do become fully aware of that resource, fully own it, and align our actions and choices with that life giving source.

The world of work may be turned upside down very soon, but if we get that core of a strong self in place and become self-aware and aware of others and the context, our actions will become flexible, active and proactive, following the flow of external events that in turn we also have the power to shape and influence.

Human aspiration, imagination, resilience, motivation, emotions and the pursuit of achievement have their roots in the oldest biological part of the brain responsible for basic survival, upon which – layer after layer – we have seen develop the higher functions of cognition, critical and symbolic thinking, creativity, purpose and meaning-making to make us who we are and what we become in the company of others, as interdependent members of the human society.

As long as the brain remains an unfathomable and magical seat of the self, individual and collective, there is great likelihood that life on earth will find endless ways to reinvent itself, well into a distant future. In the future, work may not mean a life, but the meaning of life itself will have to be reassessed, reassigned and repositioned within or outside work.

In all cases, it is due to our deep sense of identity – and our awareness of that cultural and social legacy that transcends time and brings together our past, present and future – that we will remain strong and resilient, to survive the transition and build another human society, hopefully for the better.

And so it is now time for yet another end; but it is also time for new beginnings!

Bibliography

Armsby, P., & Fillery-Travis, A. (2009). Developing the coach using work based learning masters and doctorate programmes to facilitate coaches learning. UALL Work Based Learning Network Annual Conference: The Impact of Work Based Learning for the Learner. University of the West of England, 13–14 July.

Executive Office of the President of the United States, National Science and Technology Council Committee on Technology (October 2016). Preparing for the future of artificial intelligence.

Fillery-Travis, A., & Sexton, E. Researching their own practice: The competencies required by practitioner researcher. Available from www.academia.edu/1775162/ [last accessed November 2017].

Fraser-Thill, R. (2017). Causes of low self esteem in kids: Why some children suffer from low self esteem. Available from: www.verywell.com/causes-of-low-self-esteem-in-kids-3288009 [last accessed November 2017].

Fraser-Thill. R. (2017). What is the definition of the myelination process? How the myelination process relates to your tween's impulse control. Available from: https://www.verywell.com/myelination-process-3288324 [last accessed November 2017].

Hegel, G. W. F. (1967). *Phenomenology of Mind*, J. B. Baille (Trans.). London: Harper & Row.

Keagan, R. (1983). *The Evolving Self: Problem and Process in Human Development*. Cambridge, MA: Harvard University Press.

Kohlberg, L., Levine, C., & Hewer, A. (1983). *Moral Stages: A Current Formulation and a Response to Critics*. Basel and New York: Karger.

Krumboltz, J. D., & Levin, A. S. (2004). *Luck is No Accident*. Atascadero, CA: Impact.

Lane, A. D., & Corrie, S. (2006). *The Modern Scientist-Practitioner*. Oxford: Routledge.

Loevinger, J. (Ed.). (1998). *Technical Foundations for Measuring Ego Development*. New Jersey and London: Lawrence Erlbaum.

Marx, K. (1932). *Economic and Philosophic Manuscripts of 1844*. Progress Publishers, Moscow 1959.

Messner, W., & Schäfer, N. (2012). *The ICCA Facilitator's Manual: Intercultural Communication and Collaboration Appraisal*. London: GloBus Research, p. 41.

Mitchell, K. E., Levin, S., & Krumboltz, J. D. (1999). Planned happenstance: Constructing unexpected career opportunities. *Journal of Counseling & Development*, 77(2): 115–124.

Mitleton-Kelly, E. (1998). Organisations as complex evolving systems. LSE and Warwick Conference on Organisations as Complex Evolving Systems. Warwick, December 4–5.

Mitleton-Kelly, E. (2000). Complexity: Partial support for BPR. In: P. Henderson (Ed.), *Systems Engineering for Business Process Change*. Berlin: Springer.

Mitleton-Kelly, E., & Papaefthimiou, M. C. (2000). Co-evolution and an enabling infrastructure: A solution to legacy? In: P. Henderson (Ed.), *Systems Engineering for Business Process Change*. Berlin: Springer.

Mitleton-Kelly, E., & Papaefthimiou, M. C. (2001). Co-evolution of diverse elements interacting within a social ecosystem. In: P. Henderson (Ed.), *Systems Engineering for Business Process Change*. Berlin: Springer.

Mullins, C. (2012). Retrospective analysis of technology forecasting: In-scope extension. The Tauri Group, 13 August.

Passmore, J., & Fillery-Travis, A. (2011). A critical review of executive coaching research: A decade of progress and what's to come. *Coaching: An International Journal of Theory, Practice & Research, 4*(2): 70–88.

Piaget, J. (1950). *The Psychology of Intelligence*. New York: Routledge.

Pryor, R. G., & Bright, J. (2003). The chaos theory of careers. *Australian Journal of Career Development, 12*(3): 12–20.

Pryor, R., & Bright, J. (2011). *The Chaos Theory of Careers: A New Perspective on Working in the Twenty-First Century*. Oxford: Routledge.

Riether, W. (2014). *Business Cooperation Cultural Integration as Keyfactor: Reasons for Failing and Suggestions to Improve Chances for Success*. Saarbrücken: AV Akademikerverlag.

Rooke, D., & Torbert, W. R. (2005). Seven transformations of leadership. *Harvard Business Review, 83*(4) 66–76.

Tarry, A. *Ethics and Technology: A Precarious Mix!* February 28, 2018. www.linkedin.com/pulse/ethics-technology-precarious-mix-adina-tarry/

Tarry, A. *Looking Ahead to AI and Robotics in 2018!* January 21, 2018. www.linkedin.com/pulse/looking-ahead-ai-robotics-2018-adina-tarry/

Torbert, B. (2004). *Action Inquiry: The Secret of Timely and Transforming Leadership*. San Francisco, CA: Berrett-Koehler.

Vygotsky, L. (1978). *Mind in Society: The Development of Higher Psychological Processes*. Cambridge, MA and London: Harvard University Press.

Wilber, K. (2001). *No Boundary: Eastern and Western Approaches to Personal Growth*. Boston, MA: Shambhala.

World Economic Forum. (January 2016). Global challenge insight report. The Future of Jobs Employment, Skills and Workforce Strategy for the Fourth Industrial Revolution.

Index

For Product Safety Concerns and Information please contact our EU representative GPSR@taylorandfrancis.com
Taylor & Francis Verlag GmbH, Kaufingerstraße 24, 80331 München, Germany